Thackeray
Interviews and Recollections
Volume 2

Also by Philip Collins

A Christmas Carol: The Public Reading Version (*editor*)
A Dickens Bibliography
Charles Dickens: *David Copperfield*
Charles Dickens: The Public Readings (*editor*)
Dickens and Crime
Dickens and Education
Dickens: Interviews and Recollections (*editor*) 2 vols
Dickens's *Bleak House*
Dickens: The Critical Heritage (*editor*)
English Christmas (*editor*)

Other Interviews and Recollections volumes available on

BRENDAN BEHAN (*two volumes*)   edited by E. H. Mikhail
DICKENS (*two volumes*)   edited by Philip Collins
HENRY JAMES   edited by Norman Page
KIPLING (*two volumes*)   edited by Harold Orel
D. H. LAWRENCE (*two volumes*)   edited by Norman Page
KARL MARX   edited by David McLellan
TENNYSON   edited by Norman Page
H. G. WELLS   edited by J. R. Hammond

Further titles in preparation

THACKERAY

Interviews and Recollections

Volume 2

Edited by
Philip Collins

St. Martin's Press   New York

Selection and editorial matter © Philip Collins 1983

All rights reserved. For information, write:
St. Martin's Press, Inc., 175 Fifth Avenue, New York, NY 10010
Printed in Hong Kong
First published in the United States of America in 1983

ISBN 0-312-79489-4

Library of Congress Cataloging in Publication Data

Main entry under title:

Thackeray, interviews and recollections.

   Bibliography: v. 2, p.
   Includes index.
   1. Thackeray, William Makepeace, 1811–1863 –
Biography – Addresses, essays, lectures.
2. Novelists, English – 19th century – Biography –
Addresses, essays, lectures.   I. Collins, Philip Arthur
William.
PR5631.T5   1982   823'.8   81–21327
ISBN 0-312-79488-6 (vol. 1)   AACR2
ISBN 0-312-79489-4 (vol. 2)

Contents

List of Plates   vii

INTERVIEWS AND RECOLLECTIONS
Moral Conflicts and Religious Beliefs
  Blanche Warre Cornish   193
The Tenderest-hearted Cynic   *Eliza Lynn Linton*   202
Tender-hearted, Almost Womanly   *Theodore Martin*   205
Father at Work   *Anne Thackeray Ritchie*   208
Writing and Reading *The Newcomes*   *Various*   212
The Real Thackeray   *George Augustus Sala*   218
Memories of a Right-hand Man   *George Hodder*   228
The Man with the Largest Mass of Brain
  Whitwell and Frances Elwin   242
My Hearty, Hospitable, Beloved and Honoured
  Friend   *Dean Hole*   251
'The Kindest and Truest Heart that Ever Beat'
  Emelyn and Edith Story   254
Literary Habits, Tastes and Plans   *John Esten Cooke*   256
'The Essential Manliness of his Nature'   *Bayard Taylor*   264
A Certain Boyish and Impulsive Strain   *James Payn*   273
A Man Apart, and Sad   *David Masson*   276
The Perfectly Conformist English Gentleman
  John Lothrop Motley   279
Wine and Talk in Paris   *William Allingham*   282
Imperfections Outweighed by Manly Virtues
  John Cordy Jeaffreson   284
Vexed to Hear Dickens Praised
  Lord William Pitt Lennox   299
'We Had our Differences of Opinion'   *Charles Dickens*   301
Thackeray and my Father   *Kate Dickens Perugini*   306
Thackeray and Dickens: Some Anecdotes
  George Russell   311
The Garrick Club Affair   *Edmund Yates*   313
Punch Lines   *Various*   320

'Almost Infantile Openness of Nature' *John Skelton*	326
Less Awesome than Dickens *Justin McCarthy*	328
The Softness, and the Weakness, of a Woman *Anthony Trollope*	331
Tipsy and Undignified *John Bigelow*	338
Founder-editor of the *Cornhill Magazine* *George Smith and Anne Thackeray Ritchie*	341
'Dear Old Kindly Child!' *Herman Merivale*	347
A Man of Moods *Blanchard Jerrold*	355
Glimpses *Various*	359
Intimations of Mortality *Anne Thackeray Ritchie*	369
Some Obituaries *George Venables and others*	373
A Man Not Easily Summed Up *John Blackwood*	381
Suggestions for Further Reading	383
Index	385

List of Plates

9 Sketches of Thackeray's London houses by Eyre Crowe
10 Crayon sketch of Thackeray by Samuel Laurence, 1852
11 Painting of Thackeray in his study by E. M. Ward
12 Painting of Thackeray at the Garrick Club by Sir John Gilbert, R. A. (by kind permission of the Works of Art Committee of the Garrick Club)
13 Sketches of Thackeray by Frederick Walker, 1861 (The British Library) and Richard Doyle (The British Museum)
14 Photograph of Thackeray by E. Edwards, *c*. 1863 (National Portrait Gallery)
15 Statuette by Joseph Edgar Boehm, 1864 (National Portrait Gallery)
16 Engraving from a photograph of Thackeray by Herbert Watkins, *c*. 1863 (*The Illustrated London News*)
17 Drawing of Thackeray by Samuel Laurence, 1864 (Mansell Collection)

Moral Conflicts and Religious Beliefs
BLANCHE WARRE CORNISH

(1) 'Thackeray and his Father's Family', *Cornhill Magazine*, n.s., XXXI (1911) 80–2; (2) from 'An Impression of Thackeray in his Last Years', *Dublin Review*, CL (1912) 12–26. Mrs Warre Cornish was a daughter of Thackeray's cousin William Ritchie (1817–62), of whom he was very fond. Ritchie made his career in India, from 1842, but the children returned to Europe for their education, and thus Blanche, living sometimes with members of the family in Paris, saw Thackeray there and in London. The first item was the Introduction to her collection *Some Family Letters of William Makepeace Thackeray* (1911). The special concern with religion in the second item was appropriate to its appearing in a Catholic intellectual journal.

(1) The present writer cannot have been very old when she first remembers Mr Thackeray in Paris, because when he offered her his arm on the Boulevard de la Madeleine, and said they would be taken for husband and wife, she felt sorry that French people should see such a tall stately Englishman mated to such an insignificant little wife. Her hand went straight up from the shoulder to rest upon his arm, aunts were left behind, the green Boulevard trees stretched before, the stroll seemed long with gay vistas. It cannot, however, have extended far, for there was a halt before the windows of the famous *confiseur*, Boissier, on the next Boulevard – named des Capucines. Boissier's boxes lay on a line with her eyes, and in the boxes were the *bonbons* in patterns.

'Don't you wish for that lovely blue box full of chocolates?'
'Oh yes!'

I recall my confusion still when Mr Thackeray dived into the shop, paid many francs, and ordered the large box to be sent home, as the result of my indiscreet exclamation.

After this, adoration passed all bounds. There is a straight-backed armchair of the Louis Philippe period in my possession, with cushioned arms on which I used to perch beside my grandmother, Mrs Ritchie, who was the great novelist's aunt.

In that 'Grandmother's chair' now sat Mr Thackeray, very fresh, very wise-looking behind his spectacles, very attractive with his thick curling hair and rosy cheeks. There was an element of mystery about him fascinating even to childhood. He always seemed alone. He had just been in America. He was on his way to Rome. He was meteoric. He was exceedingly sad and silent. He was wondrously droll. Above all, he was kind, so that the child perched beside him questioned him, 'Is you good?' (from the perch).

'Not so good as I should like to be' (from Mr Thackeray).

'Is you clever?'

'Well, I've written a book or two. Perhaps I am rather clever.'

'Is you pretty?'

'Oh! no, no, no! *No! No! No!*' (I recall Mr Thackeray bursting out laughing.)

'I think you's good, and you's clever, and you's pretty.'

Thackeray and childhood are linked wherever *The Rose and the Ring* is read in English nurseries and schoolrooms. It was to be drawn and written in Rome for Edith Story (Countess Peruzzi) the following New Year. At the time of which I write pictures were drawn for us Indian children in Paris. The occult Morale of Fairy Blackstick was somehow impersonated by Mr Thackeray in these pencil sketches, though to be sure he dealt poetic justice with his pencil, only in humorous moral to small heroines in well-appointed nurseries. In one of these faded sketches he appears above the steam of the evening tub looking gravely through his spectacles across a column of vapour to repress an uproar. In a pen-and-ink sketch of that time in my possession, a radiant little girl who is a foretaste of Betsinda and a lank-haired child in a shawl inhabit one slum. But she with the curls had secured a basket and a parasol. And she rides in the basket like any Park beauty, and holds her parasol aslant and knows her own dignity. And the other is the more wretched, and *she* carries a thin baby and a jug to the public-house. And in this study of temperaments we feel that when the child with the shawl is a grown woman she never *will* keep her eyes from envying a rival's happiness.

The moral conflict of everyday life, whether of rich or poor, of man or child, was never far from Thackeray's thoughts. And he ever seemed to remember not to judge lest we be judged. Once, on a later visit to Paris, naughtiness in the schoolroom, bewildering element to the culprit, was punished. A 'German tree' party was prohibited at Christmas time. Mr Thackeray called and was *told*. A kind aunt, conscious of over-severity, meant him to beg the prisoner off. But there was awful silence from the straight-backed chair. The world seemed to be coming to an end; the silence was felt by aunt and niece. Grave Mr Thackeray did not ask for another chance. But something was said about the necessity for discipline, and he spoke without a smile: 'I know some folks who were naughty when they were young and are good now.' Did he mean himself? Something in his manner suggested it and the disgrace seemed a bit lifted. But when the accused went to the party – for the informing of Mr Thackeray had apparently been considered a sufficient shock – the sting remained, he had *not* interfered.

His deliberation was awful. One day the cat of the household seemed to come in for his psychology. She leapt on to the deserted breakfast-table and stole a bit of fish. Thackeray stood alone in the room (except for the child). He watched the cat's movements contemplatively and then exclaimed with tragic intensity, 'Que voulez-vous? C'est plus fort qu'elle!'

In that Paris home of my grandmother... many literary souvenirs were gathered. But intimate things represent Thackeray better than 'gold-dust swept from the salons' – Elizabeth Barrett Browning's description of his conversation in Rome. In the following trait the home detail must appear. *The Newcomes* was finished in our house [in 1855]. My aunts left two white-capped maids for the service of Mr Thackeray and his daughters in the sunny apartment through September. And there he described the old cook, Annette, 'coming into the room one day to find me blubbering in a corner, I was writing the last page of *Newcome*'. The death of Colonel Newcome could not have been written without tears, any more than the parting of Hector and Andromache. But as for Annette, the witness of a novelist's emotion, she kept her comments on *Auteurs Anglais*, in the classic days of the *appartement*, for the subject of their gigantic tallness. 'Monsieur Thackeray était très grand et de belle carrure', but his friend, Monsieur Higgins (Jacob Omnium), 'était *encore* plus grand! C'étaient des géants et de beaux hommes pourtant.'[1]

(2) If there is a part of London still untransformed, it is the quiet green outside the precincts of Kensington Palace, where memories of Thackeray still gather for all who knew him in his later years. He lived at No. 2, Palace Green, opposite the peaceful elms which screen the outlying roofs of the Palace.... The red-brick Queen Anne mansion, one of the first examples in London of the style which Thackeray chose to build in, is associated with the writing of *Denis Duval*, those other romantic memoirs of the eighteenth century. The British admiral of so much amenity, Denis himself, became a very living person to the young visitors at Palace Green; and all around them the rooms were filled with beautiful things of the past, gathered together by the hand of Thackeray. The furniture, like the architecture of the house, was rare then; cabinets filled with old Chelsea and Dresden, old high-backed chairs and settees were not a common setting for a quiet domestic life, redolent of the methodical work of the master of the house. On the walls hung a small collection of paintings, amongst them a Watteau, a great portrait of Queen Anne by de Troye, and another of a brilliant little boy with a bird. This is the picture of Louis XVII with the ribbon of the Order of the Saint Esprit, found by Mr Thackeray in Italy. It is named today a Greuze, painted in his early manner at the Tuileries when Marie Antoinette was keeping her last sad court there. Denis Duval was to have described the French queen for us. His memoirs are not finished, for the pen was laid down as Denis concluded his description of his first naval engagement against the French, and the writer passed away in the night, as it seemed to us young ones who loved him, without a day's illness. We knew nothing of illness or fatigue in his grave and gay intercourse. The writing of *Denis Duval* was the most exciting thing imaginable....

[Mrs Warre Cornish proceeds] to describe the impression of a peaceful home where a great novelist possessed his soul, amid the distractions of two busy London seasons, with a great deal of detachment from the world.... It was not till [after their Young Street years] that both girls became old enough to be perfect companions to their father. Their social gifts were discovered with delight by Thackeray's friends in Rome, where the winter of 1854 was spent. Elizabeth Barrett Browning gave them of her best; and Mrs Kemble and

Mrs Sartoris, with the keys of art, drama, and song in their hands, found a response to their own strong English individuality in Thackeray's very English girls. Their own genuineness was their best inspiration with him. It may be said that to all who knew them, the daughters seemed made for the father, and the father for the daughters.

I now come to my own recollections of Palace Green. We ladies breakfasted alone, for Thackeray was already at work in his study – but he always came in at breakfast time, walking up and down the room as he talked. From time to time he would stride out of the study and give news of his story or consult his daughters about some detail of his work. But the mornings were full of the silent converse of work – not a cold silence that – and the converse of things and tools of work were never more attractive. Thackeray's written page was always a picture; and the drawing on wood-blocks, the revived art of the time, filled the house with beautiful vignettes for the initials of the *Roundabout Papers* or *Denis Duval*. His elder daughter had just written *The Story of Elizabeth* and kept house. Her powerful short story, 'Out of the World', was being illustrated by the young genius, Frederick Walker. Minny Thackeray, afterwards Mrs Leslie Stephen, with a complexion of milk and roses and soft wavy brown hair, had a good original vein of her own; her criticism at twenty was useful to Thackeray, and it was delivered in a voice of musical tone which was never more felt than when several people were talking. She had the gift of creating quiet about her, and withal an inimitable spirit of comedy....

But to return to the routine of the day. The morning's work was prolonged into the afternoon; the carriage came to the door to take us to the Exhibition or to a garden-party at Wimbledon or Twickenham. But daughters, and young visitors would wait dressed in the hall, and still Mr Thackeray wrote on, *their* only comment, 'Papa is getting on with his story.' Mr Thackeray was deliberate at all times and in everything. He would sit before the page and leave it blank until the fair script began to run, and he never retouched paragraphs of exquisite penmanship, showing here and there, however, as we examined them in the Centenary Exhibition, a faltering of the pen, as of the voice, in some emotional utterance.

When we reached the garden where the Thackerays were expected, what a warm welcome!... All this happy intercourse was, of course, accompanied by the strain of celebrity and appeals upon his powers which had been taxed by the editorship of the *Cornhill*. The sufferings of the unsuccessful in literature press very hardly on a man in such a position. 'In London there is nothing but fierce business, and then fierce pleasure, and then a spell of illness, during which one has leisure to think a little. I declare I have quite enjoyed two or three days this past week which kept me in bed', he wrote to my father. But from the 'spells of illness' he always arose with renewed good-will and extended helping hand.

One knew little of all this strain at the time. The memories of a girlhood may not be very valuable when all was zest and interest in the brilliant surface of life. Besides everything is known today about a great English name. But my recollections of Thackeray from childhood upwards become concerned, as I have said, with grave events, so that converse in his house was touched by the great realities of life. And I am permitted to place here in their order the facts around which all my memories turn of his grave outlook on life and beyond, in the brightness of his meridian.

From earliest years the friendship and affection of my father, William Ritchie, for his cousin, Thackeray, had been very great. [He died suddenly in 1862, in Calcutta, where he was Legal Member of the Council of India.] ... We were at that time living under the care of an aunt, whose flat in Paris was associated with Mr Thackeray's many visits there. The news of my father's death reached us in Paris before we had heard of his illness. Immediately on these events we were assembled at family-prayers, when a tall form stood in the doorway. Morning prayers were not concluded that day in the Paris salon. It was Mr Thackeray, who walked forward to the big armchair by the fire where my aunt seated herself beside him in silence. It was not the first time that he had brought her comfort and grief.... Mr Thackeray broke the silence to say that morning, 'Well, Charlotte, you know that he is now a Member of the Council of Heaven.'

In the following June, 1862, my sister, Mrs Freshfield, and I came to stay at Palace Green in the height of the London season, when the great International Exhibition was open at the South Kensington Museum, whereof the domes had just sprung into being. Mr Thackeray, whose *Roundabout Papers* were very popular, was welcomed and renowned on all sides. 'London' drove out to Kensington to find him and to compel him to come to 'London', but there was often a contemplative mood upon him. One day, as we were driving out, he began speaking of my father. 'One envies him his adoring faith', Mr Thackeray said, and his musing was as if he had found something that was not the best gift of 'adoring faith', but that amid perplexities he had found something that served him in very good stead as he faced 'the awful future to which we are all moving', his words in a letter to my aunt. He spoke of having been very near dying once, and he had felt perfectly calm. 'There is no such thing as dying hard', he said. We were driving out to a garden-party at Chief Baron Pollock's, near Twickenham. When we reached the lawns and groups of people a friend named Mr de la Pryme exclaimed, 'Here you are, Thackeray, with body enough for two and soul enough for three!'

I always see Mr Thackeray standing up under a spreading oak and saying meditatively to himself, 'Soul enough for *one*, that is all I care about. At least I believe it, I hope it.'

On another occasion of the daily drive in the July afternoon, he questioned us about our Church Catechism – 'what meaning had we been taught to give to the words "verily and indeed taken and received by the faithful in the Lord's Supper" '.

My sister and I had just been confirmed, and our instruction was very fresh in our minds, so a correct little Miss piped up, 'We were taught to lay the stress on the word faithful.'

'Oh,' said Mr Thackeray, with raised eyebrows, and a cold look, 'verily and indeed taken and received by the FAITHFUL.'

He shook his head, and his mouth closed with a very sensitive curve, and the long pause in the talk, which was so habitual to him, followed.

The teaching of this particular doctrine was very familiar to him. It is the special doctrine of the Evangelicals. Mr Thackeray heard of that whole body of doctrine from his mother, to whom he was always so tenderly and loyally attached. She was part of the family group, and must be described. Thackeray's mother was a noble figure, as I remember her. She had been . . . known as a great beauty. But not a trace of vanity was left about her dignified personality. Very tall and graceful in stature, with thick silver-grey hair, which curled naturally at the temples, she was possibly never more picturesque than in latter years. Her nose was her best feature. It was perfectly curved at the bridge, an *aesthetic* nose.

Her attitude and expressive face as she stood one day before portraits of Havelock and Outram made a granddaughter exclaim, 'Oh! Grannie you look like a Sibyl, lamenting over the fate of heroes.'

'My dear, I do not lament! I think they have gone to their crown!'

This was typical of her fine old Puritanism. With a strong individuality she had for years sunk it in that of an old man, her husband, and her young grandchildren. She had a partiality for lost causes; though a Tory in Major Carmichael-Smyth's country home, she became a Republican in Paris, and alarmed her friends during the days of the Barricades of '48 by wearing the Republican cockade on her majestic cashmere, when it was yet unsafe to do so. She had become a fervent Calvinist, under the instruction of the great Protestant Pasteur, Adolphe Monod, in Paris. . . .

William Thackeray, who had visited his mother every day when she lived in Brompton Crescent near his house in Onslow Square, had brought her to live with him at Palace Green, when she became a widow for the second time [in 1861]. I think the silent converse came to his help in his relation with his mother – the converse of deeds, not words – and in her absence of constant letters – and, better still, the silence in his soul, which he kept in the midst of busy life, and which was known to her. So that she waited for him. And in her case the peculiar converse was helped by large eyes of tender pleading, with irises of a deep blue. At his mother's wish, Thackeray went to hear the preaching in Onslow Square church, of the popular Evangelical preacher, of the day, Mr Molyneux – 'the man is very eloquent, and no doubt sincere. He has a great flow of words, but the rubbish! . . .', I heard him say. What made his eloquence folly was the isolation of one dogma, that of salvation by faith alone. . . .

Of his own Christian impressions he dwelt chiefly on the Epistle of St James, with its twofold recommendation of the widows and orphans in their affliction, and the 'keeping unspotted from the world'; and then the Anglican Liturgy, as chanted in the Temple Church or the Abbey. He often attended Morning Prayers in Kensington church at nine o'clock. One day the Anglican chant, of which he was very fond, was too much for him, even as it rose to the vaulted roof of the Abbey, in the verse 'Neither delighteth He in any man's legs.' The suggestion of men's legs, and their far removal from delight, was too much for his Hogarthian vision. Once he paid a visit to a Ritualist church. But I remember that the sight of the clergy in copes, filing in procession, with their *heads on one side*, each behind the other, sent him out....

My last visit to Palace Green was with my mother in the autumn of 1863. The life was unchanged. Mr and Mrs Charles Allston Collins were almost part of the family circle. She, Dickens's younger daughter, now Mrs Perugini, has paid her tribute at the Centenary to the memory of the great novelist by taking up her pen for the first time to depict her first acquaintance with Thackeray and his reconciliation with her father.[2] Mr Collins was the chosen friend, though many years younger, of Thackeray in his latest days; deeply in sympathy with him, one may say his disciple, in philosophy of life.... Charles Collins was a short, dignified man, with a well proportioned figure; his face and finely chiselled features had a very spiritual expression. He would remain the only one grave whilst we were convulsed with laughter at his reflections on the struggles and incongruities of life. Mr Thackeray delighted in the companionship of the younger man, who had the melancholy humour of a Jaques, with bitterness tempered by the Master. Mr Thackeray, with a consummate gift of satire and a burlesque fancy, which made humanity more grotesque to him than to the eyes of case-hardened people, was more tolerant of life than the disciple....

In general society there were pauses in Thackeray's talk, which were part of all that deliberate converse of his, so well understood at home, but embarrassing to strangers. And, again, whether in society or at home, the moral struggle of life seemed ever present with him. And this hardly made for conversational flow. All felt that he was a spectator rather than an actor in life, and this was the more alarming that his standard was very high. When men, still more women, were mediocre in feeling he hardly took it calmly. For instance, when a lady with youth, name and influence on her side, attended a dog-fight, Thackeray manifested his indignation in the presence of a young man of her circle, who gazed in wonder at the sight of a moralist in a rage. Or when a sycophantic tutor of twelve baby-noblemen was discussed, instead of being amused by the Academic favourite's bows and gestures, Thackeray shuddered, as if his spine was cold. All this sensitiveness is unknown to our generation.

Youth, however, kept its halo for the author of *Esmond*. One day, in the studio of the sculptor Foley, young men in town were being discussed. A friend of my father's had met Mr Thackeray to judge a marble bust portrait of William Ritchie. Mr Courtenay, a man of the world, was describing a young man who had just come into his estate, and was laying down wine with great judgement. 'There is nothing like him,' said Mr Thackeray, enthusiastically, 'he is what I should like to be, very handsome and very good! I don't care a bit to be clever.'

NOTES

1. 'Thackeray is the only Englishman of letters who had and retains a popular name with the Parisians at large. The restaurant where his portrait in oils, as a young man, is preserved in a small panelled dining-room is Therion's, Boulevard St Germain (Rive Gauche). Outside the restaurant hangs a sign. It represents the present Therion in the company of the novelist' [Mrs Warre Cornish's footnote]. There were many jokes current about Thackeray and the gigantic Higgins, when seen together: 'Gog and Magog', etc.
2. See below, II, 306, for her reminiscences of Thackeray.

The Tenderest-hearted Cynic
ELIZA LYNN LINTON

From *My Literary Life* (1899) pp. 59–66. Mrs Lynn Linton (1822–98) was an exceedingly prolific and professional journalist and author – 'Good for anything, and thoroughly reliable' remarked Dickens, to whose weeklies she contributed regularly – G. S. Layard, *Mrs Lynn Linton* (1901) p. 81. Of the authors in this chapter, 'Landor, Dickens, Thackeray', she best knew Landor, whose protégée and 'dear daughter' she was. Her knowledge of Thackeray was slight, though she was perceptive about him; why he was calling upon her in Paris (in 1853) I do not know.

I remember George Henry Lewes telling me the difference between Thackeray and Dickens in the way of service to a friend. Dickens, he said, would not give you a farthing of money, but he would take no end of trouble for you. He would spend a whole day, for instance, in looking for the most suitable lodgings for you, and would spare himself neither time nor fatigue. Thackeray would take two hours' grumbling indecision and hesitation in writing a two-line testimonial, but he would put his hand into his pocket and give you a handful of gold and bank-notes if you wanted them. I know of neither characteristic personally; but I repeat the illustration as Mr Lewes gave it.

Talking of Dickens and Thackeray, it is curious how continually they are put in opposition to each other. Each stood at the head of a distinct school of thought, representing different aspects of human life, and each had his followers and adherents, for the most part arrayed in self-made hostile lines, with a very small percentage of that *tertium quid* – those impartial critics who could admire both with equal favour. This kind of antagonism is very common. It was repeated in the case of Jenny Lind and Alboni, and in a minor degree with Leighton and Millais, as with Emerson and Carlyle. But it sprang in each instance from the admirers, not the principals; and in the case of Thackeray and Dickens it was emphatically made for and not by them.

Both these men illustrated the truth which so few see, or acknowledge when even they do see it, of that divorcement of intellect and character which leads to what men are pleased to call inconsistencies. Thackeray, who saw the faults and frailties of human nature so clearly, was the gentlest-hearted, most generous, most loving of men. Dickens, whose whole mind went to almost morbid tenderness and sympathy, was infinitely less plastic, less self-giving, less personally sympathetic.... He never forgave when he thought he had been slighted; and he was too proud and self-respecting for flunkeyism. He declined to be lionised, and stuck to his own order.... Hence Charles Dickens, even in the zenith of his fame, was never to be seen at the houses of the great....

Thackeray, on the contrary, like Moore, loved the grace and delicacy and inborn amenities of what is called 'good society'. He was no more of a snob than Dickens, no more of a tuft-hunter, but he was more plastic, more frankly influenced by that kind of social sensuality which finds its enjoyment in good living, good manners, pretty women, and refined talk. Dickens had no eye for beauty, *per se*. He could love a comparatively plain woman – and did; but Thackeray's fancy went out to loveliness; and cleverness alone, without beauty – which ruled Dickens – would never have stirred his passions. Both men could, and did, love deeply, passionately, madly, and the secret history of their lives has yet to be written.[1] It never will be written now, and it is best that it should not be.

But, I repeat again what was said before, in each the intellectual appreciation of life and the personal temperament and character were entirely antagonistic. The one, who wrote so tenderly, so sentimentally, so gushingly, had a strain of hardness in his nature which was like a rod of iron in his soul. The other, who took humanity as he found it, who saw its faults and appraised it at its lower value – yet did not despise what he could not admire – was of all men the most loving, the most tender-hearted, the least inflexible.

I did not know either man intimately; but if not the rose itself, I knew those who stood near. Their close friends were also mine, and I heard more than I saw. Many secret confidences were passed on to me, which, of course, I have kept sacred; and both men would have been surprised had they known how much I knew of things uncatalogued and unpublished. This consciousness of unsuspected participation gives a strange sense of secret intimacy, which adds a curious piquancy to the outward formalities *de rigueur* between those who are personally unfamiliar. I felt this keenly when Mr Thackeray did me the honour of calling on me in Paris. I was keeping house with a young Anglo-French woman, part of whose patrimony consisted of a pretty little apartment up five flights of stairs. We had only two rooms between us, each furnished in the French way of bed and sitting-room conjoined, where every piece of furniture was contrived a 'double debt to pay'. Up these five toilsome flights came the great, good, kindly man; and I well remember how he chose a box rather than a chair for his seat, and how he committed the French mistake in manners by putting his hat on the bed. His daughters were then young girls living with their grandmother, and his affection for them was one of the most touching things about him. He asked me many questions as to my life, and was beyond measure gentle and friendly.

NOTE

1. Referring, presumably, to Jane Brookfield and to Dickens's actress friend (or mistress) Ellen Ternan. Later Mrs Lynn Linton mentions how deeply Thackeray 'felt the unsoundness and instability of a certain woman, on account of whom, while smarting from his disappointment, he wrote that bitter little paragraph about dragging women's hearts as you would drag fishponds' (*My Literary Life*, p. 74).

Tender-hearted, Almost Womanly
THEODORE MARTIN

(1) from Theodore Martin, *Helena Faucit (Lady Martin)* (1900) p. 258; (2) from Herman Merivale and Frank T. Marzials, *Life of W. M. Thackeray* (1891) pp. 233–7. Martin (1816–1909), lawyer, parliamentary agent and man of letters, was knighted (1880) for his biography of the Prince Consort. Among his other writings were the 'Bon Gaultier' ballads (1845, 1849), in collaboration with William Edmonstoune Aytoun. In 1851 he married the famous actress Helen Faucit (1817–98) and settled at 31 Onslow Square, Kensington, where Thackeray became a neighbour in 1854: 'we very soon found ourselves on the most friendly footing with him' (*Helena Faucit*, p. 257), and Thackeray often referred to them as his 'dear neighbours'. His daughters, after some initial nervousness before the great actress, became and remained very friendly with her. Martin supplied Herman Merivale with memories of the novelist for his *Life*.

(1) All our recollections of Thackeray were delightful. He used to pay us long visits at breakfast, and then he talked with

frankness and unreserve, more like those of a large-hearted boy than of a man who had seen life in so many phases, many of them of a kind to induce the *pensieri stretti*, for which strangers thought he was peculiar. His nature was obviously one that yearned for sympathy. It was full of tenderness, and showed it, where he was sure it would be undertstood. In fact, of all men I have known he was the most tender-hearted; in this respect, indeed, almost womanly. He always showed a marked respect for my wife's opinion in all matters of literature and art. What he thought of her we learned from a note which came into my hands many years after his death. It was addressed to Lady Knighton, inviting her to meet the well-known Helen Faucit at dinner, in which he spoke of her as 'one of the sweetest women in Christendom' – a tribute which came to her as an agreeable surprise, as if from the lips of her old friend.

(2) The Martins were friends with whom the novelist was in thorough sympathy; and to Sir Theodore's kindness I owe some interesting facts which he allows me to publish. . . . The estrangement between Dickens and himself, rising out of the Garrick battle, ended in the hall of the Athenaeum, where Sir Theodore Martin was the witness of his going after Dickens when he had passed him one day, and saying at the foot of the stairs some words to the effect that he could not bear to be on any but the old terms. He insisted on shaking hands; and Dickens did.[1] 'The next time I saw Dickens,' (it was not long after) Sir Theodore writes to me, 'he was looking down into the grave of his great rival, in Kensal Green. How he must have rejoiced, I thought, that they had so shaken hands.' Sir Theodore, whose bond with him was nothing if not literary, thought Thackeray curiously free from literary jealousy; and certainly nothing bears this out more entirely than his casual remarks on Dickens in the Brookfield letters, such as 'Get *David Copperfield*; by Jingo, it's beautiful; it beats the yellow chap of this month [*Pendennis*] hollow.' . . . This form of literary reverence was with Thackeray always the same. A popular novelist, in the presence of a loved friend of Thackeray, one day justified something he had said, or done, or written, by remarking, 'Sir Walter Scott said, or did, or wrote, so-and-so.' 'I do not think', answered Thackeray, 'that

it becomes either you or me to speak of Sir Walter Scott as if we were his equals. Such men as you or I should take off our hats at the very mention of his name.' . . .

Another curious incident in Thackeray's intercourse with Sir Theodore Martin, which has not been published before, I tell on his authority, and with Mrs Ritchie's permission. It is interesting because it does, for once, bring home one of his character-bits to the original. The two were walking one afternoon through the playrooms at Spa – I tell the story in Sir Theodore's words, for I am not like to find better – and stopped at the Rouge et Noir table to look on. Thackeray touched his elbow, and asked him to look at a tall man, in a seedy brown frock-coat, at the other end of the table. The man's appearance was that of a broken-down gentleman, who had still the remains of a certain distinction of manner. They walked away, and Thackeray said, 'That was the original of my Deuceace; I have not seen him since the day he drove me down in his cabriolet to my broker's in the City, where I sold out my patrimony and handed it over to him.'[2] Thackeray then added that this man and another had, in the early days, knowing that he had money when he came of age, induced him to play écarté with them, letting him win at first and leading him on until they had eased him, not literally of his patrimony, but of a round fifteen hundred pounds. His losses were otherwise caused by the *Constitutional*, and an India bank, and other unlucky ventures of his own or his guardians. No doubt, in that graphic history of the Bundelcund Bank, he had his own Rummun Loll, as he had his own Deuceace.[3] But there was no bitterness in his heart or voice, says Sir Theodore, only pity, as he remarked of his old acquaintance at Spa, 'Poor devil! my money doesn't seem to have thriven with him!' The same courteous informant writes to me, 'You are quite safe in saying that Deuceace was drawn from life. I am *quite* sure of what I told you. Well do I remember, as we walked out into the soft, sweet air of a summer evening, how a sort of sadness seemed to settle upon Thackeray, as if the recollection of what he told me had been too much for him; and he said, although it was quite early, "I think I'll go home to my hotel", which he did. He told me other things in his life of a very striking kind, but I know they were meant for myself alone. Poor fellow, he had some terribly bitter experiences.'

NOTES

1. On the estrangement between Dickens and Thackeray, see below, II, 313. Ray quotes (*LPP*, I, cxxiii) an unpublished letter of Martin's (12 Oct 1906) which gives a fuller account of their reconciliation: 'There were no lookers on what passed between Thackeray & Dickens but myself. I was standing in the Athenaeum Hall chatting with Thackeray – Dickens came out of the Reading Room, passed us quite close, & taking no notice of either of us. "There's Dickens!" Thackeray exclaimed, & went so quickly after Dickens, that he caught him at the foot of the stairs. He held out his hand to Dickens, saying a few words, and then Dickens took his hand. A few words & Thackeray came back to me, and told me what had passed between them. The speaking was chiefly Thackeray's – to the [purpose that] "the estrangement must not go on, that they should shake hands, and be the friends they had used to be".' In another account, written out for Lady Priestley (who had 'heard various versions' of this anecdote, and asked him to give her the authentic one), Martin added that Dickens seemed at first rather taken aback, but he held out his hand, and some friendly words were exchanged: ' "I loved the man," said Thackeray "and could not resist the impulse." It was like his tender nature, to which the rupture of a once-cherished friendship was an unforgettable pain. A few weeks after I was reminded of the incident by seeing Dickens standing by the open grave into which Thackeray had just been lowered, and looking down into it with a look of earnest sadness. It was not difficult to imagine what thoughts were passing through his mind. The reconciliation at the Athenaeum would be among them' – Lady Priestley, *The Story of a Lifetime* (1904) p. 44.
2. Deuceace, the card-sharper, appears in *The Yellowplush Papers, Vanity Fair, Pendennis, The Newcomes*, and other stories. See Ray's 'How Thackeray Lost his Patrimony', *LPP*, I, 506–8, where it is estimated that he gambled away £3000 or more in his Cambridge days and soon afterwards.
3. Rummum Loll, the unscrupulous Indian merchant, persuades Colonel Newcome to invest in the Bundelcund Bank, disastrously (*The Newcomes*). Thackeray did indeed lose most of what remained of his patrimony through the collapse of a Calcutta bank in 1833.

Father at Work

ANNE THACKERAY RITCHIE

Sources: *Biog. Intros* (references after every item), except where otherwise stated. Thackeray was partial to writing in hotels, clubs, and other non-domestic places, but inevitably much of his work was done at home. He tried, says Anny, to write a little every day, 'were it only one line.... Sometimes he would show us a few lines and say, there has been my day's work. I have sat before it till I nearly cried – nothing would come' (MS. Reminiscences, 1864–5, in *Wisdom*, p. 365). Here are a few of her many published reminiscences of her father at work; see index for other items by her.

I can remember the morning Helen [Pendennis] died. My father was in his study in Young Street, sitting at the table at which he wrote. It stood in the middle of the room, and he used to sit facing the door. I was going into the room, but he motioned me away. An hour afterwards he came into our schoolroom, half-laughing and half-ashamed, and said to us: 'I do not know what James can have thought of me when he came in with the tax-gatherer just after you left, and found me blubbering over Helen Pendennis's death.' ...

Popular as *Pendennis* proved to be, my father did not escape criticism, and the *Examiner* especially found fault with his descriptions of literary life, and accused him of trying to win favour with the non-literary classes by decrying his own profession. The *North British Review* published an article defending him, though not altogether agreeing with his views. There seems to have been a fashion in those days for lecturing a writer about his private personal characteristics, as well as for discussing and criticising his professional writings. Few people took blame to heart more keenly than did my father, and he wrote to the *Morning Chronicle* in reply to the attack in the *Examiner* ....[1]   (II, xxxix, xlii)

One of the things I remember his saying about *Esmond* I have already put into print. It was when he exclaimed in pleasure and excitement, that a young publisher called George Smith – almost a boy, he said – had come with a liberal cheque in his pocket, to offer for the unfinished novel.[2]

I have also written of a sort of second-sight my father used sometimes to speak of. Occasionally when he described places, he said he could hardly believe he had not been there; and in one of the battles in *Esmond*, he told us that the very details of the foreground were visible to him as he wrote, even to some reeds growing by a streamlet, and the curve of the bank by which it flowed. I find a sentence in one of his letters which corroborates this impression.

'I was pleased to find Blenheim', he wrote to his mother in

August 1852, 'was just exactly the place I had figured to myself, except that the village is larger; but I fancied I had actually been there, so like the aspect of it was to what I looked for. . . .' (VII, xxv)

My father used to say that from long habit he never could think so well as when he held his pen in his hand. . . . Much of the work was done by his favourite gold pen. My father's gold pen lasted for some six years, and produced the later Christmas Books. The earlier books were drawn with pencil and with etching needle, and with fine point and brush. . . .

My father was weaving many spells with his gold pen during the winter of 1853, which we spent in Rome. *The Rose and the Ring* was begun there. There is a letter, in which he says, 'I have broke my ruby pen, which won't write upright, and finish my scrap with the gold one, which won't write slanting.' He had many gold pens, but only one that he really loved. It was with this one that he did his best work, and drew his best etchings, such as the drawings for *The Rose and the Ring*. After the pen failed him (he used it for many years) he complained that he couldn't draw comfortably any more, and only used quill pens. He liked a pair of sharp scissors to be upon his writing-table, with which to cut the nibs at a certain reverse angle to that which is generally adopted. It seems a small detail to dwell upon, but the look of my father's pens and pencils and writing-table seemed as much part of himself as his watch or his spectacles. His pencils were our admiration, so evenly cut were they, so finely pointed.   (IX, xlvii, lv)

The pictures [which he drew] were rarely preserved by himself, nor put away by us with any care. The familiar stream flowed on, loved but unheeded by us; and among the many drawings that he devised only a certain number remain in our possession. In all my remembrance he never had one of his own drawings framed, and when I was a child I remember a great scrap-book which was given me to play with and to work my will upon. I can only once remember a questioning word from him concerning some scissor-points with which I had ornamented some of his sketches. In later years, by his desire, I have washed off the drawings from many and many a wood-block; and I remember once destroying his whole day's work in my anxiety to be of use. But although he certainly never wished us to make much of his work, all that belonged to it and to his art was of vivid and serious reality to him, and of unfailing interest and suggestion.... It was only when he came to etch upon steel or to draw for the engraver upon wood that he complained of effort and want of ease; and we used often to wish that his drawings could be given as they were first made, without the various transmigrations of wood and steel, and engravers' toil and printers' ink. Once or twice experiments were tried, but they never came to anything.[3]

When my father wrote a poem he used to be more agitated than when he wrote in prose. He would come into the room worried and excited, saying, 'Here are two more days wasted. I have done nothing at all. It has taken me four mornings' work to produce six lines.' Then, after a further struggle, all would go well. There is some such account given in the life of Lady Blessington concerning the little poem called 'Piscator and Piscatrix'. He nearly gave it up in despair; but finally the pretty verses came to him. I have still some of his poems torn down the centre. They are as often as not in pencil. (XIII, xxiii)

NOTES

1. John Forster criticised Thackeray for disparaging the literary profession in *Pendennis*, in *Examiner*, 5 Jan 1850, p. 2. Thackeray replied lengthily in the *Morning Chronicle*, 12 Jan (see *LPP*, II, 629–35), and Forster responded with another *Examiner* article, 'The Dignity of Literature', 19 Jan, p. 35.

2. 'One day, as we were with our governess, my father came in, in great excitement. "There's a young fellow just come," said he; "he has brought a thousand pounds in his pocket; he has made me an offer for my book, it's the most spirited, handsome offer, I scarcely like to take him at his word; he's hardly more than a boy, his name is George Smith; he is waiting there now, and I must go back"'– *Chapters from Some Memoirs* (1894) p. 130.

3. *The Orphan of Pimlico and Other Sketches, Fragments and Drawings*, by William Makepeace Thackeray, with some notes by Anne Isabella Thackeray (1876) pp. v–vii.

Writing and Reading *The Newcomes*

VARIOUS

(1) Anne Thackeray Ritchie, in *Biog. Intros*, VIII, xxii–xxxix; (2) from Frederick Locker-Lampson, *My Confidences* (1896) pp. 300–1; (3) 'A Young Lady, Not Then Married', quoted in *Biog. Intros*, VIII, xxxvi–vii; (4) Edward Wilberforce, in Wilson, I, 166–8; (5) from James Russell Lowell, letter of 11 Aug 1855, in *Letters of James Russell Lowell*, ed. Henry James (1894) I, 265–6; (6) from Christopher P. Cranch, 'A Few Reminiscences of Thackeray', *Critic* (New York), X (1887) 315–16, in Wilson, II, 192–5. The final pages of *The Newcomes*, describing the death of Colonel Newcome, became one of the most admired instances of mid-century pathos, and, as General Wilson reports (II, 91), 'no passage in all his writings was more frequently read to American friends than [this] exquisite and touching description'.

(1) [In the postscript to *The Newcomes*, Thackeray describes] the little wood near to Berne, in Switzerland, into which he strayed one day, and where, as he tells us, 'the story was actually revealed to him'. Some moments [writes his daughter] have their special characteristics, and I can still remember that day, and the look of the fields in which we were walking, and the silence of the hour, and the faint, sultry summer mountains, with the open wood at the foot of the sloping stubble. My father had been silent and preoccupied when we first started, and was walking thoughtfully apart. We waited till he came back to us, saying he now saw his way quite clearly, and he was cheerful and in good spirits as we returned to the inn....

At home in London, in Paris sunshine, through the Roman winter (which was trying in many ways), the work kept steadily on. I can remember writing constantly to his dictation all this year, though the details only come to me in a confused sort of way. On one occasion he was at work in some room in which he slept, high up in a hotel; the windows looked out upon a wide and pleasant prospect, but I cannot put a name to my remembrance; and then he walked up and down, he paused and then he paced the room again, stopping at last at the foot of the bed, where he stood rolling his hand over the brass ball at the end of the bedstead. He was at the moment dictating that scene in which poor Jack Belsize pours out his story to Clive and J. J. at Baden. 'Yes,' my father said, with a sort of laugh, looking down at his own hand (he was very much excited at the moment), 'this is just the sort of thing a man might do at such a time.' It was in this same room, in this hotel in past-land, that he christened his heroine, still walking up and down the room, and making up his mind what her name should be. I wonder how many thousands of Ethels were christened by him, and how many have Miss Yonge for a godmother! He used, as I have said, to dictate very constantly, but when he came to a critical point he would send his secretary away and write for himself. He always said he could think best with a pen in his hand. A pen to an author is like the wand of a necromancer, it compels the spell....

I remember writing the last chapters of *The Newcomes* to my father's dictation. I wrote on as he dictated more and more slowly until he stopped short altogether, in the account of Colonel Newcome's last illness, when he said that he must now take the pen into his own hand, and he sent me away....

The manuscript of *The Newcomes* is now at Charterhouse, in the museum, and wishing to verify my own impressions, I wrote to a friend there, asking him whereabouts my father's handwriting came in, in the last chapter. He answered, that he had been to look at the manuscript, and that my writing left off, as I imagined, with the account of the illness in chapter 52. My father then continued with his own hand, and it was with his cousin Charlotte's pen and on her writing-table, that he completed his work.[1]

(2) I will now give a reminiscence of Thackeray [writes Frederick Locker-Lampson, on whom see below, II, 364] which certainly, for my own sake, I mention with reluctance; but I wish to give you a true idea of the man, and this will show you he was very sensitive. I happened to meet him as I was leaving the Travellers' Club.... He said, 'What do you think of the last number?' (No. II or III of *The Newcomes*). He himself was evidently not quite satisfied with it. 'I like it immensely' was my cordial rejoinder. A word or two more passed respecting the illustrations, which had been sharply criticised,

and just as we parted I was tactless idiot enough to add, 'But, my dear fellow, perhaps there may be some kind people who will say that *you* did the cuts and Doyle the letterpress.' On this Thackeray's jaw dropped, and he exclaimed bitterly, 'Oh! really, that's your opinion, is it?' I saw at once what a mistake I had made; but I could only reply, 'I spoke in fun, pure fun; you know perfectly well how much I admire your writings, and also Doyle's cuts.' But Thackeray would have none of it, and turned wrathfully away in the direction of Pimlico. However, his wrath, I presume, died away in the large and charitable air of the Green Park, for when I met him the day after he was as amiable as ever.

The fact is, I had so exalted an opinion of Thackeray and of his writings that it seemed impossible such a demi-god should care for aught anybody said; whereas, like Tennyson, he felt everything that everybody said.

(3) [On 23 April 1855, Thackeray was lecturing in Coventry, and stayed with Charles Bray, a friend of George Eliot's. Another close friend of George Eliot's, Sarah Hennell, was present: and an anonymous young lady left a record of the occasion.] At last he came, very quietly, but such a presence! We had to look up a long way, he was so tall. . . . He talked in a pleasant friendly way. The coming number of *The Newcomes* [No. XX, chs 62–5, published May 1855], of course, was in all our minds. Miss Hennell, as our spokeswoman, said, 'Mr Thackeray, we want you to let Clive marry Ethel. Do let them be happy.' He was surprised at our interest in his characters. 'What a fuss you make about my yellow books here in the country! In town no one cares for them. They haven't the time. The characters once created *lead me*, and I follow where they direct. I cannot tell the events that wait on Ethel and Clive.' The high world was full of Ethels who sold themselves voluntarily. 'I was talking', he said, 'to a very nice girl at a party in London, when I saw her start as a gentleman – an artist – entered the room. "Oh, that's it," I said, "is it?" She coloured and said, "What is the use? He hasn't a farthing", and walked away. They were following each other about, evidently in love, but in three weeks or so, it was announced that a marriage had been arranged between this young lady and some Lord Farintosh. . . .'[2]

He told Miss Hennell that he did not like 'dearest Laura' and that he made his women without character, or else so bad, because that was as he knew them. I was told that next morning, when they asked him whether he had had a good night, he answered, 'How could I, with Colonel Newcome making a fool of himself as he has done?'

Mrs Bray: 'But why did you let him?'

Thackeray: 'Oh, it was in him to do it. He must.'

(4) Just after the completion of *The Newcomes*, Thackeray told me he was walking to the post office in Paris to send off the concluding chapters when he came upon an old friend of his who was also known to me. 'Come into this archway,' said Thackeray to his friend, 'and I will read you a bit of *The Newcomes*.' The two went aside out of the street, and there Thackeray read the scene of the Colonel's death. The friend's emotion grew more and more intense as the reading went on, and at the close he burst out crying, and exclaimed, 'If everybody else does like that the fortune of the book is made!' 'And everybody did', was my comment. 'Not I', replied Thackeray. 'I was quite unmoved when I killed the Colonel.[3] What was nearly too much for me was the description of the "Boy" saying "Our Father". I was dictating to my daughter, and I had the greatest difficulty in controlling my voice and not let her see that I was almost breaking down. I don't think, however, that she suspected it.'

(5) Thackeray gave us (Story, Cranch – whom I brought over from Paris – and me)[4] a dinner at the Garrick Club. The ... dinner was very funny. Thackeray had ordered it for *two*, and was afraid there would not be enough – an apprehension which he expressed very forcibly to the waiter. He said something to Story which pleased me wonderfully. There were some cutlets which *did* look rather small. 'Eat one of 'em, Story,' said he; 'it will make you feel a little hungry at first, but you'll *soon* get over it.' The benevolent tone he gave to the *soon* was delightfully comic. After dinner, we went to a room over the 'Cyder Cellar' to smoke. Thackeray called for a glass of gin and water, and presently sent for the last *Newcomes*, saying that he would read us the death of Colonel Newcome. While he was reading, came in a tall man in his shirt-sleeves, and

cried, 'Well, Thack, I've read your last number. Don't like it. It's a failure. Not so good as the rest!' This was Maurice John O'Connell.[5] Thackeray was not at all disturbed, but sent him off cavalierly.[6] While reading one of the worst tirades of the 'Campaigner' he interrupted himself to say, 'That's my she-devil of a mother-in-law, you know, whom I have the good-luck to possess still.' I complained of his marrying Clive and Ethel as an artistic blunder. He acknowledged that it was so. 'But then, you see, what could a fellow do? So many people wanted 'em married. To be sure, I had to kill off poor little Rosey rather suddenly, but shall not a man do what he will with his own? Besides, we can hope they won't have any children.'

(6) [One of Lowell's fellow guests, the poet Christopher P. Cranch, also describes this occasion 'exactly as it occurred,' he claims, ' – as there has been another version published, not quite correct'. After a 'simple but excellent' dinner at the Garrick, 'spiced by our host's conversation,' Thackeray said, 'Come, let us adjourn to the Cyder Cellar.' There he ordered punch and cigars] and while we were enjoying this postprandial luxury, Thackeray said, 'By the way, have you seen the last number of *The Newcomes*?' We said we had not. 'Then,' said Thackeray, 'I should very much like to read you some of it. It is just out.'

We all of course expressed an eager pleasure in this opportunity of hearing him read anything from his own books. Whereupon he summoned a waiter and said, 'Here, waiter – here's a shilling – I want you to go out and buy for me the last number of *The Newcomes*.' It was soon brought; and Thackeray began to read, and read for an hour, I should think, in his quiet half-plaintive voice, some of the closing scenes in this novel. We were all deeply interested. I think the last page he read described the death-bed of Colonel Newcome. As he closed we thanked him cordially and Mr Lowell begged for the number from which he had read, that he might keep it as a souvenir of this delightful afternoon.... Thackeray's reading had a charm peculiar to itself. It recalled his appearance as a lecturer in New York some years before, when he gave us those delightful chapters in the *English Humourists* which are still just as delightful in print. His delivery was perfectly simple and unambitious of effect and stood in marked contrast in this respect to that of Mr Dickens.

He had hardly got through his reading from *The Newcomes*, and our thoughts were all full of the pathos of the closing scenes, and toned by his artless rendering of it, when a door opened, and in rushed half a dozen young men – artists and small authors, I think, who in a boisterous way surrounded him, and gave vent to all sorts of small shallow talk in a free and familiar style of manners – all of which jarred on my feelings. I began to remember that Thackeray had two sides to him, the thoughtful, the tender, the purely literary, and – well, call it the Bohemian. For he seemed to be on intimate terms with this noisy matter-of-fact crowd, and I could not notice that their irruption into the room had any jarring effect upon him. I remember that my two friends and I very soon took our leave: for we found nothing at all edifying in the chatter of these young Philistines, and we did not want to have the effect of the previous hour disturbed by such an uncongenial breeze, and decline upon any lower range of feeling than we had been enjoying.

NOTES

1. This manuscript is described by J. S. Sutherland in his *Thackeray at Work* (1974) ch. 4, and in 'The Inhibiting Secretary in Thackeray's Fiction', *Modern Language Quarterly*, XXXII (1971) 175–88, where it is argued that the practice of dictating harmed his art.

2. The foolish but weakly young aristocrat in *The Newcomes*, considered 'a great catch', to whom Edith Newcome is engaged for a while. The 'dearest Laura' mentioned in the next sentence is the heroine of *Pendennis*; she reappears in *The Newcomes* and other novels as Mrs Arthur Pendennis. An American friend, Maunsell B. Field, describes a walk through Paris with Thackeray, who was accosted by 'a tall and uncommonly handsome' young Englishman: 'I overheard Thackeray ask what had brought him to Paris. He answered that he had come for pleasure. "And have you found it?" drawled Thackeray, with a slight sneer in his voice, as if pleasure, as a pursuit, was an unworthy object for any man's ambition. When they parted, and Thackeray again took my arm, he said, "Of course you know the young man with whom I was just speaking?" I answered that I did not. "You don't mean to tell me," he continued, "that you, who have been so much in London, don't know him?" I assured him that I had no recollection that I had ever before met the gentleman. "Why," he said, "that is the Marquis of Farintosh." "And *who* is

the Marquis of Farintosh?" I pursued. "Why, the Marquis of Bath, of course", he replied. This led to a conversation about several other characters in his books. He told me that his own mother was the prototype of Helen Pendennis, but that the copy fell very far short of the original' – *Memories of Many Men* (New York, 1874) pp. 132–3.

3. But see above, II, 195, for Mrs Warre Cornish's account of his 'blubbering' as he wrote this scene, and *LPP*, III, 459, for his sad and solemn thoughts on finishing the novel.

4. All Americans: W. W. Story, sculptor (see below, II, 254); Christopher Pearce Cranch (1813–92), poet and Unitarian minister; Lowell (1819–91), poet and critic, who had first met Thackeray during the 1852 voyage to America, and subsequently met him there and in London.

5. Morgan, not Maurice, as Wilson notes (I, 327n): son of Daniel O'Connell, 'the Liberator'.

6. Sutherland, *Thackeray at Work*, p. 81, quotes from a magazine article of 1881 another account of Lowell's hearing Thackeray read this episode. They had met in the street, and Thackeray looked very serious and sounded weary and afflicted. 'He saw the kindly enquiry in the poet's eyes, and said, "Come into Evans's, and I'll tell you all about it. *I have killed the Colonel.*" ' He read the death-scene to Lowell, and 'When he came to the final *Adsum*, the tears which had been swelling his lids for some time trickled down his face, and the last word was almost an inarticulate sob.'

The Real Thackeray

GEORGE AUGUSTUS SALA

(1) from Wilson, II, 30–2; (2) from *Things I Have Seen and People I Have Known* (1894) ch. 1, 'The Real Thackeray', I, 22–7, 30–3, 36–44. 'Dickens and Thackeray were the friends of my youth, my editors in my maturity', wrote Sala in his Preface (I, xviii), and he was specially proud that both novelists were much impressed by the essay 'The Key of the Street' (*Household Words*, 6 Sep 1851), which effectively established him as a leading periodical-writer (see below, II, 239). Sala (1828–95), special correspondent, editor, novelist, and miscellaneous author, became 'the most active and successful journalist of the Victorian era... extremely able and courageous' (*Saturday Review*, 16 Feb 1895, pp. 223–4). He met Thackeray, whose works he had long admired, in the 1840s, through his brother. Later Thackeray helped and encouraged him, commending him to the publisher George Smith as 'a match for the best of us in light descriptive literature... a man of curious talents certainly – perhaps a genius' (*LPP*, III, 470–1), and inviting him to contribute to the *Cornhill* (see below, II, 228). Sala did so during 1860 and was invited to continue, but left to edit *Temple*

Bar, set up in imitation – even in its title – of the *Cornhill*. Thackeray was generous over Sala's leaving to establish a rival magazine.[1] It was Dickens, however, whom he regarded as 'my master in letters' (*Life and Adventures* (1895) I, 328). Flashy in style and Bohemian in habits, he was temperamentally closer to Dickens than to Thackeray. When Thackeray died, Sala was in America, covering the Civil War for the *Daily Telegraph*; extract (I) is dated from New York, 14 Jan 1864.

(1) ... I have spoken of the writer, I have spoken of the philosopher; let me add, in fear and trembling, a few words on the man. I say in fear and trembling; for conscious that this sheet may find its way to the other side of the Atlantic, I would rather a hundred times that I had never written one line on this theme, than that one friend of the departed should deem me desirous of turning my knowledge of him into materials for prurient gossip; should think me wishful of vaunting among foreigners my long acquaintance with Mr Thackeray, the constant friendship, the untiring kindness he showed me. God knows I wish to claim no hail-fellow-well-met familiarity with him. It is the sorriest of tuft-hunting to brag of the easy terms one has been on with a dead man. I never clapped him on the back and called him 'Thack', as I have seen and heard, shudderingly, some do. I always entertained for him, from the first day I met and spoke with him in 1851,[2] to the last time I pressed his hand at the Reform Club in November 1863, a feeling of admiration that was mingled with awe. He was so much bigger, wiser, older, better than I was. I always felt as a youngster in his presence, and indeed I could never forget that as a mere child I had gloated over the *Paris Sketch-book*, and *Catherine: A Story*, one of his earliest, his best, and least known works. He was to me a man whom you could address as 'Sir', without derogating from your manhood or your status. I am emboldened to think that I got on with him, during the dozen years of our friendship, much better than those who used to boast of having been his companions over night, and grumbled at having been snubbed by him the next morning, simply because I made up my mind at the outset never to toady and never to take liberties with him. He never snubbed *me*, or gave me two fingers. He gave me his whole hand, when I met him in the street, or at dinner, or at the club; if he wanted to chat and be jovial, he stopped and chatted, and was jovial; if he was in evil case, he nodded and I nodded, and we went our

several ways. When he wanted me he sought me out, and I am glad to say he wanted me frequently. When I wanted a favour at his hands, I asked him frankly, and in twelve years got but one refusal. The kindnesses and courtesies he has done for me and them I love are untold. When a dear friend of mine was lying on his death-bed, helpless and poor, the man who has been accused of 'cynicism', of 'snobbishness', followed me from my lodgings at Brompton, to my chambers in Clements' Inn, and thence to a newspaper office in the city, with a cheque for the relief of one whom he had never seen, but whom he recognised as a brother author sick and in need. His charity did not stop at a cheque. He was an influential member of the Literary Fund, and he was mainly instrumental in obtaining, from that benevolent and much maligned corporation, a munificent grant towards the object he had at heart....

The instance I have ventured to notice could be capped, I am sure, by hundreds of others within the knowledge of those who really knew Mr Thackeray. To have seen him only in social intercourse, to have met him at parties, to have listened to his jests, his songs, and his infinite whim and fancy, to have sate even at his hospitable board, was not really to know him. Under far different aspects, the real man came out. It was long ere you discovered that the so-called cynic and sybarite was the gentlest, kindest, and most lovable of creatures. My tongue is tied by discretion, by delicacy, by the hope of a speedy return to my own country. I should wish to mingle no vulgar tinsel leaf with the chaplet that will be cast on the tomb of our great novelist and essayist. I only trust that in England legions of tongues, more eloquent than mine, have already done justice to the private worth, the goodness, the benevolence, and the modesty of my dear old friend and master....

(2) [One night, early in 1855, Albert Smith – on whom see above, I, 52 – took Sala to the Fielding Club, 'to finish the evening'.] To tell the truth, I was rather frightened when I found myself with Albert Smith in the rooms of the Fielding Club – the members seemed to me, as they probably were, so immeasurably my superiors in intellect and in social rank – but I was reassured when I beheld the now blanched head and the gleaming gold-rimmed spectacles and felt the

pressure of the kind hand of Thackeray. We soon left the revellers in the larger room and adjourned to an adjacent apartment; and there Thackeray talked for a full hour, criticising in his own happy manner the capacity of those literary youngsters of the period whom he thought to be 'coming on', and among whom he distinguished pre-eminently James Hannay, essayist, reviewer, satirist, and novelist, who, at the master's death, published a delightful 'Brief Memoir of Thackeray'[3]....

I have not forgotten, I hope, one word of the wise and gentle counsel which Thackeray gave me that night, and how he bade me 'buckle my belt tight', 'hang out my sign', and ask him to come and take a chop with me....

[Later that year Sala was hoping to write a biography of Hogarth, and it struck him that he could not do better than seek Thackeray's advice.] One forenoon I called upon Thackeray at his house in Onslow Square, Brompton; and he gave me, as usual, the heartiest of receptions. He was delighted with the idea of a biography of Hogarth; and sagaciously added that the first thing to do in the matter was to secure a first-rate publisher for the work. So he sat down and wrote a letter introducing me in terms far more eulogistic than I deserved to Mr George Smith, of the firm of Smith & Elder, whose place of business was then on the Hill of Corn itself.[4] It was a fine day, and Thackeray and I walked from Brompton to Piccadilly; gossiping the whole time on a hundred and one topics, literary and artistic, foreign and domestic.

I need scarcely say that when he was not in a tetchy temper, caused by extreme physical anguish, Thackeray was one of the most delightful conversationalists it was possible to imagine. There were very few subjects indeed on which he could not talk, and talk admirably. He was as fluent in the French and in the German as in the English language. He had, I should say, a fair knowledge of Italian. He was never tired of discoursing about books and bookmen, about pictures and painters, about etchers and engravers and lithographers; and, moreover, he was a born wit and a brilliant epigrammatist. So we walked and talked by bustling Knightsbridge into crowded Piccadilly; and halting just opposite Morell's, the well-known Italian warehouse, Thackeray observed that he was about to order some wine. He made me a bow which, in its sweeping stateliness, would have done honour to Sir Charles Grandison: concurrently giving me his hand, which was cold enough to have belonged to a professor of swimming who had just emerged from his tank; and then he stalked over the way; leaving in my mind a perplexed impression that he had suddenly forgotten who I was, or, that knowing me, he had arrived at the conclusion that I was a confounded bore, and that the sooner he got rid of me the better it would be. When I came to know him intimately I fully understood the reason for these sudden reactions of apparent *hauteur* and 'stand-offishness'. It was only his way. He could not help that which probably was due either to an acute spasm of bodily pain or the sudden passing of a black cloud across the mind of one who, although he could be upon occasion full of fun and frolic, was not, I should say, on the whole, altogether a happy man. [George Smith was very encouraging, but Sala never wrote his biography of Hogarth. Thackeray, however, reminded him of it four years later when recruiting contributors for the *Cornhill*,[5] where a series of papers on Hogarth appeared in its early numbers.]

I shall always regard the ten or twelve months during which my connection with the *Cornhill* existed as one of the happiest periods of my life.... I well remember the first *Cornhill* dinner. Thackeray, of course, was in the chair; and on his left hand I think there sat a then well-known baronet, Sir Charles Taylor. On the President's right was good old Field-marshal Sir John Burgoyne. Then we had Richard Monckton Milnes, soon to be Lord Houghton; Frederick Leighton and John Everett Millais, both young, handsome men, already celebrated and promising to be speedily famous. I think George H. Lewes was there; but I am sure that Robert Browning was. Anthony Trollope was very much to the fore, contradicting everybody; afterwards saying kind things to everybody, and occasionally going to sleep on sofas or chairs.... Sir Edwin Landseer; Sikes, the designer of the *Cornhill* cover; Frederick Walker – the last a very young man with every line in his features glowing with bright artistic genius; and Matthew Higgins, the 'Jacob Omnium' of *The Times*, who was taller even than his fast friend Thackeray, were also among the guests at this memorable birthday banquet.

Naturally, Thackeray had to deliver a congratulatory

speech after the cloth was drawn. Not for the first time, perhaps, do I hint that the great author of *Vanity Fair* was not a good after-dinner speaker. He read with perfect grace and purity of intonation; and I remember being one of a densely crowded audience who had gathered to listen to the first of Thackeray's lectures on the Four Georges in the huge building erected on the site of the old Surrey Zoological Gardens. I am partially deaf, and I was a considerable distance from the platform; still I could hear every word that the lecturer uttered; and I was raised to enthusiasm not only by the interesting nature of his matter, but also by the perfection of his elocutionary manner. As a post-prandial speaker, however, Thackeray was undeniably the reverse of felicitous. I knew this; and as I cherished for the man a sentiment not only of literary cult, but of love and veneration for him personally, I rejoiced that I now knew him well enough to ask him before the dinner took place whether he was quite easy in his mind about *the* speech. So I went to him while he was at breakfast in Onslow Square, on the morning of the banquet, and asked him if the speech was 'all right'. 'As right as rain', he replied. 'I dictated it last evening to my secretary; I have learned it by heart, and I have just repeated it to my daughters.' I felt partially relieved; but I purposely arrived at Hyde Park Square in the evening ten minutes before the time appointed for the dinner, and waited for Thackeray. When he arrived I just whispered to him, 'Speech all right?' 'As right as ninepence', he made answer, laughing. 'I have repeated it twice in the brougham, and it will go trippingly.' Alas! When the master arose to make the one oration of the evening, he began capitally. 'Gentlemen,' he said, 'we have captured eighty thousand prisoners.' This was a neat and happy allusion to the circulation of the first number of the *Cornhill*; and a murmur of approval ran through the distinguished assemblage. Had it only ended in a murmur! But some occult fiend suggested to Sir Charles Taylor that he should cry, in a sonorous voice, 'Hear, hear!' and the esteemed baronet had a slight peculiarity in intonation which made him pronounce 'Hear, hear!' as 'Hyah, hyah!' Then somebody laughed. Then Thackeray, thoroughly upset, lost his temper, and exclaiming, 'Upon my word, Sir Charles Taylor, if you say another word I will sit down', proceeded to stumble through a few limping and disjointed sentences, and then resumed his seat; evidently annoyed to the stage of exasperation, although warmly sympathised with by the whole company....

During the last year of a friendship the recollection of which, full as it was of affection on both sides and of deep respect as well, on mine, I shall treasure to my dying day, I saw Thackeray at least three times a week, either at the Reform or at his own hospitable house. He had moved from Onslow Square to a tall red-brick edifice which he had purchased close to Kensington Palace, which house he bought in a somewhat dilapidated condition, but which, with a large expenditure of money, he transformed into a stately mansion. I remember in particular one dinner at which the chief guest was Mr Charles Sumner, the renowned American statesman and orator, who had been extremely kind to Thackeray during the visit of the novelist to the United States.... There was a little passage of arms between him and Thackeray at the dinner of which I speak, owing to Mr Sumner's insistence that Thackeray was bound to write a book recording his experiences of Transatlantic travel and his opinions of the American people. The only answer of the novelist to these arguments was, 'Dickens wrote a book about America, and your people didn't like it.' Mr Sumner, however, was not satisfied, and continued his protestations that the American people wanted an American book from Thackeray, and that they had had nothing except *The Virginians*, which they rather resented, inasmuch as it contained a portrait of George Washington which they thought was somewhat lacking in reverence to the Father of his Country.

Very diplomatically Thackeray changed the subject by calling for critical opinions on three different kinds of cognac, decanters of which were served with the coffee. One sample, he declared, came from the cellars of the Tuileries, and was laid down by the butler of Napoleon I. This gave him the opportunity of launching into a fierce tirade against Napoleon the Great and of relating a story that, in his childhood, being brought from Calcutta to England, the ship touched at St Helena, and he was conducted to Longwood, where through a gap in a hedge he caught sight of the exile himself. Mr Sumner was rather Bonapartist in his views; and in the discussion which followed, the question as to whether

Thackeray should have written an account of his American experiences fell happily into abeyance.

The last time I saw Thackeray in the flesh was in August 1863; and the occasion was a whitebait dinner at the Ship, Greenwich. Ladies as well as gentlemen were present at the gathering, and among the latter I especially remember William Howard Russell and Robert Chambers. Thackeray was in his brightest mood, as full of fun as a boy. He had learned from the manager that, in a room directly under the one in which we were dining, Mr Douglas Cook, then Editor of the *Saturday Review* – a journal in which at that period, about twice in every month, I was abused as though I had been a pickpocket – was entertaining Mr Beresford Hope and other personages of light and leading. Thackeray jocularly proposed that I should be tied up in a table-cloth, and by means of a rope formed of twisted napkins be lowered to the bow window of the apartment where Mr Cook and his friends were revelling, in order that I might fulfil the part of skeleton at a Greenwich–Egyptian feast.

Towards evening – and a most delicious evening it was – just one touch of melancholy overshadowed the general gaiety. Quite incidentally Thackeray said, 'I have made my mark, and my money, and said my say; and the world smiles on me; and perhaps were I to die tomorrow *The Times* newspaper would give me just three-quarters of a column of obituary notice.' I was far from England when Thackeray died, and never saw the *Times* notice of his demise. Was it a little over or a little under a column in length?[6] There was no Atlantic cable in 1863, and the first week of January 1864 had passed away when, being in New York, I learned to my inexpressible grief that William Makepeace Thackeray was no more. You will understand that, although long intervals occurred in our intercourse between the period of my boyhood and the autumn of 1863, I had many opportunities of personally studying the man, and of mentally hoarding up all that I saw and all that I thought concerning him. He was most emphatically a good man, but one continually struggling with an uneven and sometimes objectionable temperament. He was unswervingly and invariably truthful; he was kind, compassionate, charitable, and, to the best of my belief, strongly imbued with religious principle and sentiment.

L'indole era cattiva ['It was a bad temperament']. For women he had the chivalrous respect and devotion of his own Colonel Newcome.

Of his occasional propensity to treat people in a distant, stand-off, and 'Great Twamley' manner I have already incidentally and laughingly spoken. I knew him long enough and intimately enough to regard these little exhibitions of 'peskiness' as utterly unworthy of serious notice. When I strolled into the hail of the Reform, either at luncheon-time or in the evening, and saw Mr Thackeray, I never failed to take careful note of him. If, to my thinking, he was in a cantankerous humour – the expression is his own – I gave him the widest of wide berths. But when he espied me, and I saw him put his hands in his pockets and beam over his spectacles, I knew that he was in good 'form', and that he would be cheerful, tolerant, and delightful. He had an odd way of calling me the 'Reverend Dr Sala', chiefly because, I believe, I used to talk to him quite as outspokenly and seriously as in the old time he had talked to me. I never flattered nor fawned upon him, and I never took liberties with him. He knew how much I loved and revered him, and that is why we got on so well together. There were some friends of his who used to call him 'Thack', and slap him on the back. I never called him anything but 'Mr Thackeray'; and I did so because I knew he was my elder, and because I conscientiously believed that he was in every way my better.

From the bottom of my heart I contend that he was not a cynic; I mean that he entertained no morose nor contemptuous views and tenets touching human nature. The real cynic has the qualities of the surly dog; he snarls, he is captious, he is surly, currish, ill-conditioned. Bishop Berkeley speaks of 'cynical content in dirt and beggary'. Thackeray, on the contrary, loved light and culture and luxury. I have heard him say that he liked to go to his bedchamber at night with a wax taper and a silver candlestick. That was merely a frank way of saying that he preferred the elegances of life to squalor and ugliness. He has been unjustly termed a cynic, because he could not help being a satirist; but although he was a master of irony, and on occasions could use the scalpel with effect as terrible as ever it had been used by Juvenal, by Dryden, or by Pope, I never heard him say one unkindly thing of human weakness, or frailty, or misfortune. Like Fontenelle, he might have averred on his death-bed that he had never uttered the slightest word against the smallest virtue.

There have not been wanting critics of his character who have insinuated that Thackeray's own individuality might have found a niche in that great Walhalla of pomposities and prigs and 'mean cusses', *The Book of Snobs*. He was not a snob. He was a high-minded and chivalrous gentleman; but circumstances and his own peculiar temperament occasionally prompted him to say and do things which ill-natured people might have considered to be snobbish. For example, he came over to me terribly disturbed one morning at Brompton; and told me that although the London season was just drawing to a close, he had not been once asked to a dinner or a reception 'at the Jersey's', meaning that famous leader of society, the late Countess of Jersey. I said, very quietly, 'So much the worse for the Jersey.' Whereupon he put his hands in his pockets and began to talk quite sociably about things in general. The truth must out – he was of gentle extraction; had been academically educated; had inherited a modest patrimony; was intimate with the best Anglo-Indian society, county families, judges, military officers of high rank, and so forth; and even when he was poor and thought himself a Bohemian he was in reality a 'swell', although a swell in difficulties.

He liked the best society, and had always mingled with it; and if, like Tommy Moore, he 'dearly loved a lord', his partiality for patrician acquaintances never rendered him deaf to the claims of misfortune, nor regardless of the ties of friendship. His associates, for example, on the *Punch* staff – Jerrold, Mark Lemon, a Beckett, Horace Mayhew, Tenniel, Leech, and Doyle, were all essentially middle-class men, who very rarely gained, even if they sought, admission to those social circles in which Thackeray had been a welcome guest from his youth upwards. I suppose that I am not altogether myself destitute of pride. My engendrure is not of the gutter; and the parish was not at the cost of my schooling; but I frankly admit that although when I last met Thackeray I had ceased to be an obscure man, I always regarded him as much my superior in social status as he was in literary rank. Perhaps I myself was something of a snob thirty years ago, and am one, still.

NOTES

1. 'Thackeray and I parted on the best of terms, and he even said some friendly words about the rival magazine in one of his *Roundabout Papers*', wrote Sala, in his *Life and Adventures* (1895) I, 430. Cf. *LPP*, IV, 203, and *Cornhill*, II (1860) 760.
2. Sala here forgets two earlier meetings, one 'four or five' years before 1851, when his brother introduced him to Thackeray at the Deanery Club, and one in 1851 at 'Soyer's Symposium' (a restaurant), where Sala was working; Thackeray, now famous, visited it and spoke kindly to him about his work as an engraver. Then 'a few years passed before I met him again' (*Things I have Seen*, I, 10–18).
3. For Hannay, see above, I, 96.
4. 22 Sep 1855 (*LPP*, III, 470–1).
5. Thackeray's invitation (not in *LPP*) ran: 'About to start new magazine. First-rate bill of fare. Want rich collops from you.... Don't forget Hogarth' (*Things I Have Seen*, I, 28). Edward FitzGerald, however, felt that Sala's appearing in the early numbers of the *Cornhill* 'lets the Cockney in already' – *Letters and Literary Remains* (1902) II, iii.
6. Thackeray's guess was exactly right; see below, II, 319.

Memories of a Right-hand Man

GEORGE HODDER

From *Memories of My Time* (1870) pp. 238–86, 306. Hodder (1819–70), journalist and miscellaneous author, acted as Thackeray's secretary in 1855 and his tour-manager for *The Four Georges* in 1857. The impresario Willert Beale, for whom he sometimes worked, describes Hodder as 'a great favourite with everyone who knew him... naturally amiable, although amazingly peppery, sometimes at the slightest provocation' – and friends, who enjoyed these displays of irascibility, sometimes deliberately made him lose his temper – *The Light of Other Days* (1890) I, 240.

In approaching the name of William Makepeace Thackeray I feel a degree of delicacy and even timidity which his absence from the scene of his world-wide renown does not tend to diminish; for Thackeray was a man of such large mental proportions, and such far-seeing power in his mode of anatomising and criticising human character, that one seems to be treading on volcanic ground in venturing to deal with him at all. But of what is biography composed? Assuredly not of the knowledge and experience of one privileged person, but of the aggregate contributions of many, who are willing, when occasion offers, to state what they know for the information and benefit of posterity. A hundred admirers of Thackeray might undertake to write a memoir of him, and yet the task of doing full justice to his character and career must necessarily be left to a chosen future historian, who shall zealously gather together all the bits and fragments to be found scattered among books and men, and blend them into a substantial and permanent shape. But it must be admitted that there is an exceptional difficulty in regard to Thackeray, inasmuch as there were few whom he allowed to *know* him, in the true sense of the phrase – that is to say, there was a constitutional reserve in his manner, accompanied, at times, by a cold austerity which led to some misgivings as to the possibility of his being the pleasant social companion his intimates often described him to be. And yet it is well known to those who saw much of Thackeray in his familiar moments, that he could be essentially 'jolly' (a favourite term of his) when the humour suited him, and that he would on such occasions open his heart as freely as if the word 'reticence' formed no part of his vocabulary; whereas at other times he would keep himself entirely within himself, and answer a question by a monosyllable, or peradventure by a significant movement of the head. At one moment he would look you full in the face and greet you jauntily, at another he would turn from you with a peculiar waving of the hand which of course indicated that he had no desire to talk. Men who were members of the same club with him have been heard to say that sometimes he would pass them in the lobbies unnoticed, and at others he would cheerfully initiate a conversation, and leave behind him an impression that sullenness or *hauteur* was wholly foreign to his nature. It should be stated, however, that his health for many years had never been entirely unimpaired, and that his acute sensibility often rendered it irksome to him to come in contact with his fellow men. In short, he was essentially of a nervous temperament, and altogether deficient in that vigorous self-possession which enables a man to shine in public assemblies, for it was absolute pain to him to be called upon to make a speech, and even in ordinary conversation he showed no particular desire to hold a prominent place. But the above considerations apart, it would be easier to know many men in a few days than it would be thoroughly to understand Thackeray in the same number of years; for *semper idem* ['always the same'] was not his motto, and his genius was – as it undoubtedly had a perfect right to be – wayward and capricious.... But that the great novelist and satirist had a generous and sympathetic heart, can hardly, I think, be disputed; and even the few brief letters which I received from him are sufficient to prove that, however austere he sometimes appeared to be externally, he was very rarely wanting in that readiness to perform a kind office, which was one of the leading characteristics of his nature....

[In one letter quoted (*LPP*, III, 367) Thackeray remarks that he possesses copies of very few of his own books. Hodder continues:] Some time after this I received a curious confirmation of Mr Thackeray's statement that he did not possess copies of his own books. At the period now referred to he had completed *The Newcomes*, and on looking at the bookshelves in his studio one morning I observed that a newly bound copy of that novel was the only one of his works in the library. *Vanity Fair*, and *Pendennis*, and *Esmond*, were not to be seen. On Mr Thackeray entering the room, I alluded to this unexpected absence of his books, and added that I had particularly noticed that Mr Charles Dickens possessed all his own works, neatly bound, and ranged in the order in which they were successively published. 'Yes,' said Thackeray, 'I know Dickens does, and so ought I; but fellows borrow them or steal them, and I try to keep them, and can't.' ...

I cannot at this distant date precisely call to mind the circumstances under which I continued at intervals to meet Mr Thackeray, but the various letters I received from him contain the most gratifying proof that he was always well affected towards writers who could not possibly aspire to his own rank in the literary army; and the following extract is one of the best evidences of this fact I can adduce, because at the time he wrote it my knowledge of him did not extend beyond that which was derived from a few brief conversations with him at the chambers of a friend, upon matters in no way relating to business, such as afterwards brought me more closely in contact with him. The letter refers to a loss which had just befallen me in consequence of some changes which had taken place in a newspaper establishment with which I was then connected. It is dated 19 May 1855, and says, 'I am sincerely sorry to hear of your position, and send the little contribution which came so opportunely from another friend whom I was enabled once to help. When you are well to do again I know you will pay it back, and I dare say sombody else will want the money, which is meanwhile most heartily at your service.'

It was afterwards explained to me that Mr Thackeray made a practice of acting upon the principle embodied in the above note. Like many other generous men he had always a few pounds floating about amongst friends and acquaintances whom he had been able to oblige in their necessity, and whenever he received back money which he had lent, he did not put it into his pocket with a glow of satisfaction at having added so much to his exchequer; but congratulated himself that he could transfer the same sum to another person who he knew was in need of it .... [And four months later Thackeray wrote inviting Hodder to undertake some secretarial work which 'would put some money in your way'.]

To Onslow Square I accordingly went on the morning fixed upon, and found Mr Thackeray in his study ready to receive me; but instead of entering upon business in that part of the house, he took me upstairs to his bedroom, where every arrangement had been made for the convenience of writing. I then learnt that he was busily occupied in preparing his lectures on the Four Georges, and that he had need of an amanuensis to fill the place of one who was now otherwise occupied.[1] In that capacity it was my task to write to his dictation, and to make extracts from books, according to his instructions, either at his own house or at the British Museum. This duty called me to his bedchamber every morning, and as a general rule I found him up and ready to begin work, though he was sometimes in doubt and difficulty as to whether he should commence operations sitting or standing, or walking about, or lying down. Often he would light a cigar, and after pacing the room for a few minutes, would put the unsmoked remnant on the mantelpiece, and resume his work with increased cheerfulness, as if he had gathered fresh inspiration from the 'gentle odours' of the 'sublime tobacco'....

It was not a little amusing to observe the frequency with which Mr Thackeray, in the moments of dictation, would change his position, and I could not but think that he seemed most at his ease when one would suppose he was most uncomfortable. He was easy to 'follow', as his enunciation was always clear and distinct, and he generally 'weighed his words before he gave them breath', so that his amanuensis seldom received a check during the progress of his pen. He never became energetic, but spoke with that calm deliberation which distinguished his public readings; and there was one peculiarity which, amongst others, I especially remarked, viz., that when he made a humorous point, which inevitably caused me to laugh, his own countenance was unmoved, like that of the comedian Liston, who, as is well known, looked as if he wondered what had occurred to excite the risibility of his audience. Sometimes Thackeray would suddenly stop in his work to test the virtues of a pen or the quality of a particular kind of paper; and if he saw I did not write quite so fluently as he could wish, he would suggest a broader nib or a narrower nib, as the case might be, and would then direct his attention to the paper I was using, and advise me to employ a peculiar specimen before me, with a rough, ribbed surface. He proposed it, he said, because it would 'bite', and he did not like those smooth, satiny papers, as they allowed nothing for the pen to catch hold of, but let it glide along without a check when an occasional halt would seem desirable.

I refer to these trifles merely as showing that Mr Thackeray was glad to resort to any little stratagem which might afford him a moment's relaxation from his work, when the words would not spring nimbly from the lips. May it not be some consolation to the humblest labourer in the same vineyard to know that even the brightest geniuses cannot always make their light to shine? Many authors have often declared that they could not write to dictation. Thackeray was one who *could*, and liked to do so; and no better proof need be afforded of his power in that respect than is to be found in his *Four Georges*, which contain some of the most thoughtful and vigorous passages that ever emanated from his brain.

While I was thus daily engaged with Mr Thackeray, he

sometimes required my assistance on a Sunday afternoon, and I call to mind one Sunday in particular – I think it was the last before he started for America – when I found him in exceptionally high spirits, and much more inclined to talk than to write. He spoke of the journey he was about to commence, and of the money he should probably make by his readings in America. He wanted a few thousands more, he said, for he had not yet made enough. True, he added, that he possessed a small share of the world's goods, and he was happy to think that he had paid off one moiety of the cost of his house (which he then occupied), and that he should be able before he left the country to discharge the remainder of the liability. He then went on to relate some of his literary experiences, and the circumstances under which his fortunes had improved during the last few years, observing that lecturing was certainly more profitable than magazine writing. He next alluded to his friends the contributors to *Punch*, and passed in review many of their virtues and idiosyncrasies; and was at some pains to show that he held the humorous brotherhood in high esteem.

In speaking of periodical literature, he said he contemplated producing a magazine or journal in his own name after his return from America; and upon my venturing to observe that I hoped he did not intend to encourage the anonymous system in regard to his contributors, as the conductors of other publications of the day seemed resolved to do, he replied, 'No. I think that's hard lines.' Our conversation next turned upon his mission to the United States, and when he hinted at the probability of his taking a secretary with him, as he had done on his former visit to that country, I suggested that I should be delighted to fill that office if he had not already selected someone. He promised to consider my suggestion, and let me know what determination he had arrived at; but in the meantime he feared he should require a valet more than a secretary. On the following morning he said he had turned the matter over in his mind, and had come to the conclusion that, in consequence of the state of his health, he should be obliged to take a servant with him instead of a secretary; adding, dryly, 'I can ask a servant to hold a basin to me; but I doubt if I could so treat a secretary – at least, he *might* object.' He smiled as he made this droll observation, but I too well knew that it was a true word spoken in jest; for he was subject to periodical illnesses which rendered the services of a valet most essential to him; and the young man who filled that situation at the time [Charles Pearman] was fortunately one in whom he placed implicit confidence; and he was thankful for the gentle way in which his servant tended him....

[Hodder describes the farewell banquet given to Thackeray by his friends, and Thackeray's sadness when parting from his daughters.] He was to start by an early train, and when I arrived (for it had been previously arranged that I should see him before he left) I found him in his study, and his two daughters in the dining-room – all in a very tearful condition; and I do not think I am far wrong in saying that if ever man's strength was overpowered by woman's weakness it was so upon this occasion, for Mr Thackeray could not look at his daughters without betraying a moisture in his eyes, which he in vain strove to conceal. Nevertheless he was enabled to attend to several money transactions which it was necessary he should arrange before leaving; and to give me certain instructions about the four volumes of his *Miscellanies* then in course of publication, and which he begged me to watch in their passage through the press, with a view to a few footnotes that might be thought desirable. Then came the hour for parting! A cab was at the door, the luggage had all been properly disposed of, and the servants stood in the hall, to notify, by their looks, how much they regretted their master's departure. 'This is the moment I have dreaded!' said Thackeray, as he entered the dining-room to embrace his daughters; and when he hastily descended the steps of the door he *knew* that they would be at the window to 'Cast one longing, lingering look behind'. 'Goodbye!', he murmured, in a suppressed voice, as I followed him to the cab; 'keep close behind me, and let me try to jump in unseen.'

The instant the door of the vehicle was closed upon him, he threw himself back into a corner and buried his face in his hands. That was the last I saw of Mr Thackeray before he left London on his second visit to the United States; and I think I have given sufficient proof that, great as was his power of poising the shafts of ridicule at the follies and vices of the day, and coldly reserved as he sometimes was in his demeanour, he was full of that gentleness of heart to which his writings constantly bear testimony, and it was his instinct to be actuated by the kindliest impulses which do honour to our common nature....

[After this American tour, Thackeray was to tour Britain with *The Four Georges*. Hodder called upon him with the impresario Frederick Beale, to discuss terms.] Mr Thackeray was in his dressing-gown and slippers, and received us in his bedroom, where, as I have already stated, he generally passed his mornings and wrote his books. His study being a small back room behind the dining-room on the ground floor, and being exposed to the noises from the street, he had caused his writing-table and appliances to be carried upstairs to the second floor, where two rooms had been thrown into one – the back to be used as a sleeping chamber, and the front, which was considerably larger than the other, as a sitting-room. The dimensions of this apartment being capacious, Mr Thackeray was enabled to move about in the intervals of writing, and to extend his limbs on a couch, and *in fine* to change his attitude as often as his convenience demanded, for the operation of dictating necessarily spared him the pain of confining himself to a sitting posture. On the morning in question some domestic annoyance had ruffled the serenity of his mind, and it was evident, from the abruptness of his manner, that he had no idea of being other than thoroughly 'businesslike' in the negotiations we were about to commence. After a little preparatory interchange of civilities (which it was pretty evident Mr Thackeray would have described as a 'bore' had it been possible to ascertain his candid opinion at the moment), Mr Beale, in his usual courteous manner, suggested the terms himself, and Mr Thackeray, like a true diplomatist as he was, never allowed it to be supposed that he thought them more than reasonably remunerative.

The payment proposed was fifty guineas for each reading.... [Some doubt having arisen about whether it was pounds or guineas, Beale returned later to check this.] The question was simply and briefly put, and Mr Thackeray's mode of answering it was impressive in its rugged significance. 'Oh, guineas,' he said; 'decidedly *guineas*.' Mr Beale said not a word, and the bargain was complete as determined by Mr Thackeray. This was singularly characteristic of the man; for it is well known that in all his doings he took especial care never to undervalue his own powers, as more than one publishing firm of the present day can amply testify.[2] 'Always ask enough,' he said; 'they can but drop you down a bit if they don't like it.' That he was well satisfied with his arrangement with Mr Beale is best proved by the fact that, when he saw me on the following day, he exclaimed, 'What terms! fifty guineas a night! Why, I shouldn't have received one half that sum for an article in *Fraser* a few years ago.'

'I have no doubt', said I, 'that the speculation will pay sufficiently well to leave a margin of profit for Mr Beale.'

'I hope so', Mr Thackeray replied. 'At least we must do our best – Beale with his advertisements and I with my work.'[3]

My connection with the establishment of Messrs Cramer & Beale led to its being suggested that I should accompany Mr Thackeray on his tour as manager and secretary – a proposition to which I naturally had great pleasure in acceding, for I had learnt to understand and appreciate the peculiar temperament of the great Titmarsh – as many of his friends continued to call him – and had reason to believe he would not be dissatisfied with the arrangement.... It should here be stated that out of the fifty guineas per day Mr Thackeray was to defray his own expenses – so that the prospect of ultimate gain was somewhat less brilliant than it had first appeared to be; for Thackeray was not amongst those who could be said to pay the strictest regard to the social economies. He knew that money was in his brains, how quickly soever it might flow from his pockets; and it did not appear to be a matter of primary importance to him whether he saved much or little out of the enterprise.

As I was travelling entirely in an official character, and was not responsible to Mr Thackeray, I studiously avoided forcing myself on his company, but always took especial care to select a carriage he did *not* occupy, and to plant myself in an hotel he did *not* patronise. Hence – if I may speak paradoxically – we pulled remarkably well together; and although the arrangements for a public reading every evening at eight o'clock left little opportunity for social enjoyment – that is to say, at a time when it would be most in accordance with his usual habit – Mr Thackeray occasionally invited me to dine with him. 'This is a nice room', he would say, if the apartment allotted to him chanced to have a rural aspect, with trees and flowers bobbing in at the window; 'I could *write* here!' And where was it, it may be asked, that he could *not* write? [though in fact, as Hodder remarks] at the time I am now speaking of there was reason to believe that the art of writing – that is to say, the mere manual exercise of the art – had become somewhat irksome to him; for he had been often heard to complain, when engaged on one of his monthly serials, that he was behindhand with his 'copy', and that he hardly knew where or when to set about it. That some of his best things appeared in his later days is beyond question; but from the time he was about to commence *The Virginians* – when he used to exclaim in a tone almost amounting to querulousness, 'They have asked me to do another book; but I don't know what to write about; I have said all I had to say' – it could not be stated with any degree of accuracy that he wrote *currente calamo* ['with a flowing pen']. Indeed, he was apt to undervalue his own ability, and to indulge the belief that what he was doing might be done by others better than himself. But the underlying generosity of his nature was, in some degree, the cause of this self-doubting, for he was at all times ready to give the warmest praise to contemporary writers; and as I have been tempted into this digression, I must claim the privilege of relating ... a few instances, within my own experience, of Thackeray's comparing himself with others to his own disadvantage.

At the time of the publication of *Vanity Fair*, Thackeray's great contemporary, Charles Dickens (for in spite of all remonstrance it has always been the fashion to place the two writers in the same category, and often to sacrifice one at the shrine of the other, according to the particular taste of the person addressing himself to the subject), was producing, in the accustomed monthly form – the green cover in the one instance, against the yellow cover in the other – his story of *Dombey and Son*; and it was Thackeray's delight to read each number with eagerness as it issued from the press. He had often been heard to speak of the work in terms of the highest praise. When it had reached its fifth number, wherein Mr Charles Dickens described the end of little Paul with a depth of pathos which produced a vibratory emotion in the hearts of all who read it, Mr Thackeray seemed electrified at the thought that there was one man living who could exercise so complete a control over him. Putting No. v of *Dombey and*

Son in his pocket, he hastened down to Mr Punch's printing-office, and entering the Editor's room, where I chanced to be the only person present except Mr Mark Lemon himself, he dashed it on to the table with startling vehemence, and exclaimed, 'There's no writing against such power as this – one has no chance! Read that chapter describing young Paul's death: it is unsurpassed – it is stupendous!' ...

Long after this, and during the period that I acted as his amanuensis, I went into his chamber one morning, as usual, and found him in bed (for, lest it should be supposed that Mr Thackeray was what is commonly called a late riser, I should state at once that my visits to him were somewhat early, that is to say, before nine o'clock), a little pot of tea and some dry toast on a table by his side. I therefore remained at a distance from him, but Mr Thackeray called me forward, and I discovered that he had passed a very restless night. 'I am sorry', said I, 'that you do not seem very well this morning.' '*Well*,' he murmured – 'no, I am not well. I have got to make that confounded speech tonight.' I immediately recollected that he was to preside at the annual dinner of the General Theatrical Fund – an undertaking which I well knew was entirely repugnant to his taste and wishes. 'Don't let that trouble you, Mr Thackeray,' said I; 'you will be sure to be all right when the time comes.' – 'Nonsense!' he replied, 'it won't come all right – I can't make a speech. Confound it! That fellow Jackson let me in for this! Why don't they get Dickens to take the chair? He *can* make a speech, and a good one. *I'm* of no use.' I told him that I thoroughly appreciated his remark in regard to Mr Dickens, but that at the same time he was giving little credit to those whose discernment had selected him as the chairman of the evening, and they could not very well ask Mr Dickens, as he had only a year or two since occupied that position at an anniversary dinner of the same institution. 'They little think how nervous I am,' said Thackeray; 'and Dickens doesn't know the meaning of the word.' ...

The result of Mr Thackeray's chairmanship on the evening in question [29 Mar 1858] may here be recorded, with all respect to his memory and with that desire to be strictly correct, which he himself would have been the first to encourage. True to his engagement he took the post assigned to him, and commenced his duties as if he had resolved to set difficulties at defiance, and to show that the task was *not* quite impossible with him; but, unhappily for his nervous and sensitive temperament, Mr Charles Dickens, as the President of the institution, sat at his right hand, and when he came to the all-absorbing toast of the evening, the terrifying fact rushed across his mind that his great contemporary would witness all his shortcomings and his sad inferiority. He had prepared his speech, and he commenced with some learned allusions to the car of Thespis and the early history of the drama, when he suddenly collapsed, and brought his address to a close in a few common-place observations which could scarcely be called coherent. He too painfully felt the weakness of his position; and notwithstanding a particularly kind and complimentary speech in which Mr Dickens proposed his health as chairman, he could not recover the *prestige* he believed he had lost, and he left the room in company with an old friend at as early a moment as he could consistently with the respect he owed to the company.[4]

One other instance I may mention of the many which came within my own knowledge of Mr Thackeray's distrust of his own powers and his desire to exalt others at the expense of himself. I found him one morning in an unusually loquacious mood, and I had not been with him many minutes before he said he was not disposed to trouble himself with any work that day. He was more inclined to talk. Adverting, by a natural transition from the subject he had first touched upon, to the respective merits of various writers who were then daily before the world, he spoke of the great success of *Household Words*, and of the ability displayed in its pages by some of its contributors. 'There's one man', for instance, he emphatically exclaimed, 'who is a very clever fellow, and that is Sala. That paper of his, "The Key of the Street", is one of the best things I ever read.[5] I couldn't have written it. I wish I could.'

I ventured to suggest that, although there could be no doubt that the article in question possessed great merit, and that it had been talked about in the literary world as amongst the most attractive features in the publication, he was scarcely doing justice to his own powers by the observation he had made. 'No, no,' he repeated, with increased earnestness, 'I couldn't have written that article, and as I shall have a periodical of my own shortly, I shall hope for this man's co-operation.' It need hardly be said that Thackeray kept his word in this respect; for when the *Cornhill Magazine* was announced to make its appearance under his editorship, George Augustus Sala was one of the first on his list of contributors....

In regard to the routine of our daily engagements on the provincial tour (to which the reader will now return) there is little to relate, as each day's movements were as nearly as possible the same as those of the preceding – viz. to the public hall where the reading was to take place, at eight o'clock in the evening – Mr Thackeray to give his lecture, and myself to superintend the arrangements for the audience, and to take charge of the money. Mr Thackeray fulfilled his mission with the most undeviating punctuality, and always made it a special point to see me at the conclusion of the lecture, when he invariably asked me, with some eagerness, what had been the amount of the receipts. As a rule, they were more than sufficient to pay the expenses, and to allow him his honorarium; and he was always greatly pleased to learn this, as it would be disappointing to him, he said, if Mr Beale should lose by the speculation....

There was one little difficulty which presented itself in regard to the preliminary arrangements for these lectures, and that was caused by the stipulation which Mr Thackeray insisted on being made, that a desk should be prepared for him in every town he was to visit, of sufficient height to enable a man of his stature to read from it without stooping. This unusual desideratum was apparently distasteful to some of the local agents, for either they forgot to secure the exceptional dimensions of the desk, or they imagined that the letter which conveyed the instruction conveyed at the same time a mistake; and hence it occasionally happened that a little measuring and carpentering was required before the lecture could be proceeded with. It cannot be said, however, that much inconvenience arose from this indispensable preliminary, for Mr Thackeray was patient and tolerant, and the audience had no right or desire to know what was going on, provided it had not come to their time to *listen*.

Apropos of the reading-desk and the reader. Whilst I was engaged with Mr Thackeray in writing *The Four Georges* to his dictation, he was wont to ask me to constitute myself 'the audience', in order that he might test the strength of his voice and the elocutionary tone of his delivery. He would then improvise a desk of the height he required at one end of the double-room, and place me at the extremity of the other; and in this manner he read out from the manuscript before him, trying alternately three separate forms of handwriting – his own, the present writer's, and that of the amanuensis whom I had succeeded.

The result pleased him, for his voice proved clear and resonant, and his elocution unaffected and distinct. But the manner which he adopted in his own room was hardly such as could be entirely satisfactory to a public audience, and yet Mr Thackeray made little or no alteration in his tone. The consequence was that many complained that he spoke in too familiar and colloquial a style – that his idea seemed to be that it was less his business to make himself heard than it was the duty of the audience to hear him. His tall, commanding figure, however, and the imposing gravity of his countenance, generally secured respectful silence; and, excepting on occasions when he gave his reading in a building of unusual capaciousness, it was only the most remotely placed of his auditors to whom he was not sufficiently audible....

[Hodder describes the lecture tour, one of the incidents of which was Thackeray's being taken ill in Norwich. Soon after this] I saw him at his house in London, and on his making allusion to those dreadful illnesses which he said were the very bane of his life, I asked if he had ever received the best medical advice. Certainly he had, was his reply; 'but what is the use of advice, if you don't follow it?' he continued. 'They tell me not to drink, and I *do* drink. They tell me not to smoke, and I *do* smoke. They tell me not to eat, and I *do* eat. In short, I do everything that I am desired *not* to do, and, therefore, what am I to expect?' I was about to offer a trite remark which naturally suggested itself from the tenor of the conversation; but I merely said his health was of value to the world as well as to himself, and there were hundreds who had read his dedication of *Pendennis* to Dr Elliotson,[6] who would rejoice to be informed that he had never again been similarly afflicted.

NOTES

1. James Hannay; cf. *LPP*, III, 465–7.
2. For a later instance of his insisting that it was guineas, not pounds, that the firm of Beale had agreed to, see below, II, 251.
3. In fact the impresarios were disappointed with their bargain: see below, II, 250.
4. See *The Speeches of Charles Dickens*, ed. K. J. Fielding (Oxford, 1960) pp. 260–3. In his main speech, Thackeray referred to Dickens's greater felicity as a public speaker: and, replying to Dickens's speech in his honour, and moved by the loud and protracted cheering as his health was drunk, he spoke in 'a voice broken by emotion'.
5. George Augustus Sala made his début in *Household Words* with this essay (6 Sep 1851), which Dickens, Editor of the magazine, had greatly admired, too. In a letter of 1855, Thackeray called it 'almost the best magazine paper that ever was written' (*LPP*, III, 470–1).
6. Dedicating the novel to his physician Doctor John Elliotson (1791–1868), he wrote, 'Thirteen months ago, when it seemed likely that this story had come to a close, a kind friend brought you to my bedside, whence, in all probability, I never should have risen but for your constant watchfulness and skill.' Hodder concludes his chapters on Thackeray with an account of his and other friends' grief over his sudden death, and a description of the funeral.

The Man with the Largest Mass of Brain

WHITWELL AND FRANCES ELWIN

From *Some XVIII Century Men of Letters: Biographical Essays by the Revd Whitwell Elwin, with a Memoir*, ed. by his son Warwick Elwin (1902) pp. 156–8, 177–82, 186–7, 245–6. Whitwell Elwin (1815–1900), Rector of Booton, Norfolk, was a man of scholarly tastes and achievement (notably his great edition of Pope). As Editor of the *Quarterly Review*, 1854–60, he became acquainted with many notabilities, including Thackeray, and of them he would often say, 'In my life, I have only known three men whose genius seemed to tower above that of the rest of mankind. Those three were Brougham, Thackeray, and Macaulay.... [They] seemed to have been endowed by nature with a larger mass of brain than is given to other men.' And of these three, writes his son Warwick Elwin, 'he always gave the palm to Thackeray' (*XVIII Century Men of Letters*, p. 148). A warm friendship developed after Thackeray contributed to the *Quarterly*, Jan 1855, his appreciative essay on John Leech. Relishing his sweet simplicity of character, and his unworldly eccentricity, Thackeray nicknamed Elwin 'Doctor Primrose', after Goldsmith's clergyman (see below; and see *LPP*, I, cxxviii–cxxx for examples of Elwin's innocence). Towards the end of his life, Elwin began writing a biography of Thackeray, who, he thought, 'had been much misunderstood' (*XVIII Century Men of Letters*, p. 346), but he did not get far. His chapters covering Thackeray's early years were published posthumously in the *Monthly Review* (June, Sep, Oct 1904). In the extracts below, his son provides the narrative, quoting liberally from letters and memoranda by his father and – invaluably – by his mother, Frances Elwin (1815–1898). His references to the dates and recipients of letters are here mostly omitted or incorporated into the text.

It was ... one of the warmest friendships of Elwin's life. In 1855 there appeared in *The Times* a critical review of the just completed *Newcomes*, containing an attack on its 'morality and religion', which wounded Thackeray's feelings. 'With regard to religion,' he wrote to Elwin [6 Sep 1855], 'I think, please God, my books are written by a God-loving man, and the morality – the vanity of success, etc., of all but love and goodness – is not that the teaching *Domini nostri*? You once said you did not quarrel with my ethics. Perhaps, if you write about them, you will set that dull world right about them.' Elwin undertook to review the novel in the *Quarterly*, and did so in a warmly appreciative article. 'You are very good and kind to me', Thackeray wrote, on receiving the proof. 'What a pleasure my dear old mother will have in reading it!' When they met at dinner at [John] Forster's, shortly after, on 8 October, Thackeray insisted that the Editor had overpraised him. 'I told him', said Elwin, 'that there was probably more in his novels than he himself was aware of, for that I suspected he wrote by a sort of instinct, without marking the full import of his narrative as he went along. "Yes," he replied, "I have no idea where it all comes from. I have never seen the persons I describe, nor heard the conversations I put down. I am often astonished myself to read it after I have got it on paper."' 'His unbounded frankness', Elwin continued, 'surpasses what I have ever seen in any other man. His massive head looks the very symbol of intellectual power.'

Thackeray was then about to start on his lecturing tour in America.... After his return, Whitwell Elwin accidentally met him in Piccadilly, on 10 October 1856, and walked home with him, conversing. On asking if he was at work, Thackeray replied, 'I began a story, was dissatisfied with it, and burnt it. I can't jump further than I did in *The Newcomes*, but I want to jump as far.' Elwin asked what was amiss with the piece he had burnt. 'It ran in the old track', said Thackeray. 'I have exhausted all the types of character with which I am familiar, and it is very difficult to strike out anything new. I have thought of two or three schemes. One was to lay the scene in the time of Dr Johnson.' 'Don't do that', exclaimed Elwin. '*Esmond* is a good piece of imitation, but you cannot yourself tell that the accessories are correct, because you are obliged to take them at second-hand. A novelist can only describe his own age. You intimated in *The Newcomes* that you meant to give us the history of J. J.'[1] 'That', Thackeray replied, 'was what I had begun, but it was commenced in too melancholy a strain. I want to have a cheerful hero, though this is very difficult, for a cheerful character must have some deeper element to give sufficient dignity and interest. It is hardly possible to have a hero without a dash of melancholy. I think the cheerful man must be the second character – a good-humoured, pleasant rogue. But people are always complaining that my clever people are rascals, and the good people idiots.' Elwin urged him to 'describe a domestic family, enjoying the genuine blessings of calm, domestic felicity, put in contrast with the vexations and hollowness of fashionable life'. Thackeray replied pathetically, 'How can I describe that sort of domestic calm? I have never seen it. I have lived all my life in Bohemia. Besides, there would be very little to describe. It must of necessity want movement. I intended to show J. J. married, and exhibit him with the trials of a wife and children. I meant to make him in love with another man's wife, and recover him through his attachment for the little ones.' 'This story', said Elwin, 'I begged him not to write.'

There was perhaps no one at all in whose company Whitwell Elwin ever delighted so much as in Thackeray's. 'All my recollections of him are pleasant', he said in 1865; 'I can never speak of him without a pang, for I loved him. He was a fine, noble man.' 'His manners', he said, 'were simple as a child's. He had no assumption, no affectation. His conversation was in the last degree easy.'[2] Thackeray's liking for Elwin was warm. Both men were admirable conversationalists, in different veins, but with common interests and a common appreciation of humour and literature. There was, moreover, an artless simplicity of a certain kind, combined with Elwin's genius, which took Thackeray's fancy. He called him Dr Primrose, and generally addressed him so in his letters, after they became intimate. Part of the ground of his affection was indicated in a note written to Elwin at a later date. 'All people don't like me as you do,' Thackeray said; 'I think sometimes I am deservedly unpopular, and in some cases I rather like it. Why should I want to be liked by Jack and Tom? ... I know the Thackeray that those fellows have imagined to themselves – a very selfish, heartless, artful, morose, and designing man. What gall and wormwood is trickling from my pen! Well, there's no black drop in *you*, Mr Parson; but, mind you, primroses are very rare flowers by the side of Thames....'

Both he and Mrs Elwin ... greatly enjoyed a couple of days in Norwich, in May [1857], when Thackeray came there to deliver his lectures on the Four Georges. Thackeray was in a delightful mood, quite at his ease, and full of conversation. Mrs Elwin put down at the time a hastily written record of the visit, and some of its items are worth quoting as they stand:

'He speaks very low. I found it needed attention to catch each word. He does not develop his ideas much; he only puts into words just the thought that passes through his own mind. This gives a fragmentary air to his talk. He seems little to care whether it is set off fully and to advantage, or even whether those who hear him altogether take it in. He showed two manners – one very quiet, very earnest, very deep, almost pathetic; another (a general and much more common manner) is like one who played at ball with every subject, tossing them about with a light, careless, but unerring hand, taking up one thing after another – serious and gay, trifling or important – and sporting with them as though he would get pleasantry out of everything. But if any religious subject was spoken of he talked with solemnity and earnestness.

'If you did not know who he was, the first thing which would strike you would be that he was a man who looked with a magician's eye through and through everything before him. In five minutes you know he has made a complete inventory of the room, and he has weighed out everybody in it. He sits quietly watching a face for two whole minutes, and then he turns away, having spelt every letter of the character. He is constantly speaking of the sort of face a man has – "he has a bad face", "a hang-dog face", etc. Badness mars all talent in his eyes. He talks of someone who is clever, and he then adds, "But he is a bad man", as if we had no right to admire a bad clever man. On the other hand, he is always throwing in gentle, considerate excuses for everybody. "So-and-so has this and that weakness." "Ah, but then remember such and such a reason for his excuse" – "Remember such and such a good quality notwithstanding." He seems to notice the slightest specks of goodness.

'As the hour for the lecture got near, he left. I had gone soon after dinner to sit with the children. When Thackeray left the dining-room he opened the door where we were, and said in his grave, pathetic voice, "I am come to say goodnight", and took each child's hand, and lingered for a moment with their hands in his own. Then he stepped out into the balcony, took out his purse, and threw a shilling to a brass band which had been playing before the window. "Now then for the sermon", he said, turning to me, and went to his own hotel to prepare for the lecture.

'He talks quite freely and simply of his own writings – tells a story, and then adds that it suggested such and such a trait of one of his characters. He said, "People tell me such and such a character is not natural; but I *know* it is natural, that it is to the life."

'It is evident that he does not set a tremendous price on his own writings. It appears as if he did not, and could not, labour them; and, being the produce of little effort, he cannot believe they are what they are. He replied to some of Whitwell's admiration of him, "Yes, but you rave; you are a maniac." Whitwell asked him how he found out his true vein, as his earliest things were not in it. He said he began to write when his misfortunes began, and then found it.

'He said he regretted not having illustrated *The Newcomes* himself. Whitwell said the conception of the Colonel's face and figure was fine. "Oh yes," he said, "but I gave it Doyle. I drew the Colonel for him."

'He laughed at the idea of future fame. He said he could not understand why any should care for fame after they were dead.

'His mother he described as having been exquisitely handsome, and as fascinating everyone who came in her way. "When I was a child my mother took me to Exeter, to a concert. She looked like a duchess. She came splendidly dressed, in a handsome carriage, and all suitable appurtenances. That was thirty years ago.[3] The next time I went to Exeter it was I who danced on the tightrope.[4] I took the girls down with me. I could see that the waiter at the inn took them for part of the performance, and expected them to put on their trousers and spangles, and come in and sing a comic song. We went and saw the place where Pendennis kissed Miss Costigan [*Pendennis*, ch. 6], and identified it all quite satisfactorily.

'"The first literary man I ever met was Croly. I was a lad of seventeen, on the top of a coach, going to Cambridge. Somebody pointed Croly out to me. I had read *Salathiel* at sixteen, and thought it divine.[5] I turned back and gazed at him. The person who pointed him out to me said, 'I see that lad is fated!' He knew it by the way I gazed after him as a literary man.

'"I once lent a man £300 to get an outfit for India. He lived on the same stairs with me at the Temple. He was to pay me when he could, and in course of time he did pay me. He came home to England, and I went to see him, and asked him to dine with me that day three weeks – at all events, my first vacant day. I asked him three times, and he never would come. At last he said, 'The truth is, I *can't* come. If it had been in India, and you had come there, my house would have been open to you, and not to you only, but to all your friends to come and make it a home. And I come to England, and you ask me to dine with you *this day three weeks*!' The truth is, they live in India, and cherish such ideas of England, and a home, and love, that when they come to it they are disappointed. You remember, Colonel Newcome was invited to dine *that day three weeks* with his brother? [*Newcomes*, ch. 6].

'"I think I shall take the girls, and go to India next year. I should like to see my native country. I have friends in almost all the judgeships. Twelve lectures would pay for it." Whitwell expressed his astonishment at his wish, but said, "I take it, you like a roving life." "Yes," said he, "I like it. I should never be at home if I could help." "But, can you write away from home?" "I write better anywhere than at home, and I write less at home than anywhere. I did not write ten pages of *The Newcomes* in that house at Brompton [36 Onslow Square]. I wrote two lectures in it. The last half of *The Newcomes* I wrote at Paris. This" – meaning an hotel – "is the best place to write in. After a good breakfast, I make one of the girls sit down to write. It is slow work. Sometimes not a sentence for a quarter of an hour. I could not do that with a stranger. With the young ones it is different, and they are delighted. A Scotchman came to me a little while ago, and I tried him as secretary, but he was deaf. I would begin, At this moment Anna entered the room, when the Captain observed to the Countess – What? – *The Captain observed to the Countess*. – But, you know, that couldn't go on."

'Talking of the wearisomeness of going about lecturing, he said, "There is something very sweet about it, too. I meet everywhere such kindness and hospitality – taken into families, and making friends among them – so that there is quite a little heart-pang at parting." "People bring me autograph books to write my name in – books full of the autographs of singers, fiddlers – I can't conceive what they can want the autograph of a fiddler for. So I wrote my name under Signor Twankeydillo. – Now your address. – But that was too much, I would not write my address."

'He said he made £70 by the lecture for ——.[6] "I always have a charity lecture every year. It is so pleasant to feel that I always have £20 in my pocket for a poor man.

' "A lady, a blue, at New York, said to me at dinner, 'I was told I should not like you, and I don't'. 'And, I replied, I don't in the least care whether you like me or no.' She looked so surprised."

'Whitwell said it was delightful to walk with him from Norwich to Thorpe, and see his keen enjoyment of the scene and of the beautiful day. He noticed the quick, artistic eye with which he viewed everything, but Thackeray said that it distressed him to find that he did not observe as much as he formerly did.

'He told me it had been a delightful day to him, going over the old city. He said it was "a charming old city". He had thought Exeter a very fine city, but Norwich was much better. He thought the beauty of the cathedral cloisters wonderful. He went over the castle [in use as a prison]. The aspect of it "stifled" him. "The men in the zebra clothes" saddened him. He "panted to be out again". His whole expression of face was disturbed as he talked of them, and he kept shuddering.

'He wished to go and see Yarmouth, but Whitwell discouraged him, and told him there was nothing to see there. "I want to see the Great Ocean; I want to see where Peggotty lived." '[7] . . .

[Elwin was in poor health and spirits during the winter of 1857–8 but] his spirits always revived when he met Thackeray. He dined with him at Forster's, on 6 January 1858. He did not know he was to be there, and on seeing him in the room, he exclaimed, and ran up to greet him before he had spoken to Mrs Forster. Forster remonstrated, and said it was not like him to do it. 'Oh! yes, it is', said Thackeray, and then turning to him added, 'Never mind, *I* forgive you.' At dinner Elwin told Thackeray that his best poem was that on his pen ['The Pen and the Album']. 'I cannot give you the pen with which I wrote it,' Thackeray replied, 'for I let it fall at Naples, and broke it, but I will give you the pencil-case.' Thereupon he took a silver pencil-case, with a gold pen from his pocket, and put it into Elwin's hands. . . .

After the dinner at Forster's, Thackeray and Elwin left together. On their way home Thackeray talked of *The Virginians*, which was then in its early stages. He said he meant to bring in Goldsmith – 'representing him as he really was, a little, shabby, mean, shuffling Irishman' – Garrick – whose laugh he was positive he should be able to identify from the look in his portrait – Dr Johnson, and the other celebrities of the reign of Queen Anne. He thought that he should find this easy, but he afterwards told Elwin that he had discovered he could not do it. The failure of his design threw him out, and the second half of the novel dragged for lack of materials. . . .

'Won't you come to London,' Thackeray wrote, 24 May 1861, 'and see the new house I am building? – such a good, comfortable, cheerful one, all built out of *Cornhill* money.' Accordingly Elwin lunched with him when he was in town in June, and went to look at the house. As they were going over it, Thackeray said, 'An uncle of mine [Charles Carmichael]

annoyed me by saying, "It ought to be called *Vanity Fair*." '
'Why should that annoy you?' asked Elwin. 'Because it is true,'
replied the other; 'the fact is, it is too good for me.'

Elwin, on the same occasion, praised *The Adventures of Philip*,
which was then coming out in the *Cornhill*. Thackeray knew
wherein its weakness lay. He said, 'I have told my tale in the
novel department. I can repeat old things in a pleasant way,
but I have nothing fresh to say. I get sick of my task when I am
ill, and think, Good heavens! what is all this stuff about?' Miss
Thackeray asked him at lunch whether he was going to dine at
home or 'at a house by a river'. 'At a house by a river, to be
sure,' he answered; 'I shall go to Greenwich and write a bit of
Philip.' 'Write *Philip* at a tavern at Greenwich!' exclaimed
Elwin. 'Yes,' he replied, 'I cannot write comfortably in my own
room. I do most of my composition at hotels or at a club.
There is an excitement in public places which sets my brain
working.'

NOTES

1. 'J. J.'s history . . . has been revealed to me too, and may be told some of these fine summer months, or Christmas evenings, when the kind reader has leisure to hear' (*Newcomes*, ch. 80).
2. 'MS. Notes of Conversation' [Warwick Elwin's footnote]. The account of their conversation on 10 October 1856 is likewise drawn from an 'MS. Memorandum'.
3. 'In 1827 Thackeray was sixteen. His stepfather and his mother had moved into Devonshire in 1825. He must have been a boy therefore, rather than a "child"' [Warwick Elwin's note].
4. That is, as Warwick Elwin notes, gave his *Four Georges* lectures (May 1857).
5. As Warwick Elwin notes, *Salathiel: A Story of the Past, the Present and the Future* (1829) was not published when Thackeray was sixteen (1827). The Revd George Croly (1780–1860) was a novelist, poet and critic, besides being a famous preacher.
6. The impresario Willert Beale. The agreed fee was, in fact, fifty guineas, as Beale reports in *The Light of Other Days* (1890) p. 254. This was for a series of fifty appearances, in 1857. Beale, who found the contract unprofitable, tells how, after the first five lectures, he called upon Thackeray with a cheque for £250. 'Pounds?' Thackeray responded. 'Our agreement says guineas, and guineas it must be.' When Beale 'by way of apology' replied that the series had already involved him in a very heavy loss, Thackeray was

unmoved: 'That's not my affair.... Guineas, W. B.! Guineas it must be, and nothing less! I must have my shillings' (ibid., p. 262).

7. Ray (*LPP*, IV, 380n) aptly cites a conversation in which Thackeray remarked that 'while he loved Colonel Newcome... he believed a finer gentleman was Dan'l Peggotty! It was really delightful to hear him sustain this position against many dissenting voices...' (*Philadelphia Press*, 12 June 1887).

My Hearty, Hospitable, Beloved and Honoured Friend

DEAN HOLE

From *The Memories of Dean Hole*, 5th edn (1893) pp. 78–85. Samuel Reynolds Hole (1819–1904), Vicar of Caunton, 1850–87, and then Dean of Rochester, a cheerful and somewhat worldly cleric and a popular preacher, contributed to *Punch* and wrote widely on non-religious matters besides composing hymns and publishing his sermons. A familiar figure in society, he regarded it as 'a great intellectual treat to meet... Thackeray and Millais, Holman Hunt and Tenniel... Mark Lemon and Shirley Brooks, and dear old Percival Leigh', and he described Thackeray as being, from the first day they met, 'my hearty, hospitable, beloved, and honoured friend' – *Letters of Dean Hole*, ed. G. A. B. Dewar (1907) p. 29. On Thackeray's invitation, he wrote verses for the *Cornhill*, and he contributed memories of him to Dr John Brown's essay in *Horae Subsecivae*. 'In the last years of his life,' writes Ray, 'Thackeray saw much of [Hole], than whom he had no more faithful admirer' (*LPP*, IV, 174n), and Anny Thackeray said that her father had a great regard for him (*Letters*, p. 28).

I first met Thackeray at dinner, when I was staying with Leech.... He arrived in high good humour, and with a bright smile on his face. I was introduced by our host, and for his sake he gave me a cordial greeting. 'We must be about the same height,' he said; 'we'll measure.' And when, as we stood *dos-à-dos*, and the bystanders gave their verdict, 'a dead heat' (the length was six feet three inches), and I had meekly suggested 'that though there might be no difference in the size of the cases, his contained a Stradivarius, and mine a dancing-master's kit', we proceeded to talk of giants. He told me of a visit which he paid with Mr Higgins, 'Jacob Omnium', who was four or five inches the taller of the two, to see a Brobdignagian on show, and how the man at the door had inquired 'whether they were in the business, because, if so, no charge would be made'....

We had many a pleasant reunion. Whenever we met, he invited me to his house, and always, before the guests went home, he whispered in my ear, 'Stay for the fragrant weed.' He proposed me for the Garrick Club, and there we often dined together. I have few memories of his conversation. He said so many good things, being the best talker I have ever listened to, when it pleased him to talk, that they trod down and suffocated each other; but I have a distinct recollection of one most interesting discussion which he had with a learned professor from Cambridge. The subject of debate, suggested by the publication of Buckle's *History of Civilisation*, was upon the power of the human mind, and the progress of scientific discovery, to eliminate the sorrow and enlarge the happiness of mankind. The professor seemed to think that there would be hardly any limit to these attainments. Thackeray spoke, as Newton spoke about gathering pebbles on the shore, and affirmed that one of the best results of knowledge was to convince a man of his ignorance. He seemed to preach from the text, though he did not quote it, that the wisdom of this world is foolishness with God. It was a combat between pride and humility, and pride had its usual fall.

On one subject he was proud, but it was a pride which testified to his own freedom from self-conceit. He was proud of his daughter's books. 'I assure you', he said (but we tacitly declined to be sure), 'that Anny can write ten times more cleverly than I.'...

I only once heard Thackeray allude to his works, and that in a serio-comic spirit, which amused both him and us. 'I was travelling on the Rhine,' he said (in company, no doubt, with 'the Kickleburys'), 'and entering one of the hotels on the banks, exhausted and weary, I went into the salon, and threw myself on a sofa. There was a book on a little table close by, and I opened it, to find that it was *Vanity Fair*. I had not seen it since I corrected the proofs, and I read a chapter. Do you know, it seemed to me very amusing!'

He was more solicitous about his illustrations than his text, and derived more enjoyment, I believe, from his pencil than from his pen. Artists would sometimes venture upon critical comments. There was one sketch of a battle-field, which they said would have been purchased by the nation if the combatants had not been concealed beneath a canopy of smoke. But it was perilous to measure swords with one who was such a master of fence, and whose motto was *Nemo me impune lacessit* ['No one provokes me with impunity']. Sometimes there was a combination to chaff him, as swallows congregate to pursue a hawk; but 'he did bestride this narrow world like a Colossus, and those petty men walked under his huge legs to peep about, and find themselves dishonourable graves'. There was one member of the Garrick whose presence and speech seemed to irritate him, and who found pleasure in exercising his power as a gadfly on a thoroughbred horse.[1] One night, in the smoke-room, Thackeray was in the middle of a most interesting story, when his enemy suddenly entered. To everyone's surprise, Thackeray hesitated and stopped, on which his persecutor, assuming an air of the most gracious patronage, blandly encouraged him, with *'Proceed, sweet warbler; thy story interests me.'* . . .

My last interview with Thackeray took place not long before his death.[2] I went with Leech, and the servant told us that he was engaged. As we were going disappointed away, Miss Thackeray opened the door and called to us. 'Of course, papa will see you.' We went up to his study, and found him sitting, *more suo*,[3] with his face turned to the back of his chair, on which a small board was fastened for his writing materials. He sighed, and said he was wearied by his long monotonous work (it was nigh the end, for the last pages of *Denis Duval* were before him); and Leech said, 'Why don't you have a holiday, and take the girls to the seaside?' He made no verbal answer, but, rising slowly, plunged his hands to the very bottom of his pockets, brought them out, shook, replaced them, and then resumed his seat.

NOTES

1. Andrew Arcedeckne: on whom see above, I, 130.
2. Probably the occasion mentioned in a letter to his wife, 30 Sep 1863: he had called upon Thackeray that morning, and was to dine with him, Leech and Millais at the Garrick Club that night (*Letters of Dean Hole*, p. 28).
3. 'According to his wont.'

'The Kindest and Truest Heart that Ever Beat'

EMELYN AND EDITH STORY

(1) from Henry James, *William Wetmore Story and his Friends* (1903) I, 367–8; (2) from La Marchesa Peruzzi de Medici [*née* Edith Story], 'Thackeray, My Childhood's Friend', *Cornhill Magazine*, n.s. XXXI (1911) 178–81. Thackeray was first acquainted with the American poet and sculptor William Wetmore Story (1819–95) and his family in Rome, in the winter of 1853–4, when their eldest son had just died of fever and their daughter Edith was dangerously ill with it. His comfort to Edith and her parents was deeply appreciated. The friendship endured, with further meetings in Paris, London and Boston.

(1) [Henry James finds among Mrs Story's memoranda 'an affectionate reference to Thackeray', relating to their meeting in Paris, early in 1855.] 'I took [his daughter] Anny to her first ball at the Hôtel de Ville, and his interest in her dress, appearance and enjoyment was delightful to see. He sat up for her, to have the details of the evening before she had lost her fresh impression, and enjoyed to the full her enthusiasm over the splendours we had seen. He often looked in upon us during his afternoon walk, talked with Edith as she liked, and looked with her over the wardrobe, counted even the rows of socks, of *mon petit frère*, in whom he took great interest. The next winter he was with us in Boston, and dined with us, in Rowe Street I remember, on [our baby] Waldo's first birthday, calling him "Henry the Eighth" and tipping him with his first sovereign.' And she goes back to the sad winter in Rome, the time of the death of her eldest son, when 'we often urged him to forget us and not to be drawn down into the depths of our sorrow, but rather to disport himself in the cordial sunshine of appreciation, among his own people, to which he had so good a right. But he would not hear of this, and came again and again, listening to our tale of grief as if it had happened to

himself, with a kindness and sympathy never to be forgotten. Once he surprised me when I had in my hand a little worn shoe which had for me an intense association; he shed tears over it with me and understood what it meant to me as few could have done.... Under what people called his cynical exterior and manner, his was the kindest and truest heart that ever beat, large in its sympathies and gracious in its giving. I think he must have liked us – we liked *him* so much and took such endless pleasure in his society. When alone with us he talked abundantly, but when people were numerous he seemed to have little to say.'

(2) [During Edith's convalescence, Thackeray] was a constant visitor. He seemed to me [she recalled] like a great benevolent giant when he first came into the room, but even at first my child's heart went out to him. There seemed no distance between us; and I can see him today as I saw him then – his large powerful frame dominated by his great head; the steadfast eyes and his gold spectacles in my child mind the only thing that showed he was not a real giant.

It was a black day when the dear giant did not come, and my restless eyes were often turned to the door in expectancy. It seemed quite natural that he should come where he was so much wanted, and I could not then appreciate what in after-years I felt so deeply – what a great-hearted man he was, knowing all the overwhelming, all-absorbing interests of Rome and his many friends that he put aside when he came into the half-darkened room where the little feeble child lay in her white bed. He used to sit on the edge of the bed or draw his chair close up to it, and, joy of joys, he brought, chapter by chapter, to read to me *The Rose and the Ring*. After he had done reading we talked of the people in the story – they were real people to me and to him. I used to hold the pages, written in that small handwriting we all know so well, and then it did not seem to me as if a great giant could write 'so small', but I thought he must have called in a fairy scribe; and as he did not answer, but only smiled, when I told him so, I half thought it must be the case!

Sometimes he would say, 'Now you must tell me a little story to amuse me', and I tried my best to recall something he would like, that I had heard, or invent a little tale. At these times he would sit by the table and draw some illustration of what I was telling him, in pen and ink.... When he came to tell me he was going away, he promised that *The Rose and the Ring* should be printed, and then he would give me the first copy, as well as that written in the fairy writing....

The last time I remember seeing him was one day when I went to Palace Green to lunch.... At table a spasm of pain came into his face, and he went at once into the other room, where we followed. He suffered terribly, and I sat awestruck in a corner watching the others, who seemed able to help him when I could do nothing. After a time the pain subsided, he opened his eyes and saw my anxious face, silent in tears. He called, 'Edie Ochiltree, come to me at once; you see, it is nothing, child.'[1]

NOTE

1. Edie Ochiltree is a sagacious and comforting figure in Scott's *The Antiquary*.

Literary Habits, Tastes and Plans

JOHN ESTEN COOKE

From 'An Hour with Thackeray', *Appleton's Journal*, XXII (1879) 249–54. Cooke (1830–86) was just beginning to make a name for himself as a novelist with his romances of colonial Virginia (*Leather Stocking and Silk* and *The Virginian Comedians*, both 1854) when he met Thackeray during his visit to Richmond, Virginia, in January 1856. He wrote further romances and memoirs, mostly on Virginian topics, over the next thirty years. Before describing his 'hour with Thackeray' he gives his first impressions when they met at a friend's house. Everyone, he suggests, feels a strong curiosity about the character and habits of his favourite authors: but Thackeray, as a man, had a formidable and rather unendearing reputation.

What impressed me first was the remarkable difference between the real man and the malicious cartoons drawn of him by his English critics. These gentlemen seemed to have dipped their pens in gall before drawing his likeness. Their outlines were bit in with acid. There had never lived, according to them, a more unamiable human being than the author of *Vanity Fair*. Persons with any respect for themselves could not endure him. His heart was cold, his disposition cynical, and his manners so haughty and repelling that everybody thrown in contact with him became his enemy. As he strode by, he scarcely deigned to return the salutes of his friends, if he had any. He would stare, or respond with a curt nod. He would sit up hobnobbing with intimates until four in the morning, and then pass the same persons in the afternoon, as he rode toward the Park, with a movement of the head so cold and indifferent that it quite froze them. He rarely smiled; had nothing about him either natural or inviting; to quote the words of one of his critics,[1] 'His bearing is cold and uninviting, his style of conversation either openly cynical or affectedly good-natured and benevolent; his *bonhomie* is forced, his wit biting, his pride easily touched.' As to his character, that was said to be as disagreeable as his manners. He was one mass of gloom and misanthropy. Cynicism was his philosophy, and contempt his religion. Seeing nothing to love or respect in human nature, he pursued his species with merciless ridicule – especially woman. If they were good, they were feeble in intellect; if they possessed brains, they were uniformly vicious – as in the cases of Amelia Sedley and Becky Sharp. Fancying himself the English Juvenal, he had something bitter to say of everybody and everything. A mixture of Timon and Diogenes, he went about with a scowl on his brow and a sneer on his lips, refusing to see good anywhere, and spitting out his hate and venom on the whole human species.

If any reader doubts whether 'good old Thackeray', as his friends in this country used to call him, was ever thus painted, he has only to turn over the leaves of certain English periodicals published twenty years ago, where he will find that the warm-hearted gentleman was actually at that time so described....

These criticisms, or rather caricatures, were quite familiar to me when I went to call on Mr Thackeray that morning in 1856, and I was quite surprised, as I have said, to find how different that real person was from the portraits drawn of him. I saw a tall, ruddy, simple-looking Englishman, who cordially held out his hand, and met me with a friendly smile. There was nothing like a scowl on the face, and it was neither thin, bilious, nor ill-natured, but plump, rubicund, and indicative of an excellent digestion. His voice was neither curt nor ungracious, but courteous and cordial – the voice of a gentleman receiving a friend under his own roof. In person he was a 'large man' – his height I think was above six feet. His eyes were mild in expression, his hair nearly grey, his dress plain and unpretending. Everything about the individual produced the impression that pretence was hateful to him. He was quiet in his manner, and spoke slowly and deliberately in a low tone – apparently uttering his thought as it rose to his lips without selecting his words. After spending ten minutes with him, it was easy to see that he was a man of the world in the best sense of the phrase, and neither a bitter Juvenal nor a shy 'literary man', living only in books. There was, indeed, almost nothing of the typical *littérateur* about him. His face and figure indicated a decided fondness for roast beef, canvas-back ducks – of which he spoke in terms of enthusiasm – plum pudding, 'Bordeaux', of which he told me he drank a bottle daily at his dinner, and all the material good things of life. The idea of a disordered liver seems absurd in connection with him. The fact is, Mr Thackeray was a *bon vivant* – not given to wearing his heart upon his sleeve, but prone to good fellowship, fond of his ease, and liked nothing better than to loll in his armchair, tell or listen to a good story, sing a good song, smoke a good cigar, and 'have his talk out' with his chosen friends.

As to the general tone of his conversation, what impressed me most forcibly was his entire unreserve, and the genuine *bonhomie* of his air – a *bonhomie* which struck me as being anything but what his critic, Mr Yates, called it – 'forced'. The man seemed wholly simple and natural.... He smiled easily, and evidently enjoyed the humorous side of things, but in private, as in delivering his lectures on Swift and some others, there was an undertone of sadness in his voice. For whether from temperament or in consequence of the great domestic sorrow which was his lot, Mr Thackeray was not a gay man. He was kind, courteous, and good-humoured, but not a hearty, cheery person; and evidently did not look upon this as the best of all possible worlds. His comments on men and things were occasionally, half sad, half satirical. He seemed to regard life as a comedy, in which rascals, male and female, predominated – his business as a writer being to laugh at or denounce them. That he saw more vice than virtue, and had been a little soured, may have been caused by his own personal experiences. It is known that his lot had been trying. . . .

To come to my 'talk with Thackeray', which the reader may consider too slight a matter for so long a preface. It certainly was not my purpose to 'interview' Mr Thackeray on this or any other occasion. I met him in private or at the houses of friends, who gave him entertainments, and listened with great interest to his opinions of men and books; but I had no intention to make a record of anything which fell from his lips in these unreserved talks. There is no harm in doing so now when he is dead, and I find no difficulty in recalling, aided by some chance memoranda, what Mr Thackeray said in one of these interviews – to which I shall now proceed.

Having no business to engage me one morning, I went to call on him at his hotel, and found him in his private parlour, lolling in an easy-chair, and smoking. This good or bad habit, as the reader pleases, was a favourite one with him. He was a dear lover of his cigar, and I had presented him with a bundle of very good small 'Plantations', which he afterward spoke highly of, lamenting that his friend G. P. R. James,[2] then consul at Richmond, *would* come and smoke them all. On this morning he had evidently nothing to occupy him, and seemed ready for a friendly talk. Smoking was the first topic, and he said:

'I am fond of my cigar, you see. I always begin writing with one in my mouth.'

'After breakfast, I suppose. I mean that you probably write in the forenoon?'

'Yes, the morning is my time for composing. I can't write at night. I find it excites me so that I can not sleep.'

'May I ask if you ever dictate your books to an amanuensis?' I said. . . .

Mr Thackeray replied, 'I have dictated a good deal. The whole of *Esmond* was dictated to an amanuensis.'

'I should not have supposed so – the style is so terse that I would have fancied you *wrote* it. *Esmond* is one of the greatest favourites among your works in this country. I always particularly liked the chapter where Esmond returns to Lady Castlewood, "bringing his sheaves with him", as she says.'

'I am glad it pleased you. I wish the whole book was as good. But we can't play first fiddle all the time.'

'You dictated this chapter?'

'Yes – the whole work. I also dictated all of *Pendennis*. I can't say I think much of *Pendennis* – at least of the execution. It certainly drags about the middle, but I had an attack of illness about the time I reached that part of the book, and could not make it any better than it is.'

Another allusion to *Esmond*, and his portrait of Marlborough brought from Mr Thackeray's lips, in a musing tone, the single word 'Rascal!' and he then inquired in a very friendly manner what I had written. I informed him, and he said, 'Well, if I were you, I would go on writing – some day you will write a book which will make your fortune. Becky Sharp made mine. I married early, and wrote for bread; and *Vanity Fair* was my first successful work. I like Becky in that book. Sometimes I think I have myself some of her tastes. I like what are called Bohemians, and fellows of that sort. I have seen all sorts of society – dukes and duchesses, lords and ladies, authors and actors, and painters – and, taken altogether, I think I like painters the best, and "Bohemians" generally. They are more natural and unconventional; they wear their hair on their shoulders if they wish, and dress picturesquely and carelessly. You see how I made *Becky* prefer them, and that sort of life, to all the fine society she moved in. Perhaps you remember where she comes down in the world toward the end of the book, and associates with people of all sorts, Bohemians and the rest, in their garrets. . . . I like that part of the book. I think that part is well done.'

'As you speak of Becky Sharp, Mr Thackeray,' I said, 'there is one mystery about her which I should like to have cleared up. . . . Nearly at the end of the book there is a picture of Jo Sedley in his night-dress, seated – a sick old man – in his chamber; and behind the curtain is Becky, glaring and ghastly, grasping a dagger. . . . Beneath the picture is the single word "Clytemnestra" . . . . Did Becky kill him, Mr Thackeray?'

This question seemed to afford the person to whom it was

addressed, material for profound reflection. He smoked meditatively, appeared to be engaged in endeavouring to arrive at the solution of some problem, and then with a secretive expression – a 'slow smile' dawning on his face – replied, 'I don't know!'

A desultory conversation ensued on the subject of Becky Sharp, for whom, in spite of her depravity, it seemed very plain that Mr Thackeray had a secret liking, or, if not precisely a liking, at least an amused sympathy, due to the pluck and perseverance with which she pursued the objects she had in view. And then, from this lady and her sayings and doings, the conversation passed to Mr Thackeray's other *mauvais sujets*, male and female; and I said that I considered the old Earl of Crabs, in the sketches relating to 'Mr Deuceace',[3] as the most finished and altogether perfect scoundrel of the whole list. To this Mr Thackeray was disposed to assent, and I asked if the Earl was drawn from any particular person.

'I really don't know', was the reply. 'I don't remember ever meeting with any special person as the original,'

'Then you must have drawn him from your imagination, or from general observation.'

'I suppose so – I don't know – I may have seen him somewhere.'

And after smoking for several moments, with that air of silent meditation which his friends must often have observed, Mr Thackeray added, in the tone of a man indulging in soliloquy, 'I really don't know where I get all these rascals in my books. I have certainly never *lived* with such people'....

Mr Thackeray spoke of himself and his writings with entire candour and unreserve, of which I shall give an instance before concluding this brief sketch; and his opinions upon other writers were equally frank and outspoken. The elder Dumas, the author of *Monte Cristo* and the *Mousquetaire* stories, seemed to be an especial favourite with him. 'Dumas is charming,' he exclaimed; 'everything he writes interests me. I have been reading his *Mémoires*. I have read fourteen of the small volumes, all that are published, and they are delightful. Dumas is a wonderful man – wonderful. He is better than Walter Scott.'

'You refer, I suppose, to his historical novels, the *Mousquetaires*, and the rest.'

'Yes. I came near writing a book on the same subject, and taking Monseur d'Artagnan for my hero, as Dumas has done in his *Trois Mousquetaires*. D'Artagnan was a real character of the age of Louis XIV, and wrote his own *Mémoires*. I remember picking up a dingy little copy of them on an old bookstall in London, price sixpence, and intended to make something of it. But Dumas got ahead of me – he snaps up everything. He is wonderful!'

'I am glad you like him, as he was always a great favourite of my own,' I said; 'his *verve* is inflagging.'

'Yes; his good spirits seem never to change. He amuses you, and keeps you in a good humour, which is not the effect produced on me by many writers. Some books please me and enliven me, and others depress me. I never could read *Don Quixote* with pleasure. The book makes me sad.'

Further allusion to the old knight of La Mancha indicated that the source of this sadness was a profound sympathy with the crazed gentleman – a commiseration so deep for his troubles and chimeras of the brain, that the wit and farcical humour of Sancho were insufficient, in his opinion, to relieve the shadows of the picture.

Passing from these literary discussions, Mr Thackeray spoke of his tour in America, and said how much gratified he had been by his reception.... Further conversation upon Virginia, the character of the country, people, etc., led Mr Thackeray to speak of what was then a mere literary intention – the composition of *The Virginians*, which was not written, I think, or at least did not appear, until two or three years afterward.

'I shall write a novel with the scene laid here', he said.

'In America? I am very glad, and I hope you will be able to do so soon.'

'No. I shall not write it for about two years.... It will take me at least two years to collect my materials, and become acquainted with the subject. I can't write upon a subject I know nothing of. I am obliged to read up upon it, and get my ideas.'

'Your work will be a novel?'

'Yes, and relating to your State. I shall give it the title of *The Two Virginians*' – a title which, as the reader knows, was afterward changed for the shorter and simpler *The Virginians*.

As I expressed a natural pleasure at the prospect of having a novel painting Virginia life and society from the author of *Esmond*, Mr Thackeray spoke more particularly of his design, thereby exhibiting. I thought, and think still, a remarkable instance of the simplicity, directness, and absence of *secretiveness* in his character. I was nearly an entire stranger, but he spoke without reserve of his intended book, telling me his whole idea. 'I shall lay the scene in Virginia, during the Revolution', he said. 'There will be two brothers, who will be prominent characters; one will take the English side in the war, and the other the American, and they will both be in love with the same girl.'[4]

'That will be an excellent plot,' I said, 'and your novel will be a full-blooded historical one.'

'It will deal with the history of the time.'

'You have a strong *dénouement* – '

'A *dénouement*?'

'Yorktown.'

Having so said, I became suddenly aware that I had committed something closely resembling a social *faux pas*, inasmuch as I had quietly recommended to an English gentleman to take the surrender of Lord Cornwallis as the climax of his drama.

'I really must beg your pardon, Mr Thackeray', I said with some embarrassment.

'Beg my pardon?' he said, turning his head, and looking at me with a good deal of surprise.

'For my ill-breeding.'

His expression of surprise was more pronounced than before at these words, and he evidently did not understand my meaning in the least.

'I mean,' I said, 'that I quite lost sight of the fact that I was talking with an English gentleman. Yorktown was the scene of Lord Cornwallis's surrender, and might not be an agreeable *dénouement*.'

'Ah!' he said smiling, 'it is nothing. I accept Yorktown.'

'I know you admire Washington.'

'Yes, indeed. He was one of the greatest men that ever lived.'

My host had evidently no susceptibilities to wound in reference to these old historical matters, so I said, smiling, 'Everybody respects and loves Washington now; but is it not singular how the *result* changes our point of view? The English view in '76 was that Washington was a rebel, and if you had caught him you would probably have hanged him.'

To this Mr Thackeray replied in a tone of great earnestness, 'We had better have lost North America.'

This ends my brief sketch of an hour's talk with this man of great and varied genius. The man was a study, as his books are; and I might almost say that he was to me more interesting than his books. The singular commingling of humour and sadness, of sarcasm and gentleness – the contrast between his reputation as the bitterest of cynics, growling harsh anathemas at his species, and the real person, with his cordial address, and his voice which at times had a really exquisite sweetness and music in its undertone – these made up a personality of such piquant interest that the human being was a study.

NOTES

1. Edmund Yates (see below, II, 315).
2. G. P. R. James (1799–1860), lush romantic novelist, parodied by Thackeray in '*Punch*'s Prize Novelists' – '*Barbazure*, by G. P. R. Jeames, Esq.'. The New York publisher James Harper told Thackeray that James was by far the most popular British novelist in the United States. He was in the consular service there, 1850–6.
3. In *The Yellowplush Papers*.
4. This plan was later modified.

'The Essential Manliness of his Nature'

BAYARD TAYLOR

'William Makepeace Thackeray, by One who Knew Him', *Atlantic Monthly*, XIII (1864) 371–8. During his second American lecture tour Thackeray met Bayard Taylor (1825–78), prolific poet, travel-writer and novelist, later famous also for his translation of *Faust*. They immediately took to each

(a) (b)

9. Sketches of Thackeray's London houses by Eyre Crowe, from his *Thackeray's Haunts and Homes, 1897*

   (a) No. 13 Great Coram Street, Brunswick Square, where he lived from 1837 to 1840.

   (b) No. 13 Young Street, Kensington, where he lived from 1846 to 1853 and wrote *Vanity Fair.*

   (c) No. 36 Onslow Square, Brompton, his house from 1854 to 1862.

   (d) Palace Green, Kensington, which he rebuilt and where he died in 1863.

(c) (d)

10. Crayon sketch of Thackeray by Samuel Laurence, 1852

Commissioned by the publisher George Smith. 'A capital head of me', remarked Thackeray, who regarded Laurence as 'the best drawer of heads since Van Dyke' and 'the only painter in London fit to paint any man with brains in his head'. Charlotte Brontë, thanking George Smith for an engraving of this portrait, commented: 'To me the broad brow seems to express intellect. Certain lines about the nose and cheek betray the satirist and cynic; the mouth indicates the childlike simplicity – perhaps even a degree of irresoluteness, inconsistency – weakness, in short, but a weakness not unamiable. The engraving seems to me very good. A certain not quite Christian expression – "not to put too fine a point upon it" – an expression of *spite*, most vividly marked in the original, is here softened, and perhaps a little – a very little – of the power has escaped in this ameliorating process. Did it strike you thus?'

11. Painting of Thackeray in his study by E. M. Ward

When exhibited at the Royal Academy in 1864, this was entitled 'Thackeray in his Study, 1844', but Ward's biographer James Dafforne (1879) prints a letter from Thackeray (not in *LPP*) arranging for a sitting, written from 36 Onslow Square, where Thackeray resided between 1854 and 1862. The picture was 'something more than a mere portrait', Dafforne remarked: 'for though the author . . . is brought vividly to eye, just as he lived, and thought, and worked . . . the accessories of the study are introduced, even to such trivialities as slippers, cigars, and waste-paper basket'. Another letter to Ward printed by Dafforne, not in *LPP,* was written in the last week of Thackeray's life.

12. Painting of Thackeray at the Garrick Club by Sir John Gilbert, R.A.

The painting against which Thackeray is sitting is by Clarkson Stanfield, and still hangs in the Garrick Club. The portrait was executed posthumously.

13a. *(left)* **Sketch by Frederick Walker, 1861.**

George Smith, the publisher of the *Cornhill*, suggested that Walker might be employed to copy Thackeray's illustrations for *Philip*, and brought him to be interviewed. 'I'm going to shave,' said Thackeray, 'would you mind drawing my back?' – a test 'as ingenious as it was kind', Smith remarked, since Walker, then a very shy lad of twenty, would have been terrified if asked to sketch the great man's face. Thackeray was so satisfied by the result that he engaged Walker, and also asked him to execute this drawing for the initial letter of his *Roundabout* essay 'Round about the Christmas Tree', from a rough sketch he provided. Anny Thackeray thought it 'wonderfully like him – I sometimes think more like than anything else I have ever seen.'

13b. *(right)* Pencil drawing by Richard Doyle, described by F. G. Kitton as 'very characteristic'.

14. Photograph of Thackeray in his library by E. Edwards, *c.* 1863

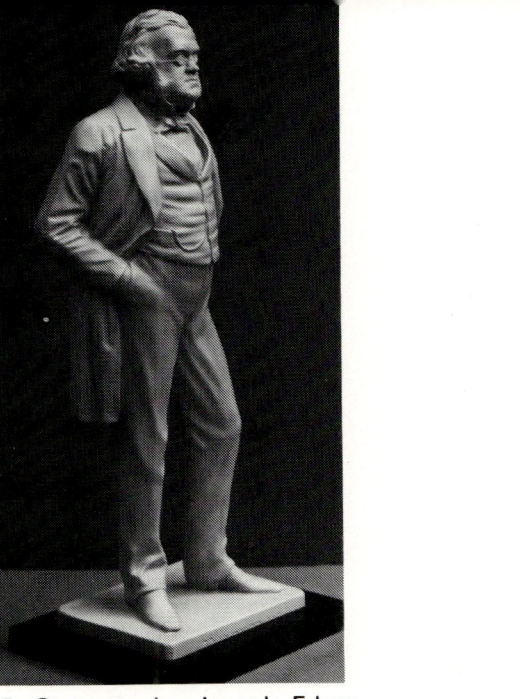

15. Statuette by Joseph Edgar Boehm, 1864

Anthony Trollope, who possessed a copy of this statuette, thought it gave a very accurate idea of the man: 'Mr Boehm has certainly not flattered, but, as far as my eye can judge, he has given the figure of the man exactly as he used to stand before us.'

16. Engraving from a photograph of Thackeray by Herbert Watkins, c. 1863

17. Drawing (executed in 1864) of Thackeray in 1862, by Samuel Laurence, after his canvas now in the National Portrait Gallery

other: Thackeray 'fell in love with Taylor at first sight', finding him 'one of the most interesting men I have ever seen in my life' – *Life and Letters of Bayard Taylor*, ed. Marie Hansen-Taylor and Horace E. Scudder (1884) I, 315n. They met subsequently during Taylor's visits to Europe.

In one sense ... he was misunderstood by the world, and he has died before that profounder recognition which he craved had time to mature. All the breadth and certainty of his fame failed to compensate him for the lack of this: the man's heart coveted that justice which was accorded only to the author's brain. Other pens may sum up the literary record he has left behind: I claim the right of a friend who knew and loved him to speak of him as a man.... During a friendship of nearly seven years, he permitted me to see that one true side of an author's nature which is never so far revealed to the public that the malignant may avail themselves of his candour to assail or the fools to annoy him....

I made Thackeray's acquaintance in New York towards the close of the year 1855. With the first grasp of his broad hand, and the first look of his large, serious grey eyes, I received an impression of the essential manliness of his nature – of his honesty, his proud, almost defiant candour, his ever-present, yet shrinking tenderness, and that sadness of the moral sentiment which the world persisted in regarding as cynicism. This impression deepened with my further acquaintance, and was never modified. Although he belonged to the sensitive, irritable genus, his only manifestations of impatience which I remember were when that which he had written with a sigh was interpreted as a sneer. When so misunderstood, he scorned to set himself right. 'I have no brain above the eyes', he was accustomed to say; 'I describe what I see.' He was quick and unerring in detecting the weaknesses of his friends, and spoke of them with a tone of disappointment sometimes bordering on exasperation; but he was equally severe upon his own shortcomings. He allowed no friend to think him better than his own deliberate estimate made him. I have never known a man whose nature was so immovably based on truth.

In a conversation upon the United States, shortly after we first met, he said, 'There is one thing in this country which astonishes me. You have a capacity for culture which contradicts all my experience. There are —— ' (mentioning two or three names well known in New York) 'who I know have arisen from nothing, yet they are fit for any society in the world. They would be just as self-possessed and entertaining in the presence of stars and garters as they are here tonight. Now, in England, a man who has made his way up, as they have, doesn't seem able to feel his social dignity. A little bit of the flunky sticks in him somewhere. I am, perhaps, as independent in this respect as any one I know, yet I'm not entirely sure of myself.'

'Do you remember', I asked him, 'what Goethe says of the boys in Venice? He explains their cleverness, grace, and self-possession as children by the possibility of any one of them becoming Doge.'

'That may be the secret, after all', said Thackeray. 'There is no country like yours for a young man who is obliged to work for his own place and fortune. If I had sons, I should send them here.'

Afterwards, in London, I visited with him the studio of Baron Marochetti,[1] the sculptor, who was then his next-door neighbour in Onslow Square, Brompton. The Baron, it appeared, had promised him an original wood-cut of Albert Dürer's, for whom Thackeray had a special admiration. Soon after our entrance, the sculptor took down a small engraving from the wall, saying, 'Now you have it, at last.'

The subject was St George and the Dragon.

Thackeray inspected it with great delight for a few minutes: then, suddenly becoming grave, he turned to me and said, 'I shall hang it near the head of my bed, where I can see it every morning. We all have our dragons to fight. Do you know yours? I know mine: I have not one, but two.'

'What are they?' I asked.

'Indolence and Luxury!'

I could not help smiling, as I thought of the prodigious amount of literary labour he had performed, and at the same time remembered the simple comfort of his dwelling, next door.

'I am serious,' he continued; 'I never take up the pen without an effort; I work only from necessity. I never walk out without seeing some pretty, useless thing which I want to buy. Sometimes I pass the same shop-window every day for months, and resist the temptation, and think I'm safe; then comes the day of weakness, and I yield. My physician tells me I must live very simply, and not dine out so much; but I cannot break off the agreeable habit. I shall look at this picture and think of my dragons, though I don't expect ever to overcome them.'

After his four lectures on the Georges had been delivered in New York, a storm of angry abuse was let loose upon him in Canada and the other British provinces. The British Americans, snubbed both by government and society when they go to England, repay the slight, like true Christians, by a rampant loyalty unknown in the mother country. Many of their newspapers accused Thackeray of pandering to the prejudices of the American public, affirming that he would not dare to repeat the same lectures in England, after his return. Of course, the papers containing the articles, duly marked to attract attention, were sent to him. He merely remarked, as he threw them contemptuously aside, 'These fellows will see that I shall not only repeat the lectures at home, but I shall make them more severe, just because the auditors will be Englishmen.' He was true to his promise. The lecture on George IV excited, not, indeed, the same amount of newspaper-abuse as he had received from Canada, but a very angry feeling in the English aristocracy, some members of which attempted to punish him by a social ostracism. When I visited him in London, in July 1856, he related this to me, with great good humour. 'There, for instance,' said he, 'is Lord —— ' (a prominent English statesman) 'who has dropped me from his dinner-parties for three months past. Well, he will find that I can do without his society better than he can do without mine.' A few days afterwards Lord —— resumed his invitations.

About the same time I witnessed an amusing interview, which explained to me the great personal respect in which Thackeray was held by the aristocratic class. He never hesitated to mention and comment upon the censure aimed against him in the presence of him who had uttered it. His fearless frankness must have seemed phenomenal. In the present instance, Lord ——, who had dabbled in literature, and held a position at Court, had expressed himself (I forget whether orally or in print) very energetically against Thackeray's picture of George IV. We had occasion to enter the shop of a fashionable tailor, and there found Lord ——. Thackeray immediately stepped up to him, bent his strong frame over the disconcerted champion of the Royal George, and said, in his full, clear, mellow voice, 'I know what you have said. Of course, you are quite right, and I am wrong. I only regret that I did not think of consulting you before my lecture was written.' The person addressed evidently did not know whether to take this for irony or truth: he stammered out an incoherent reply, and seemed greatly relieved when the giant turned to leave the shop.

At other times, however, he was kind and considerate. Reaching London one day in June 1857, I found him at home, grave and sad, having that moment returned from the funeral of Douglas Jerrold. He spoke of the periodical attacks by which his own life was threatened, and repeated what he had often said to me before – 'I shall go some day – perhaps in a year or two. I am an old man already.' ...

His mind was always occupied with some scheme of quiet benevolence. Both in America and in England, I have known him to plan ways by which he could give pecuniary assistance to some needy acquaintance or countryman without wounding his sensitive pride. He made many attempts to procure a good situation in New York for a well-known English author, who was at that time in straitened circumstances. The latter, probably, never knew of this effort to help him. In November 1857, when the financial crisis in America was at its height, I happened to say to him, playfully, that I hoped my remittances would not be stopped. He instantly picked up a note-book, ran over the leaves, and said to me, 'I find I have £300 at my banker's. Take the money now, if you are in want of it; or shall I keep it for you, in case you may need it?' Fortunately, I had no occasion to avail myself of his generous offer; but I shall never forget the impulsive, open-hearted kindness with which it was made.

I have had personal experience of Thackeray's sense of justice, as well as his generosity. And here let me say that he was that rarest of men, a cosmopolitan Englishman – loving his own land with a sturdy, enduring love, yet blind neither to its faults nor to the virtues of other lands. In fact, for the very reason that he was unsparing in dealing with his countrymen, he considered himself justified in freely criticising other nations. Yet he never joined in the popular depreciation of everything American: his principal reason for not writing a book, as every other English author does who visits us, was that it would be superficial, and might be unjust. I have seen him, in America, indignantly resent an ill-natured sneer at 'John Bull' – and, on the other hand, I have known him to take *our* part, at home. [Discussing Emerson's *English Traits*, he remarked that Emerson was] 'altogether too laudatory. He admires our best qualities so greatly that he does not scourge us for our faults as we deserve.'

Towards the end of May 1861, I saw Thackeray again in London. During our first interview, we talked of little but the war, which had then but just begun. His chief feeling on the subject was a profound regret, not only for the nation itself, whose fate seemed thus to be placed in jeopardy, but also, he said, because he had many dear friends, both North and South, who must now fight as enemies. I soon found that his ideas concerning the cause of the war were as incorrect as were those of most Englishmen at that time. He understood neither the real nature nor the extent of the conspiracy, supposing that Free Trade was the chief object of the South, and that the right of secession was tacitly admitted by the Constitution. I thereupon endeavoured to place the facts of the case before him in their true light, saying, in conclusion, 'Even if you should not believe this statement, you must admit, that, if *we* believe it, we are justified in suppressing the Rebellion by force.'

He said, 'Come, all this is exceedingly interesting. It is quite new to me, and I am sure it will be new to most of us. Take your pen and make an article out of what you have told me, and I will put it into the next number of the *Cornhill Magazine*. It is just what we want.' [The 'managing publisher' of the *Cornhill* (George Smith) refused, however, to accept such a partisan essay which would inevitably and inappropriately 'introduce a political controversy into the magazine'. Thackeray, very disappointed, offered to recommend *The Times* to accept the article; he did so, but to no avail.]

All of Thackeray's American friends will remember the feelings of pain and regret with which they read his *Roundabout Paper* in the *Cornhill Magazine*, in (February, I think) 1862,[2] – wherein he reproaches our entire people as being willing to confiscate the stocks and other property owned in this country by Englishmen, out of spite for their disappointment in relation to the Trent affair, and directs his New York bankers to sell out all his investments, and remit the proceeds to London, without delay. It was not his fierce denunciation of such national dishonesty that we deprecated, but his apparent belief in its possibility. We felt that he, of all Englishmen, should have understood us better. We regretted, for Thackeray's own sake, that he had permitted himself, in some spleenful moment, to commit an injustice, which would sooner or later be apparent to his own mind.

Three months afterwards (in May 1862), I was again in London. I had not heard from Thackeray since the publication of the *Roundabout* letter to his bankers, and was uncertain how far his evident ill-temper on that occasion had subsided; but I owed him too much kindness, I honoured him too profoundly, not to pardon him, unasked, my share of the offence. I found him installed in the new house he had built in Palace Gardens, Kensington. He received me with the frank welcome of old, and when we were alone, in the privacy of his library, made an opportunity (intentionally, I am sure) of approaching the subject, which, he knew, I could not have forgotten. I asked him why he wrote the article.

'I was unwell,' he answered, '–you know what the moral effects of my attacks are – and I was indignant that such a shameful proposition should be made in your American newspapers, and not a single voice be raised to rebuke it.'

'But you certainly knew', said I, 'that the —— —— does not represent American opinion. I assure you, that no honest, respectable man in the United States ever entertained the idea of cheating an English stockholder.'

'I should hope so, too,' he answered; 'but when I saw the same thing in the —— —— , which, you will admit, is a paper of character and influence, I lost all confidence. I know how impulsive and excitable your people are, and I really feared that some such measure might be madly advocated and carried into effect. I see, now, that I made a blunder, and I am already punished for it. I was getting 8 per cent from my American investments, and now that I have the capital here it is lying idle. I shall probably not be able to invest it at a better rate than 4 per cent.'

I said to him, playfully, that he must not expect me, as an American, to feel much sympathy with this loss: I, in common with his other friends beyond the Atlantic, expected from him a juster recognition of the national character.

'Well,' said he, 'let us say no more about it. I admit that I have made a mistake.'

Those who knew the physical torments to which Thackeray was periodically subject – spasms which not only racked his strong frame, but temporarily darkened his views of men and things – must wonder, that, with the obligation to write permanently hanging over him, he was not more frequently betrayed into impatient or petulant expressions. In his clear brain, he judged himself no less severely, and watched his own nature no less warily, than he regarded other men. His strong sense of justice was always alert and active. He sometimes tore away the protecting drapery from the world's pet heroes and heroines, but, on the other hand, he desired no one to set him beside them. He never betrayed the least sensitiveness in regard to his place in literature. The comparisons which critics sometimes instituted between himself and other prominent authors simply amused him. In 1856, he told me that he had written a play which the managers had ignominiously rejected. 'I thought I could write for the stage,' said he; 'but it seems I can't. I have a mind to have the piece privately performed, here at home. I'll take the big footman's part.' This plan, however, was given up, and the material of the play was afterwards used, I believe, in *Lovel the Widower*.

I have just read a notice of Thackeray, which asserts, as an evidence of his weakness in certain respects, that he imagined himself to be an artist, and persisted in supplying bad illustrations to his own works. This statement does injustice to his self-knowledge. He delighted in the use of the pencil, and often spoke to me of his illustrations being a pleasant relief to hand and brain, after the fatigue of writing. He had a very imperfect sense of colour, and confessed that his forte lay in caricature. Some of his sketches were charmingly drawn upon the block, but he was often unfortunate in his engraver. The original manuscript of *The Rose and the Ring*, with the illustrations, is admirable. He was fond of making groups of costumes and figures of the last century, and I have heard Engligh artists speak of his talent in this genre: but he never professed to be more than an amateur, or to exercise the art for any other reason than the pleasure it gave him.[3]

He enjoyed the popularity of his lectures, because they were out of his natural line of work. Although he made several very clever after-dinner speeches, he always assured me that it was accidental – that he had no talent whatever for thinking on his feet.

'Even when I am reading my lectures,' he said, 'I often think to myself, "What a humbug you are, and I wonder the people don't find it out!" '...

[Taylor describes the library at Thackeray's final home.] 'Here,' he said to me, when I saw him for the last time, 'here I am going to write my greatest work – a History of the Reign of Queen Anne. There are my materials' – pointing to a collection of volumes in various bindings which occupied a separate place on the shelves.

'When shall you begin it?' I asked.

'Probably as soon as I am done with *Philip*,' was his answer; 'but I am not sure: I may have to write another novel first. But the History will mature all the better for the delay. I want to *absorb* the authorities gradually, so that, when I come to write, I shall be filled with the subject, and can sit down to a continuous narrative, without jumping up every moment to consult somebody. The History has been a pet idea of mind for years past. I am slowly working up to the level of it, and know that when I once begin I shall do it well.'...

To me, there was no inconsistency in his nature. Where the careless reader may see only the cynic and the relentless satirist, I recognise his unquenchable scorn of human meanness and duplicity – the impatient wrath of a soul too frequently disappointed in its search for good. I have heard him lash the faults of others with an indignant sorrow which brought the tears to his eyes. For this reason he could not bear that ignorant homage should be given to men really unworthy of it. He said to me, once, speaking of a critic who blamed the scarcity of noble and lovable character in his novels, 'Other men can do that. I know what I can do best; and if I do good, it must be in my own way.'

NOTES

1. Carlo Marochetti (1805-67) was an Italian baron. His bust of Thackeray is in Westminster Abbey.
2. 'On Half a Loaf - A Letter to Messrs Broadway, Battery & Co., of New York, Bankers', *Cornhill Magazine*, Feb 1862. As a result of such protests as Taylor's, Thackeray omitted the essay from the reprint of the *Roundabout Papers*. The newspaper referred to below is the *New York Herald*.
3. His *Vanity Fair* illustrations were, he said 'tenth or twentieth rate performances having a meaning perhaps but a ludicrous badness of execution' (*LPP*, II, 378). By 1853 he was referring to his efforts at drawing as one of 'the flowers of one's youth' that had faded away (*LPP*, III, 288).

A Certain Boyish and Impulsive Strain

JAMES PAYN

From *Some Literary Recollections* (1884) pp. 223-33. Payn (1830-98), novelist and journalist, educated at Eton and Cambridge, made his mark in journalism in Dickens's *Household Words* and *Chambers's Journal*, which he edited 1859-74; later he edited the *Cornhill*, 1883-96. He had some slight acquaintance with Thackeray in his later years.

I first saw Thackeray at the house of my brother-in-law [Major Prower], with whom I was then staying in Gloucester Place; they had lived together as young men at Weimar, but had never seen one another since, and their meeting was very interesting. Their lines in life had been very different, but the recollection of old times drew them together closely. A curious and characteristic thing happened on the occasion in question. There were a dozen people or so at dinner, all unknown to Thackeray, but he was in good spirits and made himself very agreeable. It disappointed me excessively, when, immediately after dinner, he informed me that he had a most particular engagement and was about to wish good night to his host. 'But will you not even smoke a cigar first?' I inquired. 'A cigar? Oh, they smoke here, do they? Well, to tell you the truth, that *was* my engagement', and he remained for many hours. There was an ancient gentleman at table who had greatly distinguished himself half a century ago at college, by whom the novelist was much attracted, and especially when he told him that there was nothing really original in modern literature; everything, he said, came indirectly more or less from – I think he said – Pindar.

'But at all events Pindar did not write *Vanity Fair*', I said.

'Yes, Sir,' answered the old gentleman, 'he did. In the highest and noblest sense Pindar did write it.'

This view of affairs, which was quite new to him, delighted Thackeray, who was so pleased with his evening that he invited the whole company – fourteen in all – to dine with him the next day. I mention the circumstance not only as being a humorous thing in itself, but as illustrative of a certain boyish and impulsive strain that there was in his nature. He told me afterwards that when he subsequently went to the Club that night he had felt so dangerously hospitable that it was all he could do to prevent himself 'asking some more people'; and as a matter of fact he did ask two other guests. He had been very moderate as to wine-drinking, and was only carried away by a spirit of geniality, which now and then overmastered him. The guests who had so much taken his fancy – or perhaps it was only the ancient Classic, whom he could not well have invited without the others – were of course delighted with their invitation, but many of them had scruples about accepting it. They called the next afternoon, in pairs, to know 'what we were going to do about it', and 'whether we thought Mr Thackeray had really meant it'. For my part, I said I should go if I went alone, and go we did. An excellent dinner we got, notwithstanding the shortness of the notice; nor in our kind hostess's manner could be detected the least surprise at what must neverthless have seemed a somewhat unlooked-for incursion....

Thackeray's habits were anything but methodical, and he found the duties of editorship especially irksome. Communications from his contributors, and especially the would-be ones, annoyed and even distressed him to an almost incredible degree. I remember his complaining of one of them with a vigour and irritation which amused me exceedingly. A young fellow had sent him a long story, for which he demanded particular attention 'from the greatest of novelists', upon the ground that he had a sick sister entirely dependent upon him for support. Thackeray was touched by the appeal, and, contrary to his custom, wrote his correspondent a long letter of advice, enclosing also (which was by no means contrary to his custom) some pecuniary assistance. 'I feel for your position,' he said, 'and appreciate your motive for exertion; but I must tell you at once that you will never do anything in literature. Your contribution is worthless in every way, and it is the truest kindness, both to her for whom you are working and to yourself, to tell you so outright. Turn your mind at once to some other industry.'

This produced a reply from the young gentleman which astonished Thackeray a great deal more than it did me. It was couched in the most offensive terms conceivable, and ended by telling 'the greatest of novelists' that, though he had attained by good luck 'the top of the tree, he would one day find himself, where he deserved to be, at the bottom of it'.

'For my part,' said Thackeray (upon my showing some premonitory symptoms of suffocation), 'I see little to laugh at. What a stupid, ungrateful beast the man must be! and if ever I waste another half hour again in writing to a creature of that sort "call me horse", or worse.' He was not so accustomed to the vagaries of rejected contributors as I was....

What Thackeray – a well-qualified critic indeed – wrote of Dickens he also certainly felt. I had once a long conversation with him upon the subject: it was before the shadow (cast by a trivial matter after all) had come between them,[1] but I am sure that would not have altered his opinion. Of course there were some points on which he was less enthusiastic than on others; the height of the literary pedestal on which Dickens stood was, he thought, for some reasons, to be deplored for his own sake. 'There is nobody to tell him when anything goes wrong', he said; 'Dickens is the Sultan, and Wills[2] is his Grand Vizier'; but, on the whole, his praise was as great as it was generous.

NOTES

1. Referring to the the Garrick Club affair, 1858.
2. W. H. Wills (1810–80), journalist; Dickens's assistant editor on his weeklies. Thackeray envied Dickens's having such an able right-hand man. On undertaking to edit the *Cornhill*, he remarked, 'If there were only another Wills, my fortune would be made!' – Lady Priestley, *The Story of a Lifetime* (1904) p. 143.

A Man Apart, and Sad

DAVID MASSON

From *Memories of London in the 'Forties* (Edinburgh and London, 1908) pp. 243–8. Masson (1822–1907), a Scotsman, now best remembered for his great *Life of Milton* (1859–80), was first editor of *Macmillan's Magazine*, 1859–67, and Professor of Rhetoric and English Literature at Edinburgh, 1865–95. Earlier he had accomplished much editorial, scholarly and critical work. Living from 1847 to 1865 in London, where he held the Chair of English Literature at University College, 1853–65, he became friendly with Carlyle, Jerrold, Thackeray and other literary figures. For him, writes his daughter Flora, Thackeray always remained 'a man apart... a head taller than all his fellows', and she recalls his spending Christmas Day 1863 'writing, writing, late into the night' an obituary of him for the *Daily Telegraph*, with the printer's devil waiting – *Cornhill Magazine*, n.s. XXX (1911) 798–9. In the present chapter of his *Memories*, 'A London Club', he recalls how former members of the defunct Museum Club, led by Douglas Jerrold, established 'Our Club'. After Jerrold's death in 1857, Thackeray became its dominant figure.

Though we were members of Our Club, and had dined together there and at the Gresham, it was not till a year or two after Jerrold's death that I made Thackeray's acquaintance. As early as the year 1851 I had written an article on *Pendennis* and *David Copperfield* in the *North British Review*, and had received letters from Dickens and Thackeray in acknowledgment. I do not remember Dickens's reply – there was nothing particular about it; but Thackeray's was interesting, because in it he spoke so enthusiastically of Dickens, and of his 'divine kind of genius'.[1]

At all our meetings, at the Garrick and at Our Club, Thackeray always seemed to me – in spite of his light humour, and his habitual nickname of 'Thack' among his friends – to be a man apart; a sad and highly sensitive man; a man with whom nobody could take a liberty.

It was at one of the larger dinners of Our Club – it may have been a Shakespeare Birthday Dinner – about the year 1860 – that I chanced to sit next to Thackeray; and·in the intervals of the speeches we had a good deal of quiet talk. But, in Our Club gatherings, there was often a lapse into what we called the 'war of the nationalities', which consisted of good-humoured mutual chaff and banter between the English members and the two or three Scottish and Irish members of the club. It may have been this that somehow suggested the following bit of Thackeray's talk with me.

'D'ye know,' he said, 'that though I can describe an Irishman perfectly, I never could describe a Scotchman?'

I reminded him of Mr Binnie.[2]

'Oh,' he said, 'that's not what I mean: that's a mere facsimile of a man I know; a mere description from life. But what I mean is, I couldn't *invent* a Scotchman: I should go wrong. But oh! I'm quite at home with the Irish character! I know the Irish thoroughly. The best friend I ever had in the world – the nicest and most delightful fellow I ever knew in the world – was an Irishman. But, d'ye know, he was a great rascal! I'll tell you how he served me once. He was in low water, and was always coming to me to borrow a sovereign or two, when I hadn't many to spare. But he was such a dear delightful fellow, it was quite a pleasure to lend them to him. One day, however, he came to me and said, "I say, Thack, you're a writer for magazines. Now, I've got a paper that I think would suit a magazine, and I wish you'd get it into one of them for me, because I'm hard-up at present, and a few guineas would come in handy." I took his paper, and actually kept one of my own papers out of *Fraser's Magazine* of the coming month, though it was rather a considerable sacrifice for me at the time, in order to get my friend's paper in. Oh! you've no idea what a nice delightful fellow that was! Well, the paper appeared; and it was perhaps a week or two after the beginning of the month before I next stepped into Fraser the publisher's shop. I thought Fraser looked rather glum when I went in; but I did not know the cause till he said, "Well, this is a pretty affair, Mr Thackeray!"

' "What affair?" I asked.

' "Why, that paper of your friend's, in this number!"

' "What about it?" I said.

'He went to a drawer, and took out a newspaper clipping, and asked me to look at it. I did: and I found, to my horror, that my friend's paper was denounced as a barefaced plagiarism. It had been copied *verbatim* from an article that had appeared in some other periodical. The date and all other particulars were given. I was of course greatly annoyed, and indeed excessively angry; and I thought, "Well, I must cut the fellow for ever; there's no getting on with him." I took the clipping with me, and went straight to my friend's rooms, intending to blow him up, once for all, and have done with him. I showed him the clipping, and declared his behaviour to have been scandalous. What do you think he did? He laughed in my face, and treated the whole affair as a capital joke!'[3]

'That's how my Irish friend served me: but oh! he was the nicest friend, the dearest, most delightful fellow, I ever knew in the world!'

And then Thackeray went on to speak more seriously of the Irish, and of his intimate knowledge of, and his great liking for, them. And among other things, he said there was one most likable quality that he had observed in them, and it was this: that there would never be found an Irishman anywhere in the world so low down but there was some other Irishman still lower down, depending on him, and whom he was assisting.

NOTES

1. 'I think Mr Dickens has in many things quite a divine genius so to speak' (*LPP*, II, 771–3). Masson's distinguished essay in the *North British Review*, XV (1851) 57–89, is reprinted, with omissions, in *TCH*, pp. 111–27. He incorporated material from it in his *British Novelists and Their Styles* (1859).

2. Colonel Newcome's friend, a hard-headed Scotsman who 'was a disciple of David Hume (whom he admired more than any mortal)' (*Newcomes*, ch. 8). It is not known what actual Scotsman the novelist had in mind (see below).

3. O'Donnell, of whom Ray writes, 'Almost nothing is known of this obscure journalist, who was one of Thackeray's most intimate friends during the late 1830s and early 1840s' *(LPP,* I, 355n). For his plagiaristic exploit, see Thackeray's remarkably charitable letter about 'a starving and unsane man' (*LPP*, II, 130–1). The only O'Donnell listed in the *Wellesley Index to Victorian Periodicals* as contributing to *Fraser's* is Colonel Sir Charles Routledge O'Donnell (1794–1870), an Irish army officer; but this was in 1830, years before Thackeray's time, and cannot be the man here referred to.

The Perfectly Conformist English Gentleman

JOHN LOTHROP MOTLEY

From *The Correspondence of John Lothrop Motley*, ed. George William Curtis (1889), I, 229–30, 235, 240–1, 279. Motley (1814–77), the distinguished American historian, met Thackeray socially in London during the summer of 1858, as the following extracts from letters describe. Dining *en famille* with him, he remarked that Thackeray had been very friendly: 'I believe him to be very kindhearted and benevolent' (ibid., I, 261). A Bostonian, and, as Anny Thackeray thought, 'hardly an American' (*LPP*, IV, 231), he was made much of in London society, becoming an honorary member of the Athenaeum, etc. Thackeray commended him to Lady Stanley as 'a very agreeable presentable gnlmnlike man' (*LPP*, IV, 84).

[*25 May 1858.*] . . . I believe you have never seen Thackeray. He has the appearance of a colossal infant, smooth, white, shiny ringlety hair, flaxen, alas, with advancing years, a roundish face, with a little dab of a nose upon which it is a perpetual wonder how he keeps his spectacles, a sweet but rather piping voice, with something of the childish treble about it, and a very tall, slightly stooping figure – such are the characteristics of the great 'snob' of England. His manner is like that of everybody else in England – nothing original, all planed down into perfect uniformity with that of his fellow-creatures. There was not much more distinction in his talk than in his white choker or black coat and waistcoat. As you like detail, however, I shall endeavour to Boswellise him a little, but it is very hard work. Something was said of Carlyle the author. Thackeray said, 'Carlyle hates everybody that has arrived – if they are on the road, he may perhaps treat them civilly.' Mackintosh praised the description in the *French Revolution* of the flight of the King and Queen (which is certainly one of the most living pictures ever painted with ink), and Thackeray agreed with him, and spoke of the passages very heartily. Of the Cosmopolitan Club, Thackeray said, 'Everybody is or is supposed to be a celebrity; nobody ever says anything worth hearing; and everyone goes there with his white choker at midnight, to appear as if he had just been dining with the aristocracy. I have no doubt', he added, 'that half of us put on the white cravat after a solitary dinner at home or at our club, and so go down among the Cosmopolitans.' . . . Thackeray invited me to dine next Sunday (that is today), and he went off very soon, as he confessed, to work at *The Virginians*. . . .

This letter, begun yesterday (Sunday), has been concluded today (Monday). . . . In the evening I dined at Thackeray's. There were fifteen or sixteen people. I do not know any of their names. I sat between Thackeray's two daughters. They are both intelligent and agreeable. The youngest told me she liked *Esmond* better than any of her father's books. Thackeray, by the way, evidently considers that kind of thing his forte. He told me that he hated the *Book of Snobs*, and could not read a word of it. *The Virginians*, he said, was devilish stupid, but at the same time most admirable; but that he intended to write a novel of the time of Henry V, which would be his *capo d' opera*, in which the ancestors of all his present characters, Warringtons, Pendennises, and the rest should be introduced. It would be a most magnificent performance, he said, and nobody would read it. After the ladies had left the house, we went downstairs and smoked cigars till into the small hours.

[*30 May 1850.*] Thackeray introduced me to Lady Stanley of Alderley, at whose house he is to read the lecture tomorrow of which I told you, I think, in my last letter. . . . At five o'clock [the next day] I met Thackeray by appointment at the Athenaeum Club, and we went together to Lady Stanley's.[1] The lecture was in the back drawing-room of a very large and elegant house, and the company – not more than fifty or sixty in number – were all comfortably seated. It was on George III – one of the set of the Four Georges, first delivered in America, and which have often been read in England, but have never been printed. I was much impressed with the quiet, graceful ease with which he read – just a few notes above the conversational level – but never rising into the declamatory. This light-in-hand manner suits well the delicate, hovering rather than superficial, style of the composition. He skims lightly over the surface of the long epoch, throwing out a sketch here, exhibiting a characteristic trait there, and sprinkling about a few anecdotes, portraits, and historical allusions, running along from grave to gay, from lively to severe, moving and mocking the sensibilities in a breath, in a way which I should say was the perfection of lecturing to high-bred audiences. I suppose his manner, and his stuff also, are somewhat stronger for larger and more heterogeneous assemblies, for I have no doubt he left out a good deal which might jar upon the ears polite of his audience on this occasion. Still, I was somewhat surprised at the coolness with which he showed up the foibles and absurdities of kings, and court, and court folks in a former but not remote reign, before a small company, which consisted of the cream of London cream. They seemed to enjoy it, and to laugh heartily at all the points without wincing.

[*June 1858.*] After breakfast I went down to the British Museum. I had been immersed half-an-hour in my manuscripts, when happening to turn my head round I found seated next to me Thackeray with a file of old newspapers before him writing the ninth number of *The Virginians*. He took off his spectacles to see who I was, then immediately invited me to dinner the next day (as he seems always to do everybody he meets), which invitation I could not accept, and he then showed me the page he had been writing, a small delicate legible manuscript. After this we continued our studies. I can conceive nothing more harassing in the literary way than his way of living from hand to mouth. I mean in regard to the way in which he furnishes food for the printer's devil. Here he is just finishing the number which must appear in a few days. Of course, whether ill or well, stupid or fertile, he must produce the same amount of fun, pathos or sentiment. His gun must be regularly loaded and discharged at command. I should think it would wear his life out.[2]

NOTES

1. She was a close friend of Thackeray's: see *The Ladies of Alderley* and *The Stanleys of Alderley*, both ed. Nancy Mitford (1938, 1939); and for her daughter Katherine's account of the present occasion see *The Amberley Papers*, ed. Bertrand and Patricia Russell (1937) I, 49–51.

2. A fellow American, John Pendleton Kennedy (1795–1870), novelist and politician, records other stages of Thackeray's research on *The Virginians*. In Baltimore, on 15 January 1856, 'Thackeray tells me he is going to write a novel with the incidents of our revolution introduced into it. To give him some information he is seeking with this view, I lend him some books – Graydon's *Memoirs of the Revolution*, Heath's *Memoirs* and Garden's *Anecdotes*, which he takes away with him; I tell him he may keep them as long as he wishes, and may return them to me hereafter.' In September 1858, Kennedy was in Paris: 'Thackeray calls to see me, and sits an hour or two. He is not looking well. He tells me he has need of my assistance with his *Virginians* – and says Heaven has sent me to his aid. He wants to get his hero from Fort Duquesne, where he is confined a prisoner after Braddock's defeat, and to bring him to the coast to embark for England. "Now you know all that ground," he says to me, "and I want you to write a chapter for me to describe how he got off and what travel he made." He insists that I shall do it. I give him a doubtful promise to do it if I can find time...' – Henry T. Tuckerman, *Life of John P. Kennedy* (New York, 1871) pp. 364, 296.

Wine and Talk in Paris

WILLIAM ALLINGHAM

From *William Allingham: A Diary*, ed. H. Allingham and D. Radford (1907) pp. 76–8. Allingham (1824–89), a minor Irish poet, met Thackeray through Leigh Hunt, and received some encouragement and help from him: see *LPP*, II, 710–12, 723; IV, 171. The following is an account of their meeting in Paris in August 1858.

I found Thackeray in the Hotel Bristol with his two daughters. He not well – often in bed till midday or later – struggling with [*The Virginians*], but in the evening usually recovering himself.

I told him I had been with the Brownings (who were then in Paris, staying in the Rue Castiglioni, No. 6).

'Browning was here this morning,' Thackeray said, 'what spirits he has – almost too much for me in my weak state. He almost blew me out of bed!'

'A wonderful fellow, indeed!'

'Yes, and he doesn't drink wine.'

'He's already screwed up to concert pitch.'

'Far above it. But I can't manage his poetry. What do you say?' (I spoke highly of it).

'Well, you see, I want poetry to be musical, to run sweetly.'

'So do I'

'Then that *does for* your friend B.!'

I spoke of Browning's other qualities as so splendid as to make him, as it were, a law in himself. But Thackeray only smiled and declined further discussion.

'He has a good belief, in himself, at all events. I suppose he doesn't care whether people praise him or not.'

'I think he does, very much.'

'O does he? Then I'll say something about him in a number.'

Thackeray took me to dine with him in the Palais Royal. He noticed with quiet enjoyment every little incident – beginning with the flourish with which our waiter set down the dishes of Ostend oysters. After tasting his wine Thackeray said, looking at me solemnly through his large spectacles, 'One's first glass of wine in the day is a great event.'

That dinner was delightful. He talked to me with as much ease and familiarity as if I had been a favourite nephew.

After dinner Thackeray proposed that we should go to the Palais Royal Theatre, but on issuing forth he changed his mind, and said we would call up Father Prout.[1] 'His quarters are close by. You know him, don't you?'

'Yes, I know that singing priest a little.'

He was then Paris Correspondent of the *Globe*, and his letters were much admired. It was said that the *Globe* had been obliged to buy a fount of Greek type by reason of Mahony's fondness for classical quotations. In a narrow street at the back of the Palais Royal, in a large lowish room on the ground floor, we found the learned and witty Padre, loosely arrayed, reclining in front of a book and a bottle of Burgundy. He greeted us well, but in a low voice and said, 'Evening boys, there's a young chap asleep there in the corner.' And in a kind of recess we noted something like bed-clothes. Thackeray was anxious to know who this might be, and Prout explained that it was a young Paddy from Cork, or thereabouts, who had been on a lark in Paris and spent his money. Prout found him 'hard up', and knowing something of his friends in Ireland had taken him in to board and lodge, pending the arrival of succour.

This piece of humanity was much to Thackeray's taste, as you may suppose. Thackeray said the Burgundy was 'too strong', and had brandy and water instead.

We talked among other things of Dickens. I said how much a story of Dickens might be improved by a man of good taste with a pencil in hand, by merely scoring out this and that.

Says Thackeray (with an Irish brogue), 'Young man, your threadin' on the tail o' me coat!'

I did not understand at first.

'What you've just said applied very much to your humble servant's things.'

NOTE

1. Pen-name of the Revd Francis Sylvester Mahony (1804–66), a Catholic priest of Irish birth and Bohemian habits, who lived in Paris in his later years. Journalist and humorist, he had been prominent among the Fraserians in the 1830s; Thackeray knew him over many years.

Imperfections Outweighed by Manly Virtues

JOHN CORDY JEAFFRESON

From *A Book of Recollections* (1894) I, 195–6, 211, 224–9, 248–59, 268–75, 279–89, 297–305, 326–7. Jeaffreson (1831–1901), an Oxford graduate, journalist, novelist, biographer and miscellaneous writer, devoted to Thackeray nearly a hundred pages of his *Recollections*. His account is vivid and much cited, though Thackeray's biographers are chary about his accuracy and good faith: see Malcolm Elwin, quoted below, and Gordon Ray, who counts Jeaffreson as among Thackeray's 'old enemies' (*Adversity*, p. 4) and warns that 'everything he wrote about Thackeray... must be carefully scrutinised for bias' (*Wisdom*, p. 488). Little of Jeaffreson's account, however, is obviously hostile, much is endearing or honourable, and most sounds authentic and is in line with other – and unimpugned – observers' comments. As he remarks himself (below, II, 294), and as the present collection shows, various observers saw or experienced various aspects of the man, and 'I do not,' he adds, 'question the honesty or the discernment' of witnesses who had alleged failings and disagreeable features in Thackeray which 'he never displayed to me'. Jeaffreson there, it will be noted, presents himself as a favourable witness, not an 'old enemy'.

[Jeaffreson has been explaining how meticulously he himself planned his novels, after his first juvenile attempts.] This way of producing a novel is the reverse of the way in which Thackeray wrote his comparatively plotless novels of character and humour. His plan was to create mentally two or three of his chief characters, and then to write away from time to time, with intervals of repose between the times of industry, and go onwards from chapter to chapter, with only a general notion of the course he would be taking a few chapters later. 'I don't control my characters', he said to me. 'I am in their hands, and they take me where they please.' ...

[An *obiter dictum* of Thackeray's:] 'There's nothing new and there's nothing true, and it don't much sinnify.' ...

[In his chapter on 'Our Club' – see above, II, 276, for Thackeray's dominance there – Jeaffreson writes of his surprising fondness for its secretary, Frederick Hamstede, 'a kindly, honest, simple little man' of no great charm, grace, attainment or position: an oddity by character, and by misfortune a cripple, so much in pain that his countenance bore a very sour expression.] Some of the lighter spirits about Thackeray used to banter him about his excessive complaisance to so curious a protégé, until he silenced them by exclaiming, with a droll combination of 'gush' and irritability, 'No one shall say a word against little Hamstede in my hearing. I love little Hamstede; I tell you, I love little Hamstede; and as for his verses over which you have been making merry, all I care to say is that I take more pleasure in reading his poetry than I do in reading your prose.' Why did the scholarly and fastidious Thackeray love the old-fashioned little clerk who was singularly deficient in lovable qualities? To answer the question effectively, I must add something to what I have already said of the first secretary of Our Club. Besides being a small man, he was a hunchback, and so crippled in his limbs that he could not move across a room without the help of a stick.... Though I cannot think with Mr Herman Merivale and Mr Frank Marzials, that Thackeray was especially remarkable for religious sensibility and devotional earnestness, and that his character and career were powerfully controlled by religious influences, I concur with them in thinking that Disappointment – i.e. the deep and enduring sorrow which came to him from his various distresses – was beneficial to his generous nature and fruitful of some of his finest qualities.[1] Instead of dwarfing and deadening his sympathies, sorrow quickened them... and in the little hunchback secretary of Our Club he came upon a weakling, with several titles to his pitiful regard. Himself a sufferer from an accident, that made his countenance an example of disfigurement, the tenderhearted Thackeray found in the old city-clerk a fellow-sufferer who had been far more cruelly dealt with by accidental violence. A giant in stature, Thackeray pitied little Hamstede for being so minute.... He was 'dear Hamstede' on the lips of all of us; albeit Thackeray was the only one of us with a heart large enough and warm enough to love the simple little fellow....

[An interesting account follows of the Club's customs, which included ritual rudeness to all fellow-members, and Thackeray's habit of rendering 'Little Billee' and 'Reverend Dr Luther' at sing-songs. Two chapters on Thackeray follow. They had first met in 1857. No biography had yet appeared, and it had been suggested that Anny was an ideal biographer.] But, even though she knew the whole of his life, which is improbable, the affectionate daughter would not be the best person to produce a perfect biography of the great humorist, who was very much of a Bohemian to the last, and whose domestic infelicity was fruitful of consequences, that should be neither avoided nor glossed, but should on the contrary be displayed with equal frankness and delicacy by the final historian of a man, so supremely interesting that his foibles and errors are almost as deserving of consideration as his brightest virtues and finest faculties....

He was often heard to say that three gentle descents were needful for the production of a gentleman. 'Then you don't think much of the influence of gentle lineage?' he once said to me, by way of rejoinder to some words that had passed from my lips. [Thackeray agreed that some of the well-born were mean and nasty. He reiterated, however:] 'All the same for that, I am of opinion that it takes three generations to make a gentleman.... I give you leave, youngster, to laugh at my inordinate pride in my no family in particular, for I am fully alive to its absurdity. I was laughing at myself when I wrote of General Braddock that he was "not of high birth, yet absurdly proud of his no-ancestry". I am not exempt from the foibles of my weaker brethren, whom I lash so smartly in my books. I spoke the truth when I declared myself a snob in clear type on the title-page of a book you wot of.'[2] ...

Before he had completed his thirtieth year, Thackeray was deprived of his wife's society by her incurable mental illness, which placed him in the cruel position of a widower who might not contract a second marriage; and, as the poor lady survived him, he remained in that cruel position to the end of his life. The grief which came to the novelist from deprivation of his wife's society and from frequent broodings over her pitiful fate was probably less depressing to his spirits, and certainly less hurtful to his general health, than the indirect consequences of the domestic affliction, which broke up his home near the Foundling Hospital, and compelled him to pass the remainder of his earthly existence under the vexatious conditions of unnatural celibacy. In truth, everything that was gravely irregular and hurtful in Thackeray's way of living, from the close of 1840 to the year of his death, was mainly referable to his conjugal bereavement. Had his marriage afforded him for twenty-five years the same measure of felicity, which it yielded him before the first manifestations of his wife's nervous failure, Thackeray might and doubtless would still have been rather too fond of gaiety and good cheer, but his wife's influence would have preserved him from the habits of gustatory self-indulgence, which resulted in the physical disorders that eventually deprived the world of his splendid genius. The same influence would also have preserved him from the trouble which compelled him to go so often in his closing years to Sir Henry Thompson for surgical treatment.[3] Soon after the great novelist's death, Lord Houghton wrote to his wife, 'So Thackeray too has gone. I was not surprised, knowing how full of disease he was, and thereby accounting for much of the inequality and occasional perversity in his conduct.' The disease and the occasional perversity were consequences of the calamity that extinguished Thackeray's domestic contentment, and drove him from Great Coram Street in his thirtieth year.

Although the consequences of that calamity were deplorable, I do not say the same of all that resulted from the loss of patrimony, which several thoughtful writers have regarded as one of the grave misfortunes that befell Thackeray in his early manhood. Having regard to three of the novelist's characteristics – his pride, his sensitiveness, and his constitutional indolence – I am more disposed to rejoice than to regret that he threw away his patrimony so soon after he came into it.... It can scarcely be questioned by anyone who knew the real Thackeray, that the sharp goad of poverty, to which he used to refer so often and so feelingly in his subsequent prosperity, pricked him to exertions which he would not have made, had he been in the enjoyment of easy circumstances. To me it appears more probable that Thackeray with £500 a year of unearned income at his back would have ceased to be a candidate for literary employment, practised at the Bar with moderate success, and eventually figured as a Master in Chancery or a stipendiary magistrate, than that he would have lived to write *Vanity Fair* and *The Newcomes*....

It points to the charm of Thackeray's attractive and winning personality, that I did not know him for many months before I conceived a strong liking for him.... I had known Thackeray for a little more than a year, and for about the same time he had been in the habit of addressing me as 'youngster' and 'young 'un' (his usual way of addressing quite young men whom he regarded with favour), when the great novelist, who had hitherto shown me only his most agreeable characteristics, gave me a momentary view of one of his unamiable traits.

[It was in 1858, at the time of the Garrick Club row over Edmund Yates, on which see below, II, 313.] To me the affair was nothing more than 'Thackeray's squabble with Yates about the article in *Town Talk*', when I happened to come upon the author of *Vanity Fair*, as he was sitting alone in the dining-room of No. 16, Wimpole Street, waiting to be admitted to Henry (nowadays Sir Henry) Thompson's consulting room. [They talked; and then Thackeray] startled me by saying, 'What do people say, youngster, about my row with Yates?' Possibly because he saw in my face an indisposition to speak frankly on the delicate matter, he followed up the question quickly. 'Come, tell me what you hear.'

On being thus pressed to play the part of a reporter, I replied, 'You do not need to be told what your enemies and detractors say. Nor can there be any need for me to tell you what is being said of you by your extravagant partisans, who, though they applaud whatever you do, are scarcely to be called your friends. Your judicious admirers – all the people whose opinion on the matter is worth a rush, the people whose view of the affair will be everybody's judgement five-and-twenty-years hence – unite in saying you have made a prodigious mistake, and are forgetful of your dignity in showing so much annoyance at a few saucy words, and in condescending to quarrel with so young and unimportant a person as Mr Yates.'

The immediate consequence of these words was that Thackeray, flushing with surprise and irritation, exclaimed, 'Confound your impudence, youngster.'

Rising to my feet at this outbreak of petulance, I looked steadily into my companion's face, before I answered, slowly, 'Pardon me, Mr Thackeray, for not flattering you with an untruth, when you pressed me to give you information.'

Doubtless these words were spoken with a slight show of combativeness; for the youngster did not like being 'confounded for his impudence'. But I am sure they were not spoken in an offensive tone.

'You were quite right,' returned Thackeray, 'and it is for me to beg your pardon. You were right to tell me the truth, and I thank you for telling it. Since *Vanity Fair* people have been less quick to tell me the truth than they were before the book made me successful. But – but – ' As he said 'but – but', he rose from his seat to his full height, and looked down upon me with a face coloured with emotion. 'But – but', he continued, 'you may not think, young'un, that I am quarrelling with Mr Yates. *I am hitting the man behind him.*'

Fortunately, my *tête-a-tete* with the great man was ended at that moment by Henry Thompson's appearance in the room....[4] [Time has 'fully justified,' Jeaffreson continues, 'the discreet and dispassionate persons, who in 1858 were of opinion that Thackeray had made and was persisting in a prodigious mistake' and that his behaviour towards Yates was] harsh, passionate, vindictive, and strangely wanting in magnanimity.... As the years go by it will be much easier to prove that in the later stages of the fierce quarrel Thackeray was actuated by animosity against Dickens. The author of *Vanity Fair* was not more communicative to me, a recent and youthful acquaintance, than to several of his close and old friends about his motive in pushing his quarrel with the young journalist. He told them no less precisely than he told me that in striking Yates he was *hitting the man behind him*; and hitherto unpublished memoranda will in due course strengthen the evidence that he so spoke to them.

Though I never had any personal intercourse with Charles Dickens (albeit he wrote me two or three letters in 1858, and was so good as to give me a general invitation to visit him at Gad's Hill), I am not without grounds for holding a strong opinion that his action in the Yates–Thackeray quarrel proceeded in no degree from jealousy of Thackeray, that he never was jealous of Thackeray, that he never regarded himself as a competitor with Thackeray for literary preeminence, and that, from the dawn of Thackeray's success to the hour of his death, the rivalry of the two novelists was a one-sided rivalry. It is certain that Thackeray was keenly emulous of Dickens's literary success, and passionately desirous of surpassing it. There were times when this desire affected him so vehemently that he may be said to have suffered from Dickens-on-the-brain. He was enduring an acute visitation of the malady, when he went into Chapman & Hall's place of business, and begged to be told what was the average monthly sale of Dickens's then current story. On being shown the account of the monthly sales, he exclaimed, in a tone of mingled surprise and mortification, 'What! – so far ahead of me as all that!'

As his green leaves had a far larger circulation than Thackeray's yellow covers... one fails to see why Dickens should have been jealous of Thackeray, or have regarded him as a competitor who was running him close, and might possibly get before him. Certainly Dickens was not jealous of his literary address and peculiar ability; for, though he recognised the greatness of his genius and admired *Vanity Fair, Pendennis*, and *The Newcomes*, he rated them none too highly, and saw little to commend in Thackeray's subsequent writings. Mr Yates, who knew Dickens intimately, and studied him shrewdly, tells us in his autobiography that 'Dickens read little and thought less of Thackeray's later work' – an announcement that may cause readers to remark, 'So much the worse for Dickens!'...

On the other hand, whilst there is no sufficient reason to charge Dickens with having been jealous of Thackeray, it is certain that Thackeray, from the dawn of his celebrity to the last year of his life, was greatly desirous of surpassing Dickens in the world's favour, and at times was keenly annoyed by his inability to do so. I question whether Thackeray had a familiar friend who did not at some time or other hear the author of *Vanity Fair* speak of himself as Dickens's rival, and declare his chagrin at failing to out-rival him....

From what I have said of Thackeray's desire to surpass Dickens – a desire of which he spoke with engaging frankness to his mere acquaintances as well as his closest friends – readers may not infer that it was a passion either mean in itself or likely to degenerate into envy and hatred of the more popular novelist. An essentially and uniformly generous passion, it was attended with a cordial recognition of the genius of Charles Dickens, and with enthusiastic admiration of his finer artistic achievements. Though he often spoke to me of Dickens and his literary doings, I never heard him utter a word in disparagement of the writer whom he laboured to outshine.... He repeatedly avowed to me his desire to be thought a greater novelist than Dickens, but in doing so he always displayed a passionate admiration of the writer whom he was striving to precede. On one occasion, after descanting on the excellences of the new number of Dickens's then current book, he brought his fist down upon the table with a thump as he exclaimed, 'What is the use of my trying to run before that man, or by his side? I can't touch him – I can't get near him.' ...

On another occasion he said to me, with mingled sadness and magnanimity, that seemed to me both noble and pathetic, 'I am played out. All I can do now is to bring out my old puppets, and put new bits of riband upon them. But, if he live to be ninety, Dickens will still be creating new characters. In his art that man is marvellous.' I know him to have spoken to other persons in the same strain and almost in the same words about the novelist, whom he admired so greatly.

Though the author of *Vanity Fair* was so good as to afford me many opportunities for studying his whims and foibles, as well as his noble qualities, and talked to me about his feelings for the author of *The Tale of Two Cities* as freely as he appears to have spoken of them to any person of his acquaintance, I never discovered anything rancorous, or petty, or ignoble in his rivalry of Dickens. On the contrary, I saw much that was admirable and beautiful in it. Thackeray would have been a happier man had he done his appointed work without thinking so often and so emulously of Gushy's prodigious circulation and strong sway over the reading populace. But, as his superb power fully justified the favourite novelist of 'the classes' in pitting himself against the favourite novelist of the whole people, I honoured him for the emulation that was so generous, so magnanimous, and so pure of envious malignity.

As I walked from Wimpole Street back to my lodgings, after the interview with Thackeray, in which he told me that he was striking Yates in order to 'hit the man behind him', I was fearful that he would regret having spoken to me so frankly, and that the incident would diminish the friendliness of our intercourse. The fear was dispelled by the heartiness with which the novelist on meeting me a few days later invited me to walk with him. From that time till 25 April 1863, the day on which I spoke with Thackeray for the last time, I saw a good deal of the famous novelist, under circumstances that increased my liking for him, and made me feel that I was growing steadily in his favour. But our pleasant intercourse would not justify me in speaking of myself as one of his intimate friends, for he neither invited me to his house nor crossed my threshold during the whole course of our acquaintanceship. I was never anything more to him than an acquaintance, with whom he liked to chat, when we came upon one another in the house of a common friend, at clubs and taverns, at the British Museum, in the public ways, and at places of public amusement.

Encountering him repeatedly at No. 16, Wimpole Street, I often met him on the pavements of the town; and when we met in a public thoroughfare he usually stopped to chat with me, and sometimes asked me to walk with him. It was at *his* request that I used to look for him at Evans's, when I was passing through or near Covent Garden at night, on my way to or fro between my home in Heathcote Street and the offices of the journals to which I contributed. Had he not asked me to seek him there, I should seldom have visited the supper-room on the basement of Evans's Hotel, of which Thackeray was an *habitué*; for to me the hot, noisy cellar, in which journalists and gentlemen about town used to assemble and drink grog and toddy, and consume unwholesome suppers, when they should have been going to bed, was far from being a Cave of Harmony and Delight. Thackeray, on the contrary, enjoyed the music, the noise, and the smoky atmosphere of the hot, crowded cellar, where Herr von Joel used to whistle and 'do the farm-yard' to the lively delight of young farmers from the country. Dropping into Evans's late for 'a finish' after 'the play', or a grand dinner or a rout, the author of *Vanity Fair* used also to go there early, for the pleasure of hearing the musical boys sing glees, and madrigals, and quaint old ballads. He would listen to them, song after song, for the hour – ay, for hours together, never speaking a word during the performances. Several of the singing-boys were church-choristers; and, in reference to their ecclesiastical employment, Thackeray once said to me, 'It does me more good to listen to them in this cellar than in Westminster Abbey.' ...

I am at the more pains to say that my intercourse with Thackeray was held chiefly at taverns, because his habit of going to inns for refreshment and society, when he was a member of three such good and very different house-clubs as the Athenaeum, the Reform, and the Garrick, is an interesting illustration of one side of his social history and character.

Joining the literary cliques at a time when authors-by-profession spent much of their leisure in taverns, – when young Alfred Tennyson used to turn into the Cock in Fleet Street at 5 p.m. for 'a pint of port' – when, indeed, some of the most able and distinguished authors-by-profession would have vainly sought to be elected into a house-club of good repute – Thackeray contracted, from the habits of his early manhood, so strong a liking for tavern life, that he was to the last a frequenter of such inns as those in which he had cultivated the friendship of Maginn and Mahoney. He was, perhaps, the last greatly eminent man of letters, who preferred the old-world tavern to the modern club-house, as a place in which to take his ease and enjoy the company of his friends – the last great English man of letters, to be fairly described as a tavern-haunter, in the most agreeable and quite inoffensive sense of the term. His liking for taverns was strengthened by his familiarity with the usages, and his sympathy with the spirit and humours of Queen Anne's London....

The Thackeray with whom I used to gossip at Evans's and Clunn's, at No. 16, Wimpole Street, and during our walks about town, differed greatly from the Thackeray whose 'bearing' struck Mr. Yates as 'cold and uninviting', and in whom Mr Frith, R. A., and Serjeant Ballantine[5] discovered divers unamiable qualities. But though he charmed me by his genial manner, his conversational communicativeness, and social kindliness, and caused me to think highly of his benevolence and his habitual considerateness for the feelings of his companions, I do not question either the honesty or the discernment of the several persons, who in published words have accused him of failings which he never displayed to me during the six years of our intercourse. As Mr Yates was in his early manhood what he is at this late date of his career, a shrewd observer of human nature and a man of honour, I have no doubt that he had cause to think Thackeray 'cold and uninviting' in manner. Though I never saw anything in Thackeray to justify the severe terms in which Serjeant Ballantine declared his dislike of the novelist, I think it more probable that in some of his weak and perverse moods Thackeray displayed the alleged infirmities, than that the caustic barrister was absolutely without grounds for declaring him very egotistical, greedy of flattery, and sensitive of criticism to a ridiculous extent.... But I have grounds for thinking that my account of the author of *Vanity Fair* displays him in his most usual as well as his most agreeable moods; and I hold this opinion the more strongly, because my view of his nature closely resembled the view that was taken of him by several of my friends, who had known him for a much longer period....

I have already spoken so fully of the habits which wrecked Thackeray's health, that I shall occasion the readers of the present page no astonishment by speaking of him as an invalid, whose constitution was irrecoverably broken before I made his acquaintance. Had his appetites – especially his appetite for the pleasures of the table – been under his control, I should not be justified in using so strong an expression, to describe his bodily condition in the earlier years of my intercourse with him. Could he have acted steadily in accordance with the advice of his doctors, he might have recovered his health in 1860, or in a still later year, and kept it even to old age. But he was powerless to do as they advised him....

'At a big dinner,' he said to me, 'I behave like a child, like a schoolboy at a Christmas feast, eating everything that is offered to me, everything that comes in my way. The season plays the devil with me, because I dine out a great deal, and I am in no sense my own master at any dinner-table but my own, and even at my own table I can't control my wicked appetite, when I am entertaining a lot of people. I can be admirably prudent, so long as there is no need for prudence; but with the first glass of champagne, away goes my prudence, and I must have something of whatever is going.'

Just as he on one occasion taught me to look for revelations of himself in the subordinate touches given to the creations of his fancy, by saying he was laughing at one of his own foibles when he ridiculed General Braddock's 'absurd pride in his no-ancestry', he on another occasion gave me a similar lesson by telling me that he was thinking of his own 'contemptible gulosity' when he derided Joe Sedley for stuffing himself with different kinds of food, and then eating a lot of ratafia cakes....

Eating thus largely, he drank more than was good for him.

'You have drunk a good deal in your time,' I once observed to him.

'Enough', he answered, jollily, 'to float a seventy-four gun ship. Since I came out of my poverty, a bottle has been my daily minimum, and on three out of every four days I have taken a second bottle. I may be called a two-bottle man; and that takes no account of the two or three glasses of wine at midday, nor of the punches and grogs in the hours about midnight.'

But, though I have repeatedly seen him take in a few hours four and even six times as much alcohol as any one of his doctors would have authorised him to take in an entire day, I never saw him under the influence of the glass that used to be styled 'a glass too much'. Drinking wine as men used to drink wine in the days of Maginn and Theodore Hook, he 'carried it' like a gentleman.

As he delighted and indulged in good cheer thus freely, it is not surprising that the nervous man's stomach rebelled against a master who showed so little consideration for its weakness, and punished him with cramp and spasms, and violent fits of sickness and retching, in the last of which fits he died from the rupture of a blood-vessel in the head. Moreover, to realise fully how much the great novelist suffered in his closing years from bodily ailments, readers must bear in mind that, whilst he endured successive visitations of the stomachic disorder, that eventually put an end to his life, he was troubled by another disorder, even more wearing to the nerves and more afflicting to the spiritis. . . .

Soon after the publication of my *Live It Down: A Novel*, in March 1863, Thackeray spoke to me of the story in encouraging terms, as he sat beside me at Clunn's. He also observed, 'If you had told me of the title before you used it, I would have offered you fifty guineas for it.'

'I wish I had told you', I returned, 'in time to get the offer. I should certainly have accepted it.'

'And I wish the title were mine. It is a book in three words!' he rejoined, warmly. After a pause he added, in a sad and lower voice, 'It would be the very title for my story of my own life'–words which seemed to imply that he had some thought of writing his own biography.

Matters went thus pleasantly between me and Thackeray up

to the time when he withdrew his favour from me, under a gust of angry emotion, which I had done nothing to occasion.[6] . . .

The great man's foibles would have been less generally known, had he forborne to call attention to them in his books, his private letters, and his gossip with his friends.[7] There were moments when he was too mindful of his dignity and fame. In respect to one person of the gentler sex, who had caused him suffering, he was wanting in magnanimity. In moods of irritability, resulting more from bodily disease than from moral unsoundness, he once and again carried his private grievances and personal vexations to the public. Though he was never so obsequious to rank as Mr Andrew Arcedeckne used to declare him, he was at times more strongly affected, than a man of his natural gifts should have been, by the accidental grandeur of exalted persons. Though Charles Knight thought him 'no idolater of rank', and Harriet Martineau has been reproved for speaking sorrowfully of him as yet another example of 'the aristocracy of nature making the ko-tow to the aristocracy of accident', it must be admitted that Charles Knight was not wholly right, and that Miss Martineau was not wholly wrong.[8] It is noteworthy that, in one of the Brookfield letters – the piece of a letter written 'From the Grange' in 1851 to Mrs Brookfield – Thackeray acknowledged himself something of a rank-worshipper, and in doing so used the very expression which Miss Martineau used in her censure of the novelist, to the annoyance and resentment of so many of his admirers.

'How is it', he wrote to his correspondent, 'that I find myself humbling before her' (to wit, Lady Ashburton) 'and taking a certain parasitical air as all the rest do? There's something commanding in the woman (she was born in 1806, you'll understand), and I see we all of us bow down before her. Why don't we bow down before you, ma'am? Little Mrs Taylor is the only one who does not seem to ko-tow.'[9]

But, when the most is made of Thackeray's imperfections, they are few and small in comparison with his manly virtues and generous traits.

NOTES

1. For this judgement by Merivale and Marzials, see below, II, 351.
2. *The Book of Snobs: by One of Themselves* (1848).
3. Dr Henry Thompson (1820–1904), surgeon, knighted 1867, created Baronet 1899, often had to submit Thackeray's 'hydraulics' to surgical treatment: and the novelist possessed a copy of his *Pathology and Treatment of the Stricture of the Urethra* (1854). As Jeaffreson hints – rather boldly, for 1894 – the origin of his urethral stricture was probably a venereal complaint. See *LPP*, IV, 453–9, Appendix XXVIII, on Thackeray's medical history.
4. Malcolm Elwin regards this conversation as being 'wildly improbable' and describes as 'fatuous' Jeaffreson's suggestion (in a passage, 1.265, here omitted) that Thackeray was particularly riled by Yates's referring to his broken nose, because 'Besides being sensitive and highly nervous, Thackeray was a rather vain man' – *Thackeray: A Personality* (1932) pp. 338, 341. It is certainly a suspicious circumstance that Henry Thompson's entry comes so pat on this punch-line. Herman Merivale reports that Thackeray was 'very indifferent to banter' on the subject of his nose – adding that 'I always think of him as a man of exceeding comeliness' – Herman Merivale and Frank T. Marzials, *Life of W. M. Thackeray*, (1891) p. 47.
5. For Frith, see below, II, 360. William Ballantine (1812–87) was a serjeant-at-law; another 'old enemy' of Thackeray in Ray's opinion (*Adversity*, p. 4). Not among Thackeray's intimates, he 'met him frequently' at the Garrick and other clubs: 'I never thought him an agreeable companion. He was very egotistical, greedy of flattery, and sensitive of criticism to a ridiculous extent. He may have possessed great powers of conversation, but did not exhibit them upon the occasions when I had the opportunity of judging. He did not hesitate to introduce his associates and the members of his club into his novels', and he 'descended to most unworthy sneers at another equally great man and brother author, Sir Edward Lytton Bulwer.' In a Postscript in later editions, Ballantine referred to criticisms of these remarks on Thackeray, and mentioned 'with pleasure' a subsequent conversation with Sir Henry Thompson who 'told me that he had seen very much of him, and had never met a man more kind-hearted, more ready to listen to a tale of sorrow or want, or possessing more extended benevolence' – *Some Experiences of a Barrister's Life*, 6th edn (1884 reprint) pp. 93–8.
6. Jeaffreson here recounts, at some length, Thackeray's wrath over the unkind review of his daughter Anny's novel *The Story of Elizabeth* in the *Athenaeum*, 25 Apr 1863. Jeaffreson was associated with this journal and Thackeray, wrongly informed that he had written the review (Geraldine Jewsbury had done so), publicly snubbed him. Thackeray eventually discovered that Jeaffreson was not guilty of the offence, but died before any apology or reconciliation could occur. Later in 1863 the National Shakespeare Tercentenary Celebration Committee was established with the Editor of the *Athenaeum*, William Hepworth Dixon, and Jeaffreson prominent among its organisers; Thackeray ignored their letters inviting him to be a vice-president. A scandal arose, and Thackeray's death at this time caused

further recriminations, explanations, breast-beating, and so on. The affair, which soured the Tercentenary atmosphere, was a final instance of Thackeray's combativeness, or sensitivity, or poor judgement, or 'the final test of Thackeray's forbearance' (Ray, *Wisdom*, p. 407), according to taste, and/or of his proclivity for getting involved in literary gang-warfare. For Ray's account, see *LPP*, IV, 416–17.

7. As Jeaffreson remarks later, 'he often startled his hearers by the candour with which he spoke of the petty misadventures and vexations he experienced from time to time in the pursuit of his chief vocation' (*Recollections*, II, 240).

8. In her *Autobiography*, 2nd edn (1877) II, 375–7, Harriet Martineau remarks that she met Thackeray only once, at the Bullers' house in 1851. 'He seemed cynical,' she recalled, and she had been unable to read *Vanity Fair*, 'from the moral disgust it occasions', though she greatly admired *Pendennis* and *Esmond*. Among her criticisms of him is this: 'Mr Thackeray has said more, and more effectually, about snobs and snobbism than any other man; and yet his frittered life, and his obedience to the call of the great are the observed of all observers. As it is so, so it must be; but "O! the pity of it! the pity of it!" Great and unusual allowance is to be made in his case, I am aware; but this does not lessen the concern occasioned by the spectacle of one after another of the aristocracy of nature making the ko-tow to the aristocracy of accident.'

9. *LPP*, II, 698. Mrs Taylor was the wife of Henry (later Sir Henry) Taylor, the author and civil servant.

Vexed to Hear Dickens Praised

LORD WILLIAM PITT LENNOX

From *My Recollections from 1806 to 1873* (1874) II, 164–9. Lennox (1799–1881), novelist, journalist and miscellaneous author, edited the *Review* newspaper, 1858. He is here recollecting Garrick Club friends.

... having often met him at the table of private friends, at the Garrick, at the Beef-steak Club, at civic feasts and banquets, I certainly had a fair opportunity of judging of his social qualities, which to my mind, when he 'was in the vein', were equal, if not superior to those of any writer of his day. There was one feeling about the author of *Vanity Fair* which tried him sorely, and ever proved a thorn in his side, and that was the adulation paid to Dickens. One day when dining in company, at a friend's house, with the above two intellectual giants of a race now nearly extinct, the conversation, after the ladies had left the room, took a literary turn; and a young man who sat next to Charles Dickens, and immediately opposite Thackeray and myself, began to praise Dickens to his face in a most fulsome manner. All of a sudden Thackeray stopped in the midst of a sentence, turned his chair round, as if to escape from the sound of the flatterer's tongue, and, addressing me in a voice full of bitterness, said, 'Did you hear that? I go nowhere but I am subject to it. I should not mind to hear Lytton Bulwer praised to the skies, for I own my inferiority, but – ' he then held down his head, evidently tortured at mind, and was silent for some minutes.[1]

After a time I ventured to say, 'If you had been sitting where Dickens was, the same remark would probably have been made to you, for the young man that made it evidently drawled it out in the most Dundreary[2] fashion.' Nothing, however, that I could say seemed to rouse Thackeray from his lethargy, and he shortly afterwards abruptly left the room.

NOTES

1. Making this comparison, in another mood, in 1854, he asserted that Dickens was 'undoubtedly the greatest *genius*' of the three – 'not that I have read him of late' (*LPP*, III, 407, 409). The French novelist Paul Feval, in an obituary of Dickens, wrote that 'Dickens regarded *Vanity Fair* as a masterpiece. Thackeray, with a modesty a little less genuine perhaps than his master's, used to say, "I'm less than half of Charles"' (*Le Gaulois*, 13 June 1870, p. 1).

2. Lord Dundreary was the vacuous young aristocrat in the play *Our American Cousin* (1858). Edward Southern's performance in this role made the character achieve classic status; thus, long side-whiskers became 'dundrearies'.

'We Had our Differences of Opinion'

CHARLES DICKENS

From 'In Memoriam', *Cornhill Magazine*, IX (1864) 129-32. Dickens (1812-70) knew Thackeray from 1836, when he applied unsuccessfully to become illustrator on *Pickwick Papers*, and in 1837, as Editor of *Bentley's Miscellany*, he published Thackeray's first story, 'The Professor'. A friendly though never very close relationship developed, interrupted by various squabbles, mostly occasioned by their associates' having offended or been offended by Thackeray. The Garrick Club row of 1858, caused by Edmund Yates (see below, II, 313), was the most resounding and lasting of these, and led to a cessation of their friendship until a reconciliation took place shortly before Thackeray's death. When, with the success of *Vanity Fair*, Thackeray had suddenly and at last become Dickens's rival, he inevitably measured himself for size against Dickens (who seems to have been very little concerned by the entry of a rival). See the Index for the many instances of Thackeray's awareness of Dickens, and for contemporaries' comparing and contrasting them; and see the next item, by Dickens's daughter Kate. Thackeray's friend B. W. Procter reported that he had never seen signs of his being jealous of Dickens; Malcolm Elwin, quoting this, remarks that it was envy, not jealousy, that Thackeray felt – *Thackeray: A Personality* (1932), p. 186. Some awkwardness, at least, was inevitable between two such literary rivals, who were also considered leaders of antagonistic literary factions. John Kenyon, the socialite and minor poet, 'had a fine sense of the fitness of things', reports Mrs Andrew Crosse; ' "I never ask Dickens and Thackeray together now", said Kenyon, "I did so once, and found it was a mistake" ' – *Red-letter Days of My Life* (1892) I, 124. Thackeray had often reviewed Dickens, almost always warmly and generously. Dickens is on record very sparsely about Thackeray or his books, though his conviction that *Vanity Fair* was a masterpiece is well attested. He was uneasy about what he took to be Thackeray's 'jesting much too lightly between what was true and what was false, and what he owed to both, and not being sufficiently steady to the former', as he wrote to John Forster in 1847; and in this letter he expressed his 'strong opinion' that Thackeray's *'Punch's* Prize Novelists' lampoons 'did no honor to literature or literary men, and should be left to very inferior and miserable hands: which I desired Thackeray to know' – *Letters*, ed. Walter Dexter (1938) II, 28–9. He told Thackeray so, 'candidly', in a letter of 1848 (*LPP*, II, 336-7); Thackeray meanwhile had been warned by Bradbury & Evans not to include Dickens in this series of parodies. This was an episode in the 'Dignity of Literature' controversy, over which they often crossed swords. Having to write the following obituary appreciation of Thackeray embarrassed Dickens, who confided to Wilkie Collins, 'At the solicitation of Mr Smith and some of his friends, I have done what I would most gladly have excused myself from doing, if I felt I could – written a couple of pages about him in what was his own magazine' (*Letters*, III, 379).

It has been desired by some of the personal friends of the great English writer who established this magazine, that its brief record of his having been stricken from among men should be written by the old comrade and brother-in-arms who pens these lines, and of whom he often wrote himself, and always with the warmest generosity.

I saw him first, nearly twenty-eight years ago, when he proposed to become the illustrator of my earliest book.[1] I saw him last, shortly before Christmas, at the Athenaeum Club, when he told me that he had been in bed three days – that, after these attacks, he was troubled with cold shiverings, 'which quite took the power of work out of him' – and that he had it in his mind to try a new remedy which he laughingly described. He was very cheerful, and looked very bright. In the night of that day week, he died.

The long interval between those two periods is marked in my remembrance of him by many occasions when he was supremely humorous, when he was irresistibly extravagant, when he was softened and serious, when he was charming with children. But, by none do I recall him more tenderly than by two or three that start out of the crowd, when he unexpectedly presented himself in my room, announcing how that some passage in a certain book had made him cry yesterday, and how that he had come to dinner, 'because he couldn't help it', and must talk such passage over.[2] No one can ever have seen him more genial, natural, cordial, fresh, and honestly impulsive, than I have seen him at those times. No one can be surer than I, of the greatness and the goodness of the heart that then disclosed itself.

We had our differences of opinion. I thought that he too much feigned a want of earnestness, and that he made a pretence of undervaluing his art, which was not good for the art that he held in trust. But, when we fell upon these topics, it was never very gravely, and I have a lively image of him in my mind, twisting both his hands in his hair, and stamping about, laughing, to make an end of the discussion.

When we were associated in remembrance of the late Mr Douglas Jerrold, he delivered a public lecture in London, in the course of which, he read his very best contribution to *Punch*, describing the grown-up cares of a poor family of young children.[3] No one hearing him could have doubted his natural gentleness, or his thoroughly unaffected manly sympathy with the weak and lowly. He read the paper most pathetically, and with a simplicity of tenderness that certainly moved one of his audience to tears. This was presently after his standing for Oxford, from which place he had dispatched his agent to me, with a droll note (to which he afterwards added a verbal postscript), urging me to 'come down and make a speech, and tell them who he was, for he doubted whether more than two of the electors had ever heard of him, and he thought there might be as many as six or eight who had heard of me'. He introduced the lecture just mentioned, with a reference to his late electioneering failure, which was full of good sense, good spirits, and good humour.

He had a particular delight in boys, and an excellent way with them. I remember his once asking me with fantastic gravity, when he had been to Eton where my eldest son then was, whether I felt as he did in regard of never seeing a boy without wanting instantly to give him a sovereign?[4] I thought of this when I looked down into his grave, after he was laid there, for I looked down into it over the shoulder of a boy to whom he had been kind.[5]

These are slight remembrances; but it is to little familiar things suggestive of the voice, look, manner, never, never more to be encountered on this earth, that the mind first turns in a bereavement. And greater things that are known of him, in the way of his warm affections, his quiet endurance, his unselfish thoughtfulness for others, and his munificent hand, may not be told.

If, in the reckless vivacity of his youth, his satirical pen had ever gone astray or done amiss, he had caused it to prefer its own petition for forgiveness, long before:

> I've writ the foolish fancy of his brain;
> The aimless jest that, striking, hath caused pain;
> The idle word that he'd wish back again.
>
>   ['The Pen and the Album', ll. 22–4]

In no pages should I take it upon myself at this time to discourse of his books, of his refined knowledge of character, of his subtle acquaintance with the weaknesses of human nature, of his delightful playfulness as an essayist, of his quaint and touching ballads, of his mastery over the English language. Least of all, in these pages, enriched by his brilliant qualities from the first of the series, and beforehand accepted by the Public through the strength of his great name.

But, on the table before me, there lies all that he had written of his latest and last story.... The pain ... that I have felt in perusing it, has not been deeper than the conviction that he was in the healthiest vigour of his powers when he wrought on this last labour.... The last line he wrote, and the last proof he corrected, are among these papers through which I have so sorrowfully made my way. The condition of the little pages of manuscript where Death stopped his hand, shows that he had carried them about, and often taken them out of his pocket here and there, for patient revision and interlineation. The last words he corrected in print, were, 'And my heart throbbed with an exquisite bliss.' God grant that on that Christmas Eve when he laid his head back on his pillow and threw up his arms as he had been wont to do when very weary, some consciousness of duty done and Christian hope throughout life humbly cherished, may have caused his own heart so to throb, when he passed away to his Redeemer's rest!

He was found peacefully lying as above described, composed, undisturbed, and to all appearance asleep, on 24 December 1863.[6] He was only in his fifty-third year; so young a man, that the mother who blessed him in his first sleep, blessed him in his last. Twenty years before, he had written, after being in a white squall,

> And when, its force expended,
> The harmless storm was ended,
> And, as the sunrise splendid
>   Came blushing o'er the sea;
> I thought, as day was breaking,
> My little girls were waking,
> And smiling, and making
>   A prayer at home for me.
>
>   ['The White Squall']

Those little girls had grown to be women when the mournful day broke that saw their father lying dead. In those twenty years of companionship with him, they had learned much from him; and one of them has a literary course before her, worthy of her famous name.

On the bright wintry day, the last but one of the old year, he was laid in his grave at Kensal Green, there to mingle the dust to which the mortal part of him had returned, with that of a third child, lost in her infancy, years ago. The heads of a great concourse of his fellow-workers in the Arts, were bowed around his tomb.

NOTES

1. Thackeray referred amusingly to 'that unfortunate blight which came over my artistical experience' at the 1858 Royal Academy banquet, where Dickens was a fellow guest: see Lewis Melville, *William Makepeace Thackeray: Biography* (1910) II, 115. At the time, he had been so sure that he had got the job that he gave a celebratory sausage-and-mash supper to – ironically, as it proved – Hablot Browne, who did become Dickens's illustrator.
2. Probably *Dombey and Son* (1846–8), where the death of Paul Dombey had much affected him: see above, II, 237–8.
3. 'The Curate's Walk', Dickens's great admiration for which he had expressed to Thackeray in 1848 (*LPP*, II, 337). The lecture was 'Charity and Humour', given in 1857 for the Jerrold Fund. Dickens had been 'profoundly touched' by the generous reference to himself in this lecture (*LPP*, III, 431).
4. Cf. *Newcomes* (ch. 16): 'What money is better bestowed than that of a schoolboy's tip?'
5. Dickens's eldest son, Charles. One of his younger brothers, Alfred, recalled a similar episode: 'When my brothers, Frank and Sydney, and myself were at school at Boulogne, Thackeray upon one occasion, which I shall never forget, called and took us for an outing. He made us row him up the Liane to the Pont de Briques, where we had tea. Then on our return he fed us with pastry at the fashionable pastry-cook's in the town..., and finally, when we got back to the school, solemnly presented each of us with a napoleon, thus practising his doctrine as to how schoolboys should be treated. He was indeed most charming to us boys, and that was a red-letter day in our lives, never, never to be forgotten' – Alfred Tennyson Dickens, 'My Father and his Friends', *Nash's Magazine*, IV (1911) 639.
6. Some kindly suppression of fact here. 'Dickens told me', wrote James T. Fields, 'that, looking on [Thackeray] as he lay in his coffin, he wondered that the figure he had known in life as one of such noble presence could seem so shrunken and wasted' – *Yesterdays with Authors* (1872) pp. 36–7.

Sir William Hardman further contradicts Dickens's, and others', account: 'The papers say he died peaceably and his corpse was calm. Poor fellow! I regret to contradict this on the authority of Leech (the *Punch* artist), who, living near, was the first person sent for by the family. The features were much distorted and discoloured by the bursting of the blood-vessel, of course. Moreover, both arms were bent, the hands clutching at the collar of his night-shirt, and were so rigidly fixed that he was buried in that position' – *Letters and Memoirs: Second Series: 1863–1865*, ed. S. M. Ellis (1925) p. 120. Another report – second-hand – is Browning's: 'I am told he looked grandly in his coffin: Thackeray with all the nonsense gone would be grand indeed...' (above, I, 106).

Thackeray and my Father

KATE DICKENS PERUGINI

From *Pall Mall Magazine*, n.s., XIV (1911) 212–19. Kate (1839–1929), Dickens's younger daughter, married Charles Alston Collins (1828–73), brother of Wilkie Collins, and a minor member of the Pre-Raphaelites: he was also a journalist and author. Kate and her husband were among Thackeray's closest friends in his final years. 'He liked few people better than Charles Alston Collins' (*Wisdom*, p. 398), and when he was found dead on 24 December 1863 it was the Collinses that Anny and Minny first sent for: see *LPP*, IV, 296n. After Collins's death, Kate married another artist, Charles Edward Perugini.

My sister and I had known Thackeray's two daughters ever since we were children ... but it was not until soon after I was married that I came to know their great father.... I had been to Palace Green, Kensington several times before I had any real talk with its master, for notwithstanding my immense admiration for his work, or perhaps, because of it, I felt a little shy and reserved with him, for I too was young and had been brought up with a wholesome awe of men so great as Thackeray; but one morning as I was walking rapidly towards the High Street with head held low to shield my eyes from the sun, I became conscious of a large tall obstacle in front of me and of a cheery voice saying, 'Where are you going to, my pretty maid?' I looked up, startled, and there stood Thackeray. 'I'm going a-shopping, kind sir', I said. 'May I go with you, my pretty maid?' And he offered me his arm with a courtly air and led me, not a-shopping, but into Kensington Gardens, where, as we walked up and down his 'favourite path', he said, 'Now that I have captured the fair Princess, and brought her to my Enchanted Garden, like the wicked old ogre I am, I want her to tell me about that other ogre she knows who lives shut up in his castle near Gravesend.'

And this was the beginning of countless conversations we had concerning my father, a subject that deeply interested Thackeray. My father's way of life, his daily habits of writing, his likes and dislikes – his friends – and, above everything, his written books, all held for Thackeray a singular fascination, and he never seemed to tire of what I had to tell him. Sometimes, but that was later on, he would criticise my father's work, while I, grown bolder as I knew him better and always keen in defence of one who in my eyes seemed little short of perfection, would hotly oppose his never very severe but always wise and reasonable objections. At any sign of resentment on my part his eyes twinkled merrily, and I soon learned to understand that he took a sly pleasure in teasing me; but before I arrived at this just conclusion I recollect how one day, having greatly offended me by strongly objecting to something I particularly admired in one of my father's stories, I rose from my seat and with all the dignity my foolish youth could muster I told him that never, *never* again would I discuss with him any of my father's work; and I daresay I meant this awful threat for the moment, and no doubt was very flushed and indignant when he gravely kissed my hand and left me. And I remember also how gratefully (in my heart) I accepted his reappearance next day, when he immediately began talking of *David Copperfield* (as though nothing had happened), and while he spoke of Traddles cutting the mutton into slices and of Mr Micawber covering them with pepper, mustard, salt and cayenne, I was inwardly registering a solemn vow that never, *never* again would I be so silly. But there were times when he said things about my father that satisfied even my craving for appreciation of his genius – times when more than ever I liked and admired him for the large simplicity and generosity of his character, and those moments made ample amends for any little irritation I may have felt in listening to his criticism.

The feeling of friendship and good-will Thackeray felt for my father he extended to my father's daughter, who has never ceased to bless the happy accident of birth that, having already given her so much, added to the gift a great and never-to-be-forgotten friend; to three of her brothers, at school for a time at Boulogne, Thackeray had the opportunity which he did not miss of showing various substantial little kindnesses such as are generally appreciated by small boys away from home, who always seem to require a very large allowance of bodily sustenance and a great amount of mental diversion to enable them to cope with the apparently unnatural and desperate task of learning. Thackeray had indeed a remarkable insight into the minds and hearts of young people, and had also a gift for teaching, of which he was probably unaware. No small prejudices, nor affectations of any kind, flourished for long in the school of which he was master, and his pupils always left him wiser and better than before they came under his influence. One of the few remaining pupils of that school, alas, and the one who has done him most honour, is his daughter, Anne Thackeray Ritchie – now Lady Ritchie – of whom and of her younger sister Minny – afterwards Mrs Leslie Stephen – he was fond of talking, and I recollect a phrase of his that fell so pleasantly upon the ear as to give one delight in repeating it: 'Anny is golden', he would say with a smile, while his manner of saying it implied that no praise ever imagined could reach beyond the meaning of those three little words.

At one period of their friendship there came a misunderstanding between Thackeray and my father, that perhaps never would have existed had it not been fanned into flame by the mistaken interference of two or three friends, who believed they were doing a kindness in attempting to set matters straight. The cloud persisted, however, and was like a dreary mist after a warm and genial day, dividing the pleasant companionship of the past from the cold estrangement rising in its place. Thackeray, I knew, pondered this disagreement a good deal, although for some time it was a subject he carefully avoided; but one day while paying me a visit he suddenly spoke: 'It is ridiculous that your father and I should be placed in a position of positive enmity towards one another.' 'It is quite ridiculous', said I, with emphasis. 'How can reconciliation be brought about?' said he. 'Indeed, I don't know – unless you were to – ' 'Oh, you mean I should apologise', said Thackeray, turning quickly upon me.

'No, I don't mean that, exactly,' said I, hesitating; 'still – if you could say a few words –'

'You know he is more in the wrong than I am', said he.

'Even if that were so,' I said, 'he is more shy of speaking than you are, and perhaps he mightn't know you would be nice to him. He cannot apologise, I fear.'

'In that case there will be no reconciliation', said Thackeray decisively, looking at me severely through the glare of his glasses.

'I am very sorry', said I, sadly.

There was a pause that lasted quite a long time. 'And how do I know he would be nice to me?' mused Thackeray, presently.

'Oh, I can answer for him', said I, joyfully. 'There is no need for me even to tell him what has passed between us, I shall not say a word; try him, dear Mr Thackeray, only try him, and you will see.' And later on Thackeray did try him, and came to our house with radiant face to tell me the result. 'How did it happen?' said I.

'Oh,' he said gaily, 'your father knew he was wrong and was full of apologies – '

It was now my turn to look severe.

'You know you are not telling me the truth, you wicked man. Please let me hear immediately what really did happen.'

Thackeray's eyes were very kind as he said quite simply, 'I met him at the Athenaeum Club and held out my hand, saying we had been foolish long enough – or words to that effect; your father grasped it very cordially – and – and we are friends again, thank God!'

Thackeray had his moments of depression occasionally, although he did not suffer from 'moods' to a more alarming extent than did 'that other ogre shut up in his castle near Gravesend', but one afternoon when on his way to the club he called in to see me; he was not in his usual serene frame of mind, for after a few attempts at small talk he sat silently by looking sombre and preoccupied. As it happened I had just been reading a collection of poetry in which were some of his verses; I told him of these, and after quoting the lines said how much I liked them. Thackeray was not a vain man but he was very human, and always frankly pleased by any genuine admiration of his work; he asked me to repeat the words again, and then told me when and where they were written. From this our talk fell upon those charming verses in *Vanity Fair* that Becky sang in the private theatricals at Gaunt House. 'I am glad you like my verse', said he, with the candid delight of a boy. 'I am thinking of writing some more soon'; and he rose to go, but after saying goodbye and reaching the door he turned back. 'I am not feeling quite myself,' said he, 'I think I shall go and see what Dr Brighton can do for me; perhaps after swallowing a few of his delicious draughts I may feel better – and if I do and am at my very best – I will write to you.' [He did so, enclosing the verses to her, later published as 'Mrs Katherine's Lantern'.] They will no doubt be remembered by those who met with them in the pages of the *Cornhill Magazine* and elsewhere, where I quote the last six lines:

> And a man – I let the truth out –
> Who's had almost every tooth out
> Cannot sing as once he sung
> When he was young, as you are young:
> When he was young, and lutes were strung
> And love lamp in the casement hung....

Thackeray's interest in my father never ceased, but continued until the last day I saw him – a day that came all too soon, for a very few years after I first grew to know him he died, at the early age of fifty-two years.

But before that sad event occurred, I remember many pleasant hours spent with him and his daughters in the charming Palace Green House, and particularly well do I remember a certain evening when the dinner was to be prepared by his two girls and their guests, who wore white aprons and caps for the occasion. The guests were nearly all young people, and among them were Herman Merivale, afterwards the author of *All for Her*, and his pretty sister Ella, who became Mrs Freeman, and Frederick Walker, the young painter, who turned out to be the best amateur cook among us. I should like to think, for the sake of the company, that something was cooked by a professional, though at this distance of time I cannot say, nor do I recollect whether the cooks partook of their own broth; but I do remember that Thackeray tried everything that was set before him, and I am convinced he must have suffered dreadfully, for if ever sacrifices were made to friendship it was upon that evening, and our dear host was one of the kindest and most obliging of victims.

Thackeray and Dickens: Some Anecdotes

GEORGE RUSSELL

From Lady [Constance] Russell, *Swallowfield and Its Owners* (1901) pp. 303–6. George Russell (1818–98), barrister, succeeded to a baronetcy in 1883, inheriting the family seat, Swallowfield Park, and became an M. P. soon afterwards. In his earlier years he was a keen member of the Garrick Club and thus became intimate with Thackeray, Dickens and other literary and artistic celebrities, being particularly fond of Dickens, his widow states. He had 'a never-failing fund of anecdotes' about both novelists; these are among the few that he wrote down.

'One evening at Thackeray's house, about two years before his death, when I was talking with him and his daughters, I said, "Tell me, Thackeray, which is your own favourite amongst your own works." He said, "Tell me first which is yours." I replied *The Newcomes*. Miss Thackeray expressed her preference for *Pendennis*, and her sister, I think, shared her opinion. Thackeray, after a pause, said with emphasis – I give his very words – "Well, I should like to stand or fall by *Esmond*."

'One night I was dining with Thackeray, and Hallé the pianist was of the party. After dinner Thackeray said, "Now, Hallé, give us a tune." Halle sat down to the piano and struck a chord, and a terrible chord it was! Before, however, he could give vent in words to the despair which his countenance only too clearly portrayed, Thackeray cried out, "Come, come, Hallé, it is a bad workman who finds fault with his tools." Halle laughed, accepted the jest in good part, and illustrated the truth of the adage by making us all forget the indifference of the instrument in the marvellous skill of the master.

'Thackeray complaining to me of feeling ill on the day succeeding a Richmond dinner, "*O tempora!*" I said. "Oh! more ease is what I require", he rejoined.[1]

'On expressing my regret to Thackeray that the jackals that followed their heels had been able to separate him and Dickens, I found him inflexible. "It is a quarrel, I wish it to be a quarrel, and it always will be a quarrel", he said with great warmth.

'I was being driven by Dickens in his pony carriage from the station to Gad's Hill after we had attended Thackeray's funeral, when he expressed his great satisfaction that he and Thackeray had been reconciled before death separated them. He described their reconciliation thus: "I and another member accidentally went to the same peg in the hall of the Athenaeum to hang up our hats. I turned and found myself face to face with Thackeray! I was startled and distressed at his changed appearance, and putting out my hand said, 'Thackeray, have you been ill?' He said, 'Yes, and I am still very ill.' I expressed the sympathy that I felt, and we then sat down on a settee in the hall and had a long and cordial talk as in old days, and that was the last time we ever met."[2] I then', writes Sir George, 'expressed my regret to Dickens, as I had before done to Thackeray, that they had allowed the malice of talebearers to poison the mind of each against the other, instead of using their own direct and honest judgement. He made no reply for some moments, and I can still recall the tinkling of the pony's bells which alone broke in upon our silence. At last he exclaimed in his own emphatic way, "Well, I am bound to say nothing ever took place between Thackeray and me face to face which was not to his honour." During the rest of our drive to Gad's Hill he spoke much of Thackeray, with admiration of him both as a man and a writer, and was warm in praise of his last and unfinished book *Philip*, which he thought promised to be among the greatest of his works.[3] . . .

'Unlike Thackeray, Dickens was not a great admirer of Fielding. . . . I heard Thackeray speak disparagingly of Walter Scott, and even contemptuously of his heroic, as distinguished from his love novels. Dickens, on the contrary, after criticising the undue length of his descriptions as "too constantly interrupting the thread of his narrative", added, "But after all, who is there like him?"'

NOTES

1. 'O tempora! O mores!' ('Oh, the times! Oh, the manners!') – Cicero, *In Catilinam*.
2. See above, II, 309, for Thackeray's notably different account of this meeting.
3. Russell misremembers: *Philip* had of course been completed. As Dickens states in his obituary article (above, II, 304), he had seen 'all that [Thackeray] had written of his latest, and last story' – *Denis Duval*, published during 1864 – which he describes very favourably.

The Garrick Club Affair

EDMUND YATES

(1) from *Edmund Yates: His Recollections and Experiences*, 4th edn (1885) pp. 190, 238–41, 248, 255, 258–9; (2) from obituary of Thackeray. in *Northern Whig*, repr. by 'Theodore Taylor' (J. C. Hotten), *Thackeray the Humorist and Man of Letters* (1864) pp. 182–3; (3) from letter to Herman Merivale, 25 May 1889, *LPP*, IV, 133n. Yates (1831–94), journalist, novelist, Post Office official and one-man-show performer, was the son of the popular theatrical couple, Frederick and Mrs Yates. *Pendennis* had fired his ambitions 'to be a member of that wonderful Corporation of the Goosequill' (*Recollections*, p. 148), and he became a prolific contributor to – and later editor of – magazines, being associated, from 1856, with Dickens's weeklies, among others. One of 'Mr Dickens's young men' (i.e. journalistic colleagues and imitators), he became also a confidential friend; and this was of particular importance in 1858, for the much-bruited break-up of Dickens's marriage, precipitated by his fondness for a young actress, Ellen Ternan, occurred in the weeks just before the Garrick Club row, and these events were connected in complex and not altogether intelligible ways. Certainly, over this Yates was partisan for Dickens, and Thackeray for Mrs Dickens, though Thackeray had also unintentionally offended Dickens through a maladroit effort to rebut sinister rumours about him (*LPP*, IV, 86).

Yates had been acquainted with Thackeray since the early 1850s, and they were fellow members of the Garrick Club, to which 'Dickens came rarely...; but Thackeray was dearly fond of it, and was always there' (*Reminiscences*, p. 237). Thackeray was indeed its 'Dictator', so it was unsurprising that Yates and his supporters came off worse when Thackeray complained of him to the Club's committee and members. The wonder is that Thackeray acted so severely over Yates's 'profile' of him in an insignificant new journal. Yates was a vulgar fellow and, as he and his supporters came to agree, his article on Thackeray was a regrettable folly, to say the least; but, as Yates pointed out to him, the article did not mention the Garrick nor draw upon Club tittle-tattle, and Thackeray was wide open to a *tu quoque* for publicly attacking and ridiculing fellow authors (*LPP*, IV, 94–6; *Reminiscences*, pp. 242–3). Not coming to this squabble with clean hands, nor devoid of a wish to damage Dickens through Yates, Thackeray was odiously self-important and self-righteous in his conduct: and its after-effects rankled (*LPP*, IV, 133–5). But nobody involved in this affair comes out of it well. To an extent, as was said at the time, Yates simply provided an occasion for the two great novelists and their gangs to have a scrap, in which pent-up distastes could be given vent. Gordon Ray and Dickens's biographer Edgar Johnson state the case for their respective men in *PMLA*, LXIX (1954) 815–32; LXXI (1956) 256–9. Ray presents important new letters, not available in *LPP* or the *PMLA* essay, in *Wisdom*, especially pp. 285–6, 312–13; and see *Wisdom*, pp. 289, 306–7, 415, for Yates's further attacks on Thackeray, and p. 374 for Thackeray's ripostes in novels and elsewhere. As Ray shows, the remaining years of Thackeray's life were bedevilled with ongoing nastinesses between the two camps, in which the combatants were drawn up largely on class lines, Thackeray being one of the 'gentlemanly' party.

(1) [In 1855, in Henry Vizetelly's *Illustrated Times*, Yates had been a pioneer in 'gossip-column' journalism, as it was later called. His 'The Lounger at the Clubs' series was, he wrote ironically, 'the commencement of that style of "personal" journalism which is so very much to be deprecated and so enormously popular'. It was on 22 May 1858, only weeks before his fatal essay on Thackeray, that Yates was invited to contribute likewise to 'a quiet harmless little paper', *Town Talk*, which had just begun publication.] About the third week of my engagement I went over to the printer's, which was in Aldersgate Street, close by the Post Office, at the close of my official work, to 'make up' the paper. All my contribution was in type, and I thought I should only have to remain half an hour to 'see all straight', when I was horrified at hearing from the head-printer that in consequence of illness Mr Watts Phillips [a main contributor] had not sent in his usual amount, and that another column of original matter was absolutely requisite. There was no help for it; I took off my coat –

literally, I remember, for it was a warm evening – mounted a high stool at a high desk, and commenced to cudgel my brains.

It happened that in the previous week's number I had written a pen-and-ink sketch of Dickens, which had given satisfaction; I thought I could not do better than follow on with a similar portrait of his great rival. And this is what I wrote:

> Mr Thackeray is forty-six years old, though, from the silvery whiteness of his hair, he appears somewhat older. He is very tall, standing upwards of six feet two inches, and as he walks erect his height makes him conspicuous in every assembly. His face is bloodless, and not particularly expressive, but remarkable for the fracture of the bridge of the nose, the result of an accident in youth. He wears a small grey whisker, but otherwise is clean-shaven. No one meeting him could fail to recognise in him a gentleman; his bearing is cold and uninviting, his style of conversation either openly cynical or affectedly good-natured and benevolent; his *bonhomie* is forced, his wit biting, his pride easily touched; but his appearance is invariably that of the cool, suave, well-bred gentleman, who, whatever may be rankling within, suffers no surface display of his emotion. [A survey of his literary career follows.] His success, commencing with *Vanity Fair*, culminated with his *Lectures on the English Humourists of the Eighteenth Century*, which were attended by all the court and fashion of London. The prices were extravagant, the lecturer's adulation of birth and position was extravagant, the success was extravagant. No one succeeds better than Mr Thackeray in cutting his coat according to his cloth. Here he flattered the aristocracy; but when he crossed the Atlantic, George Washington became the idol of his worship, the 'Four Georges' the objects of his bitterest attacks. These last-named lectures have been dead failures in England, though as literary compositions they are most excellent. Our own opinion is that his success is on the wane. His writings never were understood or appreciated even by the middle classes; the aristocracy have been alienated by his American onslaught on their body; and the educated and refined are not sufficiently numerous to constitute an audience. Moreover, there is a want of heart

in all he writes, which is not to be balanced by the most brilliant sarcasm and the most perfect knowledge of the workings of the human heart.

As soon as this little sketch was written, and while the ink was scarcely dry, I handed the slips to the printer, and went off. I never saw it in proof, I never thought of it again. That it was offensive or objectionable, or likely to bring me into trouble, I *could* not have thought, for that very evening I mentioned at the Garrick Club to a well-known *littérateur*, whom I at that time believed to be a friend of mine, the fact of my new engagement, with a general idea of what I was doing for it. I have not the least doubt it was from this person that Thackeray had his information as to the writer.

Two days after, I received the following letter [from Thackeray (*LPP*, IV, 89–90), characterising his article as 'not offensive and unfriendly merely, but slanderous and untrue', and ending:]

> We meet at a club, where, before you were born, I believe, I and other gentlemen have been in the habit of talking without any idea that our conversation would supply paragraphs for professional vendors of 'Literary Talk'; and I don't remember that out of that club I have ever exchanged six words with you. Allow me to inform you that the talk which you have heard there is not intended for newspaper remark; and to beg – as I have a right to do – that you will refrain from printing comments upon my private conversations; that you will forego discussions, however blundering, upon my private affairs; and that you will henceforth please to consider any question of my personal truth and sincerity as quite out of the province of your criticism.

Now it must, I think, be admitted by the most impartial reader that this letter is severe to the point of cruelty; that whatever the silliness and impertinence of the article, it was scarcely calculated to have provoked so curiously bitter an outburst of personal feeling against its writer; that, in comparison with the offence committed by me, the censure administered by

Mr Thackeray is almost ludicrously exaggerated. The question naturally suggests itself, how such a disparity between the peccant composition and the witheringly wrathful and rancorous reply is to be accounted for? To that matter I may presently revert. Here I will only say that Mr Thackeray's letter, as it well might have done, came upon me with a sense of amazement. But although I had at the moment no idea of the motive which impelled Thackeray to insist so strongly upon the fact that the Club was our only common meeting-ground, and that it was thence my presumed knowledge of him was derived, I felt that the sentence in which he emphasised the fact afforded me a legitimate opportunity for a tolerably effective retort.

I therefore sat down at once, and wrote Mr Thackeray a letter in which I not only disclaimed the motives by which he had accused me of being actuated, but took the liberty of reminding him of some past errors of his own. . . . [If sent, this might have closed the matter; but unfortunately, as he later felt, Yates consulted Dickens, who, regarding this letter as 'too violent and too flippant', persuaded him to send a more formal protest (*LPP*, IV, 91–2). Thackeray referred Yates's letter, and the whole affair, to the Garrick Club committee, which on 26 June upheld Thackeray's complaint and instructed Yates to apologise or face the judgement of a General Meeting of the Club.] This was an anxious time; there were frequent councils, at which John Forster, W. H. Wills, Albert and Arthur Smith, as well as Dickens and myself were present. Just then out came the (I think) seventh number of *The Virginians*, containing a wholly irrelevant and ridiculously lugged-in-by-the-shoulders allusion to me, as 'Young Grub Street', in its pages.[1] This was generally considered to be hitting below the belt while pretending to fight on the square, and to be unworthy of a man in Mr Thackeray's position. . . . [On 10 July, Yates was in effect expelled from the Club. He initiated legal proceedings but, finding that he could not afford the expenses involved, withdrew the action. Meanwhile Dickens wrote personally to Thackeray, on 24 November, urging that the matter be resolved out of court. Thackeray replied, grieving to discover 'that you were Mr Yates's adviser in the dispute between me and him', stating that the matter was now out of his hands, and signing himself

'Yours, etc.' – 'He be damned', burst out Dickens's friend John Forster, 'with his "Yours etc"!']

There is no doubt it was pretty generally said at the time, as it has been said since, and is said even now, that this whole affair was a struggle for supremacy, or an outburst of jealousy, between Thackeray and Dickens, and that my part was merely that of the scapegoat or shuttlecock.

There was no intimacy, nor anything really like friendship, between the two men, though an outward show of cordiality had been maintained in public. Dickens had taken the chair at the dinner to Thackeray in '55, and had alluded to the 'treasures of wit and wisdom within the yellow covers': Thackeray, in his lectures on 'Weekday Preachers', declared that he thought Dickens was specially commissioned by Divine Benevolence to delight mankind. But Dickens read little, and thought less, of Thackeray's later work; and once, when I was speaking of the ruthless strictures of the *Saturday Review* on *Little Dorrit*, Thackeray, agreeing with me in the main, added, with that strange, half-humorous, half-serious look, 'though, between ourselves, my dear Yates, *Little D.* is Deed stupid.' ...

Such is the history, with nothing extenuated nor aught set down in malice, of a most important event in my life.... I have told it, not to vindicate myself – for no one can see more clearly than I do the silliness and bad taste of the original article – nor, most assuredly, to cast any slur upon Mr Thackeray's memory; for I firmly believe that, had he lived, he would have been led to acknowledge that the severity of my punishment was out of proportion to the offence committed.

(2) Thackeray was dead; and the purest English prose writer of the nineteenth century, and the novelist with a greater knowledge of the human heart as it really is than any one – with the exception, perhaps, of Shakespeare and Balzac – was suddenly struck down in the midst of us. In the midst of us! ... No other celebrity, be he writer, statesman, artist, actor, seemed so thoroughly a portion of London. That 'good grey head which all men knew' was as easy of recognition as his to whom the term applied, the Duke of Wellington. Scarcely a day passed without his being seen in the Pall Mall districts; and a Londoner showing country cousins the

wonders of the metropolis, generally knew how to arrange for them to have a sight of the great English writer.... One would have thought that *The Times* could have spared more space than a bare three-quarters of a column for the record of such a man's life and death. One would have thought that Westminster Abbey might have opened her doors for the reception of the earthly remains of one whose name will echo to the end of time. And, as I write, the thought occurs to me that the same man was, perhaps, the last to wish for either of such distinctions.

(3) Please bear in mind, first, the circumstances under which the offending little article was written. While the press waited, to supply 'short copy', at a desk in a printing office, with the master-printer at my elbow, urging me on, slip by slip being carried off to the compositors, as it was written. Think that I was then only 27 years old, with wife & three children, supplementing a small Post Office salary by journalistic labour, sitting down at my desk, three or four nights a week, after my day's official grind, sitting down at 8 pm. & steadily writing till midnight. Remember what the social degradation inflicted upon me at Thackeray's instance, not the fury of a moment but deliberately insisted on through six weeks, meant to an unknown man, who had not made any mark then, but was merely pulling the devil by the tail, in a struggle for bread. Think of being 'expelled' from a club, as tho' one had been a card-sharper, a cheat, a thief, a braggart about women! 'He was expelled from the Garrick': for 30 years that has been the cry, no one caring to ask why or wherefore, the kindest among the speakers allowing that it must have been for printing revelations of what I had heard in the club circle! ... Then, taking the article on the ground of its 'personality', the huge stone with which I was smashed to earth, compare it not merely with W M T's own early writings, but with the articles of now-a-days. In my wretched nonsense, there is no single reference to Thackeray's home-life, no mention of his Club, no 'gossip' of any kind, no hint – God forbid! – at his domestic trouble, no word of anything that was not thoroughly patent & well known at the time. Then, look at the persistent malignity with which I was hunted down! all offer of compromise rejected, nothing but bitter insatiable revenge. I am, by

constitution & fibre, a strong man, & I 'lived it down': but in those days I too was sensitive, & it nearly broke me down: what was suffered by my wife and my mother, I shall never forget.

Throughout all these 30 years, Thackeray, as author, has had no more devoted worshipper: even now, I wd go through a stiff examination paper, with innumerable quotations from his works: do your paper without any reading *Vanity Fair, Pendennis, The Newcomes*: & constantly dipping into the *Miscellanies* & the Ballads. But for Thackeray, the man, I shall think, & say, to my dying day, that his treatment of me was one of the wickedest, cruellest, & most damnable acts of tyranny, ever perpetrated.

NOTE

1. Opening paragraphs of ch. 35 (No. IX, July 1858). Dickens commented, after a narrative of events at the Garrick, 'Thackeray *thereupon*, by way of showing what an ill thing it is for writers to attack one another in print, denounces E. Y. (in *Virginians*, as Young Grubstreet)...' – *Letters*, ed. Walter Dexter (1938) III, 31-2.

Punch Lines

VARIOUS

Sources indicated after items: mainly M. H. Spielmann, *The History of 'Punch'* (1895); F. C. Burnand, *Records and Reminiscences, Personal and General* (1899); R. G. G. Price, *A History of 'Punch'* (1957); Arthur A. Adrian, *Mark Lemon: First Editor of 'Punch'* (1966); and works listed in 'Abbreviations' (above). *Punch* began in July 1841, and within a year Thackeray was contributing; he had indeed been involved in the abortive 1835 discussions about the London *Charivari* which eventually resulted in *Punch*. He joined 'the Table' – i.e. became a member of staff attending the weekly business dinners – in February 1844, contributed (as the 'Fat Contributor' and otherwise) various series including *Snobs*, thus consolidating his position as a leading periodical journalist, and was the most distinguished though not the most prolific writer for *Punch* in its first decade, besides being an illustrator.

'It was a good day for himself, the journal, and the world, when Thackeray found *Punch*', said Shirley Brooks, its editor 1870–4 (Spielmann, *History of 'Punch'*, p. 308): and Thackeray himself remarked to the *Punch* engraver Joseph Swain, 'Ah, Swain! if it had not been for *Punch*, I wonder where I should be!' (ibid., p. 253). It was 'chiefly under his influence', writes Spielmann (ibid., p. 422), that *Punch* 'raised its eyes from Bloomsbury [i.e. Bohemia] to Belgravia', becoming an agreeably conformist comic journal instead of mordantly radical, as Thackeray's antagonist Douglas Jerrold desired. Jerrold was, in these years, 'the only rival whom he feared' – Walter Jerrold, *Douglas Jerrold and 'Punch'* (1910) p. 27 – and their rivalry was political as much as literary: 'Jerrold represented the extreme left, and Thackeray the most pronounced right' on the *Punch* Table – Arthur William à Beckett, *The à Becketts of 'Punch'* (1903) p. 64. By 1847 he could report, 'Jerrold and I had a sort of war and I came off conqueror' (*LPP*, II, 274), and in 1850 he nearly resigned from the staff because of Jerrold's continued radicalism: 'I don't think I ought to pull any longer in the same boat with such a savage little Robespierre' (*LPP*, II, 681). As in his altercation with the Dickens group, Thackeray at *Punch* led the 'gentlemenly' public-school party. He respected his colleague Gilbert Abbott à Beckett 'on account of his school', Westminster (A. W. à Beckett, *The à Becketts of 'Punch'*, p. 43), and with his fellow Old Carthusian and main ally, John Leech, twitted their editor, Mark Lemon, for his low 'potboy' origins (Adrian, *Mark Lemon*, p. 48) – in a 'gentlemanly' way, no doubt. As Spielmann observes (*History of 'Punch'*, p. 319), Jerrold was justified at least in regarding Thackeray as 'a little – if ever so little – of a snob himself'. He finally resigned from *Punch* in December 1851 (see *LPP*, II, 823; III, 432), over its foreign policy, though Lemon maintained that it was over salary. 'I am sure that it is best for my reputation and the comfort of some of that crew that I should be out of it', he told its proprietor. 'I fancied myself too big to pull in the boat; and it wasn't in the nature of things that Lemon and Jerrold should like me' (Price, *History of 'Punch'*, p. 51; not in *LPP*).

Ray's account, *Adversity*, ch. 13, 'The *Punch* Connexion', is informative but strongly biassed; Price offers a more balanced assessment. An invaluable record of *Punch* Table conversations, 1858–70, occurs in the diary of Henry Silver, unpublished but drawn upon by Spielmann and later commentators. It does little to warrant Arthur A. Adrian's judgement that these Table-talkers were 'some of the best-informed men of their time' (*Mark Lemon*, p. 68): they appear as politically naive, lacking in compassion, generally self-satisfied, and dirty-minded at a schoolboy level. Thackeray wrote their anthem 'The Mahogany Tree' (*Punch*, 9 Jan 1847): '... Here let us sport, Boys, as we sit; / Laughter and wit / Flashing so free', etc. 'Boys' seems right; 'mahogany' was wrong, the famous Table being made of deal (Price, *History of 'Punch'*, p. 50). His last contribution to *Punch* was in 1854, but he remained a fairly constant attender at the weekly dinners, and was at the Table a week before he died.

[Anny is commenting upon her father's 'fury' over what he considered errors in *Punch's* politics.] One peculiarity which has always struck me in my father, and which I have never noticed in any one else to the same extent, was his personal interest in others and in their actions. He seemed to feel in a measure responsible for the doings of anyone he was concerned with. His admiration, his appreciation, were extraordinarily keen for things which he approved and loved; in the same way, his feeling of real suffering and emotion over the failures and lapses of those with whom he lived was intensely vivid. This made his relations with others anxious at times – indifferent, never. (*Biog. Intros*, VI, xxiv)

During this period [the 1840s] many literary men and artists connected with *Punch*, including Mark Lemon, Douglas Jerrold, Henry and Horace Mayhew, G à Beckett, John Gilbert, Alfred Forrester (A. Crowquill), H. K. Browne (Phiz), and William Harvey, frequently called at Landells's establishment [where the illustrations were engraved], and all had a cheery word to say to his employees; but Thackeray, who drew on wood-blocks as well as wrote for *Punch*, used to march past them with his long strides, without uttering a word.[1]

[*Silver diary, 2 March 1859.*] Thackeray leaves early, to go to an 'episcopal tea-fight', as he tells us – a jump 'from lively to severe', to Fulham Palace from the *Punch* Table. Tom [Taylor] merely looks in 'to hear what you fellows say about the Reform Bill', which Dizzy introduced on Monday.[2] So we begin discussing politics even with venison. 'Ponny' [Horace] Mayhew condemns the Bill: does nothing for the working man, he says. Tom thinks that people look to *Punch* for guidance, and that we ought to be plain-speaking, and take a decided course. 'Professor' [Percival] Leigh and Mark [Lemon] agree in thinking that we rather should stand by awhile, and see how the stream runs....

Seria mista jocis [a mixture of the serious and the frivolous] being Mr Punch's motto... Shirley [Brooks], apropos of money, asks, 'Why is Lord Overstone[3] like a copper?' 'Because he is a Lloyd with tin.' Whereat Thackeray laughs heartily.

Odd that there should now be three old Carthusians in Mr Punch's Council of Ten. Thackeray observes this to the other two of them [John Leech and Henry Silver], and proceeds to say, 'I went to Charterhouse the other day. Hadn't seen School come out since I left. Saw a touching scene there – a little fellow with his hands held tenderly behind him, and a tear or two still trickling down his rosy cheeks, and two little cronies with their arms round his neck; and I well knew what had happened, and how they'd take him away *privily*, and make him show his cuts!'[4]

'Talking of cuts, Mark, how about the Large one?'[5] Thackeray suggests Lawyer, Doctor, and Schoolmaster, standing in a row as prize boys, and Dizzy presenting them with votes.... Mark suggests D. joining hands of artisan and yeoman, giving each of them a vote. Thackeray thinks of workman coming among gentlemen of Parliament and asking, 'What have you done for *me*?'[6]

[*Silver diary, 1861.*] Thackeray calls Tennyson the greatest man of the age – 'has thrown the quoit furthest'. [Shirley] Brooks says *Vanity Fair* ranks higher than anything of Tennyson's. 'Would you change your reputation for his?' 'Yes.' 'I don't believe you.' Thackeray, Brooks and Leigh all praise Scott, Brooks and Leigh the most – stirs the blood – but, says Thackeray, I don't want my blood stirred. Says Brooks, Bulwer might much improve Scott's language. Curious felicity of words, says Thackeray. (Thackeray often talks just as he writes....)...

War talk predominates.[7] Leigh throwing cold water on the fire of indignation. Thinks people too prone to fight.... Thackeray says, British ships are British soil – and if we submit the Yankees will get the notion that British Bottoms are made to be kicked.... Has 5000 dear relations (invested) in the States: 'but yet I, Makepeace, declare for War...'. (Price, *History of 'Punch'*, p. 102)

[F. C. Burnand (1837–1917), later to edit *Punch*, joined the Table in 1863. Thackeray remained a fairly regular attender, he writes, 'and took his share in the political discussions, invariably commencing with a sort of apology, describing himself as one not having present authority, but as "one of the past scribes"' (*Reminiscences*, II, 7). He met, and was generously welcomed by, Thackeray at one such dinner.] Thackeray, as I remember, had to leave early and after bidding them all good-night with a comprehensive wave of the hand, he paused by my chair, put out his hand, and, as I rose from my seat, shook mine most cordially. Then releasing it, he placed his right hand on my shoulder, and, as it were, introduced me to the assemblage, saying, 'Gentlemen, allow the old boy to present to you "the new boy", and I wish him every success. He's sure of it.' Whereat his short speech was loudly acclaimed, my health was drunk informally, I was not required to respond, and with another hearty shake of the hand, Thackeray quitted the room, turning once to nod encouragingly at me and to wave his adieux to the others. That was to me a memorable night....

I must not omit the only night that I ever saw Thackeray lose his temper; and he did, with a vengeance. [They were relaxing, after completing the evening's business, when Horace Mayhew 'dragged in the name of Edmund Yates'. Lemon tried to change the subject, in vain.] Thackeray frowningly asked a question; somebody replied. Another question, Thackeray becoming hotter. Mark attempted to throw oil on the troubled waters, which would have been effective had they been only waters. But, as it was, he threw the oil on smouldering fire, and – phew! –what a blaze!! Down came Thackeray's fist like a sledge-hammer on the arm of the chair, as, in quite unmeasured terms, he denounced the man who had written of him in a Sunday paper, describing him as 'a broken-nosed satirist'. Then after this lightning flash and peal of thunder, which made even Mark Lemon quiver, there came a pause. It was the pause after Virgil's 'Quos ego'[8] – and Thackeray, without another word, rose quickly, left the room, and the house.

Then Mark told me the story about Edmund Yates, Thackeray, Dickens, and the Garrick Club, and I was sorry for every one mixed up in that affair, especially for Thackeray, who, I rather fancy, was not absolutely satisfied with the line he had taken, although he could not subsequently retract.... My notion of it, in my Gospel 'according to Mark', is that Edmund Yates was wrong to begin with, that Thackeray was wrong to go on with, and that Charles Dickens acted impulsively and rather more hastily than he would otherwise have done, had it been against anyone except Thackeray.[9]

Thackeray was the only man upon the *Punch* staff with whom

Mark Lemon was not upon thoroughly easy terms [writes Joseph Hatton]. 'I never felt quite at home with him,' he said to me during one of our numerous gossips, 'he was always so infernally wise. He was genial; but whatever you talked about, you felt that he would have the wisest views upon the subject. He seemed too great for ordinary conversation. Now Dickens was very different. He was full of fun, merry and wise, buoyant with animal spirits. I always, however, liked Thackeray, in addition to other reasons, because he liked Dickens, and never showed a spark of jealousy about his work, which he always openly and honestly admired.'[10]

[Thackeray attended his last *Punch* dinner on 16 December 1863 (*Wisdom*, p. 414). A fortnight later, almost all the 'Table' were present at his funeral, all feeling 'as if the glory of *Punch* had been irremediably dimmed'. Horace Mayhew had brought the news of Thackeray's death to the previous weekly dinner and, as Frederick Greenwood told Spielmann,] he proceeded, 'I tell you what we'll do. We'll sing the dear old boy's "Mahogany Tree"; he'd like it.' Accordingly we all stood up, and with such memory of the words as each possessed ... and a catching of the breath here and there by about all of us, the song was sung. (Spielmann, *History of 'Punch'*, pp. 326, 86–7)

NOTES

1. H. M. Cundall, *Birket Foster* (1906) p. 36. Cundall was drawing here on the recollections of the Foster family.
2. The Derby–Disraeli administration was defeated on this Bill, and resigned soon afterwards.
3. Samuel Jones Loyd, eminent banker and financier, became first Baron Overstone in 1850.
4. It was traditional to repair to the toilets, to show one's scars. 'It hurt like h—ll', Thackeray recalled, in another conversation with Silver (*Adversity*, p. 82).
5. The week's main political cartoon.
6. Spielmann, *History of 'Punch'*, pp. 68–70. The cartoon (*Punch*, 12 Mar 1859, p. 105) was eventually based on a suggestion from Percival Leigh. A heated argument ensued about whether *Punch* had become politically too conservative and complacent; Thackeray did not participate, probably

having left for Fulham Palace. Spielmann, who gives the seating plans at the Table over the years (ibid., pp. 65–8), remarks that Thackeray 'seldom made a suggestion' about the subject of the weekly 'Big Cut' (ibid., p. 170).

7. In November 1861 an American warship seized some Confederate envoys from a British ship, the *Trent*. An American observer in London wrote home about British reactions to what was regarded as an act of piracy: 'The people are frantic with rage, and were the country polled, I fear 999 men out of every thousand would declare for immediate war' – quoted in E. L. Woodward, *The Age of Reform 1815–1870* (1946) p. 297. On Thackeray's dollar investments, mentioned below, see II, 270.

8. Neptune's wrathful uncompleted threat against whoever had caused the storm which beset Aeneas (*Aeneid*, I, 135).

9. Burnand, *Reminiscences*, II, 2–4, 11–14. Henry Silver's account of this episode (Aug 1863) is summarised by Adrian (*Mark Lemon*, p. 135): 'Thackeray exploded, "Damn it, you fellows still seem to think it was because of my nose that I fell foul of him. But he imputed dishonourable conduct to me – and for that I got him kicked out of the Garrick." "Ponny" only fanned the flame by retorting, "With your strength you might have been more generous." A terse note in Silver's diary records the conclusion of this scene: "And Thackeray blazes up, and finally bolts." '

10. Joseph Hatton, 'The True History of *Punch*: Chapter VIII', *London Society*, XXIX (1867) 255. Another *Punch* colleague, Shirley Brooks, has different memories of Thackeray on Dickens. 'And what delightful English [Thackeray] wrote!' he recalled. 'He knew this and was proud and said that Dickens might be a greater "moralist", but that he was the best grammarian, and "anybody could be moral!" ' – George Soames Layard, *A Great 'Punch' Editor: Shirley Brooks* (1907) p. 555.

'Almost Infantile Openness of Nature'

JOHN SKELTON

From *The Table-talk of Shirley* (1895) pp. 25–35. Skelton (1831–97), knighted 1897, civil servant and author (under the pseudonym 'Shirley'). He met Thackeray through a letter of introduction from Doctor John Brown, and was later invited to contribute to the *Cornhill*.

The notion that he was an utterly heartless worldling, curt, cynical, unsympathetic, finding his chief joy in eating and drinking and the assiduous cultivation of social 'swells', must be dismissed. But a false impression once formed has a malignant vitality which time does not impair. I should say that Thackeray was constitutionally a shy man, and that his shyness accounts for a good many traits (foibles, if you like) which have been gravely rebuked by superior moralists. For myself, I can only testify that on the rare occasions when I met him in the snuggery at Onslow Square, or elsewhere, I found him one of the gentlest of satirists. At the same time he was extremely outspoken; he had a childish inability to conceal, and, like a child, he sometimes repeated what was not intended for repetition. In an old diary I find it written, 'I found him sitting in his den at the top of his house in Onslow Square. He has suffered much and long, and the traces of suffering are visible in his face. I fancy that even in his brightest moods it is possible to detect these traces, sometimes in the eyes, more frequently above the grave curves of the mouth. Of course I was ushered into his den – of course he told me how and from what he was suffering. This perfect unreserve, this almost infantile openness of nature, is characteristic of Thackeray. He is willing that his whole life should be laid bare and looked through. The clear, transparent simplicity of the boy at the Charterhouse never deserts him. In fact, there is much of the boy about him, in spite of the grey hairs and the spectacles. On this very day he wore an old shooting-coat much too short for him; it fitted the giant as a boy's jacket would fit an ordinary mortal. Yet, with all his boyishness of manner, there is something leonine about Thackeray.' . . .

There was no one of his standing so quick to appreciate what he held to be a really sincere and kindly greeting as Thackeray. He was essentially a humble-minded man who was rather astonished at the fuss the world was beginning to make about him. I had made the most casual allusion to him in a *Fraser* article . . . and I had no thought that they would meet his eye. But within a week of their publication there came a letter [from Thackeray, *LPP*, IV. 216] to 'Dr John' – the ever dear 'J. B.' – in which grateful allusion was made to the half-dozen lines. Even now one wonders how he came to light upon them, or how they should have made the most fleeting impression on his mind. . . .

He had been a sufferer for years; but he treated his sufferings with a touch of humorous exaggeration that was apt to mislead; and his friends had looked forward with confidence to an Indian summer. Possibly with due vigilance he need not have died at fifty-two. He knew 'Syme's method and high reputation', he wrote me; but he shrank from the cruel knife, however deftly handed. 'We shall see', he added, writing on the last day of 1861. Perhaps the old year was dying while he wrote; for there is a brief postscript which seems to belong to 1862. 'What a sad New Year with war to open it!' In these last months I fancy he was taking a silent farewell of much.

Less Awesome than Dickens

JUSTIN McCARTHY

From *Reminiscences* (1899) I, 32–43. McCarthy (1830–1912), later to become journalist, novelist and politician, arrived in London, a young Irishman, in 1852.

When I first settled in London, England was under the sway of a great literary triumvirate: Dickens, Thackeray and Tennyson. [He became acquainted with both novelists, and with Carlyle. In their different ways, and for quite different reasons, both Dickens and Carlyle] made me feel rather afraid.... I cannot explain why it was that I never felt the same kind of awe or awkwardness in the presence of Thackeray. One might have thought that Thackeray's presence would have been more inspiring of awe to a young and thoroughly obscure man. Thackeray was much taller than Dickens; his form, indeed, approached to the gigantic in its proportions; he looked far older, although the two men were much about the same age; his immense head, his broad forehead, and his prematurely white hair, gave him an appearance of authority, and even of severity, which one might have thought would prove intimidating to a stranger. Yet I at least never felt it so. He seemed to me to be less self-assertive, less conscious of his superiority, than Dickens appeared to be. I never had the good fortune of approaching to intimacy with Thackeray – the chance that at one time opened upon me was reduced to nothing by the Fates, and its memory has left an indelible impression on my mind. I had met Thackeray in a casual way several times; but I never was a pushing sort of person, and indeed I idolised Thackeray and Dickens far too much to think of pushing myself on either of them. A literary controversy on some question which has now lost all its importance sprang up in 1863, and I wrote something anonymously in the *Morning Star* which had the good luck to please the author of *Vanity Fair*. Thackeray asked a friend of mine and of his to find out who the writer was; and the friend had no difficulty in accomplishing this task. For myself, I was almost in a humour to think I had lived long enough, since I had lived to write anything which was worthy of Thackeray's favourable notice. [Thackeray invited him to dinner, but died before the occasion came.]

Of course, I heard all Thackeray's lectures; and to hear them was a delightful experience for me. I remember that I was rather nervous about going to hear his first lecture on the Georges, because of my fear lest my author should be undertaking a task outside his proper range and should disappoint me; for I could not bear the idea of Thackeray's attempting to do anything and not distinctly succeeding in the attempt. All my fears vanished when I did hear that first lecture. Thackeray was not a magnificent declaimer like Dickens; he made no attempt at dramatic effect of any kind; his voice, though clear and penetrating and sometimes thrilling, had nothing like the variety and richness of intonation which the voice of Dickens could always command; he was simply an educated gentleman reading aloud to an educated assembly. But he had to the full the unstudied art of expression in all that he read; and after a long and vast variety of experiences in the hearing of all manner of public men addressing audiences from platforms, from pulpits, from judicial benches, and from the benches of the Houses of Parliament, I can remember no instance of an audience kept more thoroughly in hushed and anxious delight – delight blended with terror lest a single word should be lost – than was the audience that listened to the closing passage of Thackeray's lecture on George III. I heard that lecture again and again, and each time towards the close there came that enraptured stillness over the audience which made me understand what people meant when they said 'you might have heard a pin drop'. I was impressed in much the same way by Thackeray's reading of Hood's 'Bridge of Sighs' in one of his other lectures, and by his reading of that charming poem of Bishop Heber's which begins with the line 'If thou, my love, wert by my side.'

I remember that towards the close of Thackeray's life we used to have great discussions as to whether Thackeray was or was not a great admirer of rank – whether he was not, in fact, as some ill-natured critics declared him to be, a personage who ought to have had a place in the collection of characters represented by his own *Book of Snobs*. So far as I knew or could observe Thackeray, I had no reason to believe that he had any defect of the kind. I had known him to be on the most kindly and friendly terms with men and women who had nothing whatever of rank or station to recommend them to his notice. One anecdote, however, which was told to me as a proof of Thackeray's alleged weakness for aristocratic rank, I feel bound to narrate – it is so whimsical an illustration of an utterly perverse reading of character by an oddly prejudiced observer. Among my casual acquaintances at the time was a man who was, like myself, struggling to get into literature. He was a man who claimed to belong to a good family, and who was always boasting of the fact and telling you of his high connections, bringing out the names of his first cousin the marquis, and his second cousin the duchess, and his aunt in the country whose father had been in the Royal Household. We all understood the weakness of our poor friend, and made fun of him when his back was turned. He had been lucky enough to make the acquaintance of Thackeray, and was fond of alluding to the fact. One day I met him at the Garrick Club, and he suddenly began to talk to me about Thackeray. 'Now look here,' he said, 'you always refuse to believe that Thackeray worships the aristocracy. I'll give you a convincing proof that he does, a proof that I got only this very day. Do you see this cigar?' He held one out between his fingers, and I admitted that I did see it. 'Well,' he said, 'that cigar was given me by Thackeray; and do you know what he said when he was giving it to me?' I had to admit that I could not form any guess as to what Thackeray might have said. So he went on with an air of triumph. 'Well,' he said, 'Thackeray's words to me were these: "Now, my dear fellow, here is a cigar which I know you will be delighted to have, because it is one of a box that was given to me by a marquis." Now what have you to say?' I had nothing to say. I could have said 'I really didn't know that Thackeray was as well acquainted with you as all that', but I controlled my tongue, and the conversation dropped. Thackeray, too, had evidently seen the weakness of our poor friend, and was making merciless fun of it.

The Softness, and the Weakness, of a Woman

ANTHONY TROLLOPE

(1) from 'W. M. Thackeray', *Cornhill Magazine*, IX (1864) 134–6; (2) from *Thackeray* (1879) pp. 15–20, 30–2, 50, 54–60. Trollope (1815–82) regarded Thackeray as undoubtedly the greatest of contemporary novelists, with the 'purest' and 'most harmonious' prose style in all English fiction, and at fault only in that, in his later years, 'he allowed his mind to become idle' (*Autobiography*, ch. 13); *Esmond* was the finest novel, and Colonel Newcome the finest single character, in English fiction. Trollope was beginning to make his name, with the Barsetshire novels, when, in October 1859, he wrote to Thackeray offering to contribute stories to the *Cornhill*. He became for several years its leading serialist – his novel *Castle Richmond* held pride of place in No. 1 – and it was thus that he met Thackeray (ibid., ch. 8). See below, II, 342–3, for George Smith's account of their unhappy first encounter. He last saw him 'about ten days before his death, and ... I never knew him pleasanter or more at ease as to his bodily ailments. How I seem to have loved that dear head of his now that he is gone' – *Letters of Anthony Trollope*, ed. Bradford Allen Booth (Oxford, 1951) p. 142. With Dickens and Houghton (Monckton Milnes) he shared the task of providing the obsequies in the *Cornhill* (Feb 1864),[1] and he wrote the English Men of Letters volume on Thackeray (1879), finding this 'a terrible job', partly because neither Anny Thackeray nor Edward FitzGerald would help him with materials: 'There is absolutely nothing to say – except washed out criticism [he wrote]. But it had to be done, and no one could do it more lovingly' – James Pope Hennessy, *Anthony Trollope* (1973 reprint) p. 196.

(1) He who knew Thackeray will have a vacancy in his heart's inmost casket, which must remain vacant till he dies. One loved him almost as one loves a woman, tenderly and with thoughtfulness – thinking of him when away from him as a source of joy which cannot be analysed, but is full of comfort. One who loved him, loved him thus because his heart was tender, as is the heart of a woman.[2]

It need be told to no one that four years ago – four years and one month at the day on which these words will come before the reader – this magazine was commenced under the guidance, and in the hands, of Mr Thackeray. It is not for any of us who were connected with him in the enterprise to say whether this was done successfully or not; but it is for us – for us of all men – to declare that he was the kindest of guides, the gentlest of rulers, and, as a fellow-workman, liberal, unselfish, considerate, beyond compare. It has been said of him that he was jealous as a writer. We of the *Cornhill* knew nothing of such jealousy. At the end of two years Mr Thackeray gave up the management of the magazine, finding that there was much in the very nature of the task which embarrassed and annoyed him. He could not bear to tell an ambitious aspirant that his aspirations were in vain; and, worse again, he could not endure to do so when a lady was his suppliant.... He lacked hardness for the place, and therefore, at the end of two years, he relinquished it.

But he did not on that account in any way sever himself from the magazine.... It was only in November last, as our readers may remember, that a paper appeared from his hand, entitled, 'Strange to Say, on Club Paper'. In this he ridiculed a silly report as to Lord Clyde, which had spread itself about the town – doing so with that mingled tenderness and sarcasm for which he was noted – the tenderness being ever for those named, and the sarcasm for those unknown. As far as we know, they were the last words he lived to publish. Speaking of the old hero who was just gone he bids us remember that 'censure and praise are alike to him; "The music warbling to the deafened ear,/The incense wasted on the funeral bier!"' How strange and how sad that these, his last words, should now come home to us as so fitted for himself!... He, of whom we speak, loved such incense when living. If that be an infirmity he was so far infirm. But we hold it to be no infirmity.

Who is the man who loves it not? Where is the public character to whom it is not as the breath of his nostrils? But there are men to whom it is given to conceal their feelings. Of such Thackeray was not one. He carried his heart-strings in a crystal case, and when they were wrung or when they were soothed all their workings were seen by friend and foe.

When he died he was still at work for this magazine. He was writing yet another novel for the delight of its readers.... The leisure time of which he was thinking never came to him. That presently was denied to him, nor had he lived would it have been his for many a year to come. He was young in power, young in heart as a child, young even in constitution in spite of that malady which carried him off. But, though it was so, Thackeray ever spoke of himself, and thought of himself, as of one that was old. He in truth believed that the time for letting others speak was speedily coming to him. But they who knew him did not believe it....

(2) He was not a man capable of feeling at any time quite assured in his position, and when that occurred he was very far from assurance. I think that at no time did he doubt the sufficiency of his own mental qualification for the work he had taken in hand; but he doubted all else. He doubted the appreciation of the world; he doubted his fitness for turning his intellect to valuable account; he doubted his physical capacity – dreading his own lack of industry; he doubted his luck; he doubted the continual absence of some of those misfortunes on which the works of literary men are shipwrecked. Though he was aware of his own power, he always, to the last, was afraid that his own deficiencies should be too strong against him. It was his nature to be idle – to put off his work – and then to be angry with himself for putting it off. Ginger was hot in the mouth with him, and all the allurements of the world were strong upon him. To find on Monday morning an excuse why he should not on Monday do Monday's work was, at the time, an inexpressible relief to him, but had become a deep regret – almost a remorse – before the Monday was over. To such a one it was not given to believe in himself with that sturdy rock-bound foundation which we see to have belonged to some men from the earliest struggles of their career. To him, them, must have come an inexpressible

pang when he was told that his story must be curtailed.

Who else would have told such a story of himself to the first acquaintance he chanced to meet? Of Thackeray it might be predicted that he certainly would do so. No little wound of the kind ever came to him but what he disclosed it at once. 'They have only bought so many of my new book.' 'Have you seen the abuse of my last number?' 'What am I to turn my hand to? They are getting tired of my novels.' 'They don't read it', he said to me of *Esmond*. 'So you don't mean to publish my work?' he said once to a publisher in an open company. Other men keep their little troubles to themselves. I have heard even of authors who have declared how all the publishers were running after their books; I have heard some discourse freely of their fourth and fifth editions; I have known an author to boast of his thousands sold in this country, and his tens of thousands in America; but I never heard anyone else declare that no one would read his *chef-d'oeuvre*, and that the world was becoming tired of him. It was he who said, when he was fifty, that a man past fifty should never write a novel....

It may almost be said Thackeray was the very opposite of [Dickens, in temperament]. Unsteadfast, idle, changeable of purpose, aware of his own intellect but not trusting it, no man ever failed more generally than he to put his best foot foremost. Full as his works are of pathos, full of humour, full of love and charity, tending, as they always do, to truth and honour and manly worth and womanly modesty, excelling, as they seem to me to do, most other written precepts that I know, they always seem to lack something that might have been there. There is a touch of vagueness which indicates that his pen was not firm while he was using it. He seems to me to have been dreaming ever of some high flight, and then to have told himself, with a half-broken heart, that it was beyond his power to soar up into those bright regions. I can fancy as the sheets went from him every day he told himself, in regard to every sheet, that it was a failure. Dickens was quite sure of his sheets....

Thackeray was a man of no great power of conversation. I doubt whether he ever shone in what is called general society. He was not a man to be valuable at a dinner-table as a good talker. It was when there were but two or three together that he was happy himself and made others happy; and then it would rather be from some special piece of drollery that the joy of the moment would come, than from the discussion of ordinary topics. After so many years his old friends remember the fag-ends of the doggerel lines which used to drop from him without any effort on all occasions of jollity. And though he could be very sad – laden with melancholy, as I think must have been the case with him always – the feeling of fun would quickly come to him, and the queer rhymes would be poured out as plentifully as the sketches were made.... He was always versifying. He once owed me £5 17s. 6d., his share of a dinner bill at Richmond. He sent me a cheque for the amount in rhyme, giving the proper financial document on the second half of a sheet of note paper. I gave the poem away as an autograph, and now forget the lines. This was all trifling, the reader will say. No doubt. Thackeray was always trifling, and yet always serious. In attempting to understand his character it is necessary for you to bear within your own mind the idea that he was always, within his own bosom, encountering melancholy with buffoonery, and meanness with satire. The very spirit of burlesque dwelt within him – a spirit which does not see the grand the less because of the travesties which it is always engendering....

[Serialisation] though easy... is seductive, and leads to idleness. An author by means of it can raise money and reputation on his book before he has written it, and when the pang of parturition is over in regard to one part, he feels himself entitled to a period of ease because the amount required for the next division will occupy him only half the month. This to Thackeray was so alluring that the entirety of the final half was not always given to the task. His self-reproaches and bemoanings when sometimes the day for reappearing would come terribly nigh, while yet the necessary amount of copy was far from being ready, were often very ludicrous and very sad – ludicrous because he never told of his distress without adding to it something of ridicule which was irresistible, and sad because those who loved him best were aware that physical suffering had already fallen upon him, and that he was deterred by illness from the exercise of continuous energy. I myself did not know him till after the time now in question. My acquaintance with him was quite late in his life. But he has told me something of it, and I have heard from those who lived with him how continual were his sufferings....

The [*Cornhill*] was a great success, but justice compels me to say that Thackeray was not a good editor. As he would have been an indifferent civil servant, an indifferent member of Parliament, so was he perfunctory as an editor.... I think it may be doubted whether Thackeray did bring himself to read the basketfuls of manuscripts with which he was deluged.... Nor, in truth, do I think that he did much of the editorial work. I had once made an arrangement, not with Thackeray, but with the proprietors, as to some little story. The story was sent back to me by Thackeray – rejected. *Virginibus puerisque!* That was the gist of his objection. There was a project in a gentleman's mind, – as told in my story, – to run away with a married woman! Thackeray's letter was very kind, very regretful, – full of apology for such treatment to such a contributor. But – *Virginibus puerisque!* I was quite sure that Thackeray had not taken the trouble to read the story himself. Some moral deputy had read it, and disapproving, no doubt properly, of the little project to which I have alluded, had incited the Editor to use his authority. That Thackeray had suffered when he wrote it was easy to see, fearing that he was giving pain to one he would fain have pleased. I wrote him a long letter in return, as full of drollery as I knew how to make it. In four or five days there came a reply in the same spirit – boiling over with fun.[3] ...

It has been said of Thackeray that he was a cynic.... A public man should of course be judged from his public work. If he wrote as a cynic – a point which I will not discuss here – it may be fair that he who is to be known as a writer should be so called. But, as a man, I protest that it would be hard to find an individual farther removed from the character. Over and outside his fancy, which was the gift which made him so remarkable – a certain feminine softness was the most remarkable trait about him. To give some inmediate pleasure was the great delight of his life – a sovereign to a schoolboy, gloves to a girl, a dinner to a man, a compliment to a woman. His charity was overflowing. His generosity excessive. I heard once a story of woe from a man who was the dear friend of both of us.[4] The gentleman wanted a large sum of money instantly – something under £2000 – had no natural friends who could provide it, but must go utterly to the wall without it. Pondering over this sad condition of things just revealed to me, I met Thackeray between the two mounted heroes at the Horse Guards, and told him the story. 'Do you mean to say that I am to find £2000?' he said, angrily, with some expletives. I explained that I had not even suggested the doing of anything – only that we might discuss the matter. Then there came over his face a peculiar smile, and a wink in his eye, and he whispered his suggestion, as though half ashamed of his meanness. 'I'll go half,' he said, 'if anybody will do the rest.' And he did go half, at a day or two's notice, though the gentleman was no more than simply a friend. I am glad to be able to add that the money was quickly repaid. I could tell various stories of the same kind, only that I lack space, and that they, if simply added one to the other, would lack interest....

Such is my idea of the man whom many call a cynic, but whom I regard as one of the most soft-hearted of human beings, sweet as Charity itself, who went about the world dropping pearls, doing good, and never wilfully inflicting a wound.

NOTES

1. He had written to George Smith, 25 Dec 1863, asking who would provide the *Cornhill* obituary appreciation, and offering to do it 'if you have no one better.... Of course ... [as] a work of love', though W. H. Russell, G. H. Lewes or Robert Bell 'would do it better', he suggested (*Letters of Trollope*, pp. 213–14).

2. He put this point more sharply in a letter, Aug 1864: 'He was a man to be loved even more than liked. He was tender-hearted in the extreme, and had much of the softness and sometimes also ... of the weakness of a woman' (*Wisdom*, p. 425).

3. For this correspondence about Trollope's story 'Mrs General Talboys', see *LPP*, IV, 206–8.

4. The man was William Webb Follett Synge (on whom see below, II, 355), and it was Trollope who lent the other thousand pounds. The loan, made in May 1862, was mostly still unrepaid when Thackeray died: see *Letters of Trollope*, p. 143.

Tipsy and Undignified

JOHN BIGELOW

From *Retrospections of an Active Life* (New York, 1909) I, 254–5, 263–4, 278–9. Bigelow (1817–1911), politician, newspaper-editor, diplomat, author and historian, presided at the New York Press Club dinner in Thackeray's honour, 4 Dec 1852, and met him subsequently in London and elsewhere. Thackeray, encountering him in 1862 in Paris, where he was American Consul-general, found him 'as jolly as ever' (*LPP*, IV. 265).

[*20 Jan 1860*. Thackeray calls upon him, exultant over the high circulation of the *Cornhill's* opening number, and reporting that] he told Lord Palmerston at Lady Palmerston's reception, a few nights ago, that he was now a power in the state.... In the next number, he told me, he means to give the true version of the story about Mrs King of Charleston and himself.[1] As I heard that story, Thackeray was reported to have said to her, 'Mrs King, I thought you were a fast woman.' To which she replied, 'Mr Thackeray, I thought you were a gentleman.' Thackeray said 'nothing of the kind ever passed between them'; that she was eternally teasing him with her attentions till finally she said to him one day, 'Mr Thackeray, I was told I should like you, but I don't.' 'I replied,' said Thackeray, ' "Well, I don't care a pin if you don't." The other story', he said emphatically, 'is a lie....'

On 10 March [1860] we dined with Thackeray, and the company consisted entirely of strangers, exclusive of his family. Among them were Mrs Charles Dickens; Dr Quin, the earliest homeopathic physician, as he claimed to be; Mrs Caulfield, a very pretty and unaffected woman whom I was permitted to take down to dinner; Sir Henry Havelock, son of the famous defender of Lucknow; Mr Oliphant, the eccentric though gifted husband of an eccentric wife; and some half-dozen others whose names I did not learn. Thackeray, at whose side I was seated, was suffering with chills and fever. He drank a great deal, as it seemed to me, and garnished his food with red pepper and curry to excess, for the purpose, as he said, of staving off or drawing off the chills. He succeeded in bringing on a profuse perspiration about eleven o'clock; at the same time he said he was tipsy, and talked a little to verify his diagnosis.

He and Quin[2] throughout the dinner kept sparring with each other, at the expense to both of a good deal of personal dignity. Quin frequently called him a humbug, and other names of that ilk, with a degree of familiarity which could well have been spared. Thackeray said at an early stage of the dinner, 'Look here, Quin, you must not be so familiar. My daughter told me the other day that you were too familiar.' He also said that the advertisements in the first number of his magazine, the *Cornhill*, were a loss to him, as they had calculated on a sale of but 40,000 and they sold 100,000 so that the extra paper consumed all the profits of that number.

[On 28 April 1860 Bigelow called on Thackeray's neighbour W. H. Russell, and the novelist dropped in. The fifth number of the *Cornhill* had just appeared.] It at once became the subject of conversation. Each in turn expressed his opinion of the merits and demerits of the several articles in the number. After they had all pretty much said their say, my wife, who had been silent, said, 'Well, for my part, I enjoyed the story about the school of girls better than anything else in the number.' 'Did you?' shrieked Thackeray, jumping up and seizing both her hands. 'Did you? My daughter [Anny] wrote that.'[3] He was completely overcome by the genuineness and unaffected sincerity of the compliment, for of course he knew that no one in the room but himself was aware of the authorship of the story, nor had any of the other persons present alluded to it. I doubt if Thackeray ever received a compliment for anything he wrote himself that gave him the pleasure he got from this involuntary tribute to the maiden effort of Miss [Anny].

He said he thought the verses about Washington Irving in that number[4] rather small beer – a kind of beer of which he admitted he was very fond.

I am here [in a footnote] tempted to quote a paragraph from a letter which Miss [Anny] Thackeray wrote to my wife shortly after our return to the United States,[5] because of its allusion to some of the penalties Thackeray's family paid for the pleasure his labours gave to the public:

> Papa I'm thankful to say has been pretty well this summer, ill indeed but not quite so ill as usual. He's going to work very hard at another book. Yet if anybody knew how I hate the sight of a 'new book by Mr Thackeray', I think they wd be kind enough not to buy a single copy. I'm sure 'writing-books-&-going-out-to-dinner-to-shake-them-off' is the real name of his illness. However when he's well the work runs famously on wheels & then its pleasant enough. Our new house is coming to life & costing O! such a deal of money; so this is another little incubus, though indeed we are such fortunate people with such good luck & so happy a home for us young women & so kind a Papa to take care of us that I have to make the most of any little disagreeables if I want to get any pity.

NOTES

1. *Roundabout Papers*, 'On Two Children in Black' (*Cornhill Magazine*, Mar 1860), where she is described as 'a clever and candid woman' in America. Thackeray often retold this anecdote and, as the conversation with Bigelow implies, various other versions of it were current. On Mrs King, see also above, I, 175–6, 177.

2. Dr Frederick Quin (1799–1878), homeopathic physician and socialite, with whom Thackeray had long been acquainted, socially and professionally; he came to regard him as 'a humbug and quack' though 'a very kind and good natured and serviceable man' (*LPP*, II, 360).

3. Anny Thackeray's 'Little Scholars' (*Cornhill Magazine*, May 1860), her first published work, was not a 'story' in the fictional sense but an account of her visiting some Industrial Schools for the poor in London.

4. A poem by, not about, Washington Irving: his 'Children in the Deepdene', dated 24 June 1822.

5. The Bigelows sailed for home on 30 May 1860. The 'new book' on which Thackeray was working that summer (referred to below) was *Philip*, serialised in the *Cornhill* from January 1861.

Founder-editor of the *Cornhill Magazine*

GEORGE SMITH AND ANNE THACKERAY RITCHIE

(1) from Leonard Huxley, *The House of Smith, Elder* (privately printed, 1923) pp. 71-2, 104-9, 160; (2) from *Biog. Intros*, XI, xvii, and 'The First Number of *The Cornhill*', by Mrs Richmond Ritchie, *Cornhill Magazine* n.s.I (1896) 10. George Smith II (1824-1901) took editorial control of the firm of Smith, Elder & Co. in 1843, at the age of nineteen, and during his long career made it illustrious; he was indeed arguably the most important Victorian publisher. An early admirer of Thackeray, he had sent him a message, long before he was famous, inviting him to publish with the firm, but to no avail; later he reproached Thackeray for not offering them *Vanity Fair*. They first met in 1849, through Charlotte Brontë's visit to London (see above, I, 107), and Smith subsequently published *The Kickleburys on the Rhine* (1850), *The English Humourists* (1853), *The Rose and the Ring* (1854) and *Esmond* (1852). The latter collaboration between author and publisher was of special importance: see J. A. Sutherland, *Victorian Novelists and Publishers* (1976) ch. 4, '*Henry Esmond*: The Shaping Power of Contract'. In 1859 the idea of founding a magazine 'flashed upon me suddenly', as Smith recalled. He secured Thackeray, on generous terms, as its main serial contributor and then, having failed to find a suitable editor, persuaded him to undertake that task too, again for an excellent salary, though aware that Thackeray's business qualifications were slight. (There was a vogue for eminent authors' editing such periodicals, Dickens being the most notable instance.) But Thackeray was not its only star. 'Our terms', Smith recalled, 'were lavish almost to the point of recklessness. No pains and no cost were spared to make the new magazine the best periodical yet known in English literature.' As Leonard Huxley says, 'No other group of writers equally brilliant had ever before been brought together within the covers of one magazine' (*House of Smith, Elder*, pp. 95, 100).

From its inception in January 1860 it was an enormous success; for a full account, see Spencer L. Eddy, Jr, *The Founding of 'The Cornhill Magazine'* (Muncie, Ind., 1970). Smith's warm friendship with Thackeray survived the latter's shortcomings as an editor and his resignation in 1862, and Smith Elder became the publishers of his works in the decades after his death. Smith's manuscript 'Reminiscences', quoted here, appears in Huxley's history of the firm. Earlier in his 'Reminiscences', describing the progress of *Esmond*, Smith mentions 'Thackeray's scrupulous dealings in matters of business', instancing his returning a cheque when he had failed to finish the book by the contracted date, and he adds that 'After his death, there was found in his desk a slip of paper which supplies an odd proof of this trait of his character. On it were written the words: "I.O. S.E. & Co., 35 pp." (i.e. pages of the *Cornhill* still to be written)' (Huxley, *House of Smith Elder*, p. 70).

(1) When [the *Cornhill*] proved a great success, and I felt that its editor ought to share in that success, I accordingly told Thackeray that I proposed to send him a cheque for double the payment that had been agreed upon for the editorship. This was so totally unexpected by Thackeray that, for a moment, he lost his balance. His lips quivered, and then he broke into tears.[1] This was an experience, he said, to which he was not accustomed. A touch of kindness, however, would always melt Thackeray. Our friendship became very close and unrestrained. Thackeray was not a good business manager of his own affairs, and would confide to me his difficulties. 'Well,' I would say to him jestingly, 'you know a bank whereon the wild thyme grows.' But his self-respect was too keen to permit him to lean too much on others. His mode of suggesting to me that a cheque would be convenient was characteristic. He would walk into my room in Pall Mall with both his trouser pockets turned inside out, a silent and expressive proof of their emptiness. I used to take out my cheque-book and look at him enquiringly. He mentioned the sum required and the transaction was completed....

We lightened our labours in the service of the *Cornhill* by monthly dinners. The principal contributors used to assemble at my table in Gloucester Square every month while we were in London; and these 'Cornhill dinners' were very delightful and interesting. Thackeray always attended, though he was often in an indifferent state of health. At one of these dinners Trollope was to meet Thackeray for the first time and was equally looking forward to an introduction to him. Just before dinner I took him up to Thackeray and introduced him with all the suitable *empressement*. Thackeray curtly said, 'How do?' and, to my wonder and Trollope's anger, turned on his heel! He was suffering at the time from a malady which at that particular moment caused him a sudden spasm of pain; though we, of course, could not know this. I well remember the expression on Trollope's face at that moment, and no one who knew Trollope will doubt that he *could* look furious on an adequate – and sometimes on an inadequate – occasion! He came to me the next morning in a very wrathful mood, and said, that had it not been that he was in my house for the first time, he would have walked out of it. He vowed he would never speak to Thackeray again, etc., etc. I did my best to soothe him; and, though rather violent and irritable, he had a fine nature with a substratum of great kindliness, and I believe he left my room in a happier frame of mind than when he entered it. He and Thackeray became afterwards close friends....

The monthly dinners were not our only alleviations of the regular routine of business. Whenever any new literary arrangement with Mr Thackeray was pending, he would playfully suggest that he always found his mind clearer for business at Greenwich than elsewhere, especially if his digestion were assisted by a certain brown hock at fifteen shillings a bottle, which Mr Hart, the landlord, used to produce. On these occasions Sir Charles Taylor, a very agreeable and prominent member of the Garrick Club, a friend of Thackeray and an acquaintance of mine, was always present. Beyond an occasional witticism, Sir Charles Taylor did not take part in our negotiations (and, indeed, there was no negotiation, for I cannot remember a single instance in which Mr Thackeray demurred to any proposal that I made to him), but his social gifts made our little dinners very pleasant....

The *Cornhill* was edited by Thackeray from 1860 to May 1862. I cannot truly say that he was, in a business sense, a good editor, and I had to do some part of the work myself. This was a pleasure to me, for I had the greatest possible admiration and affection for him. I had taken the precaution to arrange that I should have a veto on contributions; for I had a sufficient knowledge of Thackeray's wayward and erratic judgement, which made him liable as Editor to be influenced by totally irrelevant circumstances, to know that this was absolutely necessary. Such a relation between editor and publisher would have worked ill in the case of some men; but Thackeray's nature was so generous, and my regard for him was so sincere, that no misunderstanding between us ever occurred.

I used to drive round to his house in Onslow Square nearly every morning, and we discussed manuscripts and subjects together. He handed me one morning a manuscript and said, 'I hope, Smith, you won't exercise your veto upon that.' I asked, 'Why? Is it in your opinion so very good?' 'No,' he answered, 'I can't say it is really good; but it is written by such a pretty woman! She has such lovely eyes and such a sweet voice.' To my more prosaic nature these did not seem to be quite adequate reasons for accepting an article for the *Cornhill*. I read the manuscript and, not being under the glamour of the writer's beauty, I said to Thackeray the next morning, 'This will never do for us.' 'Very well,' said Thackeray, with a sigh, 'I am very sorry.' Before I left – and, as I supposed, to show he was not offended with my obstinacy – he asked me to dine with him on a given day. When the dinner came off he sent me down with the writer of the article in question, and a most agreeable evening I passed. 'What do you say *now* about that article, my young friend?' he asked in a tone of triumph the next time we met. I replied I preferred the writer to the article. If it was a question of putting the *writer*, instead of the article, into the *Cornhill*, I might yield. As this was not possible the article was sent back.

Thackeray was far too tender-hearted to be happy as Editor. He could not say 'No' without himself suffering a pang as keen as was inflicted by that 'No' on the rejected contributor himself. He would take pains – such as I believe few editors have ever taken – to soften his refusal.... Thackeray poured out his own sorrows as an editor in one of his 'Roundabout Papers'. It is entitled 'Thorns in the Cushion', and is a good example of Thackeray's humour and an illustration of the effect upon him of editorial duties. No one can read the article without realising as I did that Mr Thackeray came to a wise decision when he resigned the editorship of the magazine, and thus consulted his own comfort and peace of mind. I like to think that the tender heart of this noble man of genius was not troubled by editorial thorns during the remainder of his life. But in looking back it sometimes comes to me with a feeling akin to remorse that I was the instrument of imposing on him an uncongenial task, and that I might have done more than I did to relieve him of its burden....

[Smith recalls Anne Thackeray's first contribution to the *Cornhill*, an essay 'Little Scholars', published in April 1860.] Thackeray sent it to me with a letter containing the following passage: 'And in the meantime comes a little contribution called "Little Scholars", which I send you and which moistened my paternal spectacles. It is the article I talked of sending to *Blackwood*, but why should *Cornhill* lose such a sweet paper because it was my dear girl who wrote it? Papas, however, are bad judges – you decide whether we shall have it or not.' [Three further essays appeared, and then in 1862–3 her novel *The Story of Elizabeth*, which established her reputation. Smith recalls:] As I was going away from the house in Onslow Square one night, Anny, who had been watching for me, thrust a little parcel into my hand, whispered, 'Do you mind looking at that?' and then vanished into the diningroom. I put the parcel into my pocket and opened it on reaching my home. It was *The Story of Elizabeth*. ... I sent Thackeray the proofs of the story, and when we met I asked him if he had read them. 'No,' he said, 'I *could* not. I read some of them and then broke down so thoroughly I could not face the rest. She is such a dear girl.' "[2]

(2) I can still see my father walking about the house, coming in and out of the rooms, and sitting down and getting up again as he thought over his plans and the name of the forthcoming magazine. ...[3]

I can remember messengers arriving during the day when that first number was published to tell the Editor of fresh thousands being wanted by the public; then more messengers came, and we were told how the printers were kept working till all hours of the night. I can also remember one little fact that Mr George Smith mentioned at the time, and which happened to impress me. The calculations for the advertisements were all put out by the enormous sale. The price which pays for 10,000 announcements and the paper and the printing ceases to be remunerative when 120,000 notices are put forth. The proprietors actually lost upon transaction after a certain number had been reached. ...

With the third number there was published a fly-leaf from the Editor, in which he appeals to his contributors, and requests them not to send their contributions to his private house, but to the office of the magazine. As my father's health failed, the mechanical part of the work became more and more irksome to him, and he found – in common, I believe, with most editors – that it is not that which appears in print, but that which does not appear, which proves the really trying part of the editor's duty. [Like George Smith, she refers to her father's 'Thorns in the Cushion' paper.] Only a week or two ago I burnt a whole armful of these dusty thorns, and I can well imagine what it must have been for a man of sensitive nerves and vivid imagination to have to answer and dismiss all this mass of correspondence, suggestion, and petition arriving by every post.[4]

NOTES

1. Thackeray's £1000 a year was doubled to £2000. In a more restrained version of these reminiscences, Smith writes that Thackeray 'seemed much touched by my communication' – 'Our Birth and Parentage', *Cornhill Magazine*, n.s., x (1901) 10.

2. Another witness to his extreme emotionality over his daughter's literary achievement – which occasioned the last of his Grub Street quarrels, when she was adversely reviewed (see above, II, 298) – is the actress Fanny Kemble, who, meeting Thackeray soon after *The Story of Elizabeth* was published, complimented the father on having such a talented daughter: 'He looked at me for a moment with a beaming face, and then said, "Do you know, I have never read a word of that thing?" "Oh," cried I, "Thackeray! Why don't you? It is excellent! It would give you so much pleasure!" "My dear lady, I couldn't, I couldn't!" said he with the tears in his eyes, "It would *tear my guts out!*"' – Frances Anne Kemble, *Records of Later Life* (1882) III, 362–3.

3. It was Thackeray who suggested using the name of the street in which Smith Elders' offices were situated as the title of the magazine: 'It has a sound of jollity and abundance about it', he said. Though initially derided, his suggestion was accepted, and it set a fashion for periodicals' being named after streets or areas of London (Huxley, *House of Smith, Elder*, pp. 95–6).

4. She gives sundry examples. She reminisces further in her *From the Porch* (1913) pp. 227–36, 'Concerning the Founding of the *Cornhill Magazine*'.

'Dear Old Kindly Child!'

HERMAN MERIVALE

(1) from Herman Merivale, 'About Two Great Novelists', *Temple Bar*, LXXXIII (1888) 189–98; (2) from Herman Merivale and Frank T. Marzials, *Life of W. M. Thackeray* (1891) pp. 12–13, 237, 240–8. Herman Charles Merivale (1836–1906), dramatist and novelist, was the son of Herman Merivale (1806–74), academic and distinguished civil servant, who was a close friend of Thackeray's – 'my father held, I know, a large place in his heart' (ibid., p. 233) – and thus Merivale *fils* was only a child when he first met the novelist: 'my first memory of him goes back as far as memory can' (ibid., p. 11). In his 1888 article, outraged by Jane Brookfield's recent publication of some Thackeray letters, he urged that a full biography now be issued, despite Thackeray's wishes: 'There is no cause for scruple left.' Moved by this plea, Anny Ritchie authorised him to write one (see *Adversity*, p. 4) and gave him access to some family papers. He collected reminiscences from various people, but his health broke down and, after writing the opening chapters and a chapter on Thackeray's friendships, he abandoned the task, which was completed by (Sir) Frank T. Marzials. Merivale's first item opens with the exclamation, 'Four-and-twenty dear little girls! They must have four-and-twenty sixpences!' Thackeray, at the 1862 Exhibition, has just encountered a school crocodile of small girls.

(1) My stout old friend's attention was at once diverted from all other sources of interest. He spoke to the teachers, counted the heads, and stopped the procession. It was not enough for him that they should have sixpence apiece, to spend each upon a favourite fancy. He must himself get the full change in new sixpences, and personally present each baby with her particular coin and particular pat on the head. So said, so done; and it was like looking at one of Leech's pictures to see the same procession trotting off, this time in a picturesque disorder which rather baffled the teachers, with a view to investing their capital in such securities as might seem to them respectively the soundest. If the kindness of an action may be tested by the pleasure it gives, Sterne's Recording Angel had a good time over this one. How much it pleased the giver, I guessed from the moisture on his spectacles. If I had worn a

pair, I doubt if they would have been quite dry. This is my most characteristic memory of a man who was not only, as all know, one of the greatest and wisest of Englishmen, but was also – what all do *not* know – one of the very kindest-hearted....

Like all good and unspoiled souls, he loved 'the play'. Asking a listless friend one day if he liked it, he got the usual answer, 'Ye-es – I like a good play.' 'Oh! get out,' said Thackeray. 'I said *the* play; you don't even understand what I mean.' He liked to hear the fiddlers tune up, and to be well set in his place before each act began, and see it all out.... When a mere slip of a boy, I remember his asking me and a brother-boy who was staying at my father's house (just like him – he invited me, and when I hinted at a guest he said, 'Oh, bring him too – bring six boys if you've got them, I love boys') to dine with him at the old historic Garrick in King Street, and to go afterwards to another extinct institution – the Victoria in the New Cut – Queen Victoria's own theayter as Mrs Brown called it – to see the transpontine melodrama of the day.[1] ... Our host delighted more than his young guests did, I think, in the actions and passions of 'The Vic'. We were just old enough to resent such a 'tissue of improbabilities from beginning to end', as the late Baron Martin once described *Romeo and Juliet*. Not so the novelist, who would rather have written a Victoria melodrama than *Vanity Fair*, I believe. He was always wanting to write plays....

Thackeray's hair was of that loveliest shade in man: fine of texture and of pure white silk. In his deep interest in the sufferings of Queen Victoria's own heroine, he was leaning over the dress-circle with his head between his hands (there were no stalls at the Vic). A Vickite from the gallery took steady aim, and expectorated exactly in the middle of it. The dear old man did not look up. He merely had recourse to his handkerchief, and observed, 'The heathen gods, I believe, never used to do that.' Ah! that was an Ambrosian night.... When he treated boys, it was with no ungenerous views about bed. After the play he carried us off to Evans's to be greeted by Paddy Green with 'Dear boy, dear boy', to eat such baked potatoes as never have been baked since, and listen well into the small hours to the divine voices of the boys, in a framework of rich portraiture of bygone heroes of the stage.

How Thackeray loved the boys' voices!...

Some years afterwards, I asked my dear old host if he remembered our dining with him at the Garrick that night. 'Oh, yes,' he said, 'and I remember what I gave you for dinner. Beefsteak and apricot omelette.' I felt immensely pleased that he should remember us in such detail, and grew in my own esteem at once, and said so. 'Yes,' said he, twinkling in his inimitable way. 'I always give boys beefsteak and apricot omelette.'

Once, and once only, the great novelist had a play produced. It ran one night, and I had the honour of being among the players. For, in truth, he had to do what lesser men than he have done, and produce it himself as his own manager. It was, in fact, an amateur performance by way of house-warming.[2] The play had been submitted to Alfred Wigan, the comedy-manager of the day, who had decided that it was impossible for the stage. I think that Wigan was right. Needless to say that it was splendidly written, and full of the touches of language and character which only its author could give. But there was a lack of dramatic incident and movement.... I have the Thackeray playbill before me as I write, [headed] 'W. EMPTY HOUSE THEATRICALS'.... Of all things Thackeray loved a pun – and the worse it was, the better he loved it. He drew up his playbill himself, and two things he insisted on. First that there must be an announcement to this effect – 'During this piece the theatre will *not* be perfumed by Rimmel's patent vaporiser' – an invention which at that period was stupefying half the theatres in London – and, secondly, that W. Empty House must head the bill. Humbly I tried to persuade the great man that the joke was unworthy of him; but he insisted that it was very much wittier than anything in the play, and he would have it. W. M. T. were his initials, that is all. Dear old kindly child!

The play closed with a graceful rhymed epilogue of his own (unpublished, I believe, as I can't find it), through which he promised that, in his new house, he 'hoped to raise two or three *stories* more'....

Of the usual criticisms, obituaries, and other outpourings which followed Thackeray's death, one was noteworthy. It was by Anthony Trollope[3].... Of Thackeray, the man, he said one very true thing – that those who loved him felt for him something of the tenderness which attached to their feeling for a woman. That was so: and it was, I think, because he had in himself something of a woman's tender delicacy.... When one was with him it was impossible not to feel it. It had its little touch of petulance, too.

[Merivale ends by referring to the death of Helen Pendennis (*Pendennis*, ch. 57).] If Thackeray could write such prose as this, it is because he was a poet.... Thackeray was no mere verse-writer; he was a poet. Helen Pendennis's death is poetry. Rather than dilate much upon the author, I have tried to show something of the man. The man himself, as I knew him, is in that passage.

(2) He was the most sensitive of mortals. Conscious probably of certain defects of manner – of a certain shyness, of a certain incapacity for the 'jolly good fellow' business with every first comer – he liked to be liked, and he loved to be loved. To be well thought of and well spoken of was a great desire with him; and he chafed and winced a good deal, at times, under the feeling that the world at large misunderstood him much. It could scarcely be otherwise. He had all the nervous susceptibilities, as he had all the loving-kindness, of a woman; having, indeed, about him more than any other man I have known, of Goethe's untranslatable *Ewigweiblichkeit*. He froze in an ungenial atmosphere. One unwelcome presence silenced him. He was not a good talker, in the common sense, or a brilliant. Of all things his delight was to be among a small circle of his intimates, and to be allowed, if we may use the phrase, to play the fool. *Desipere in loco* ['to be silly at the right moment' – Horace] was his favourite pursuit; and he fretted under a companion who could not understand or join in it. It is on record that in *Cornhill* days – when he was labouring at the uncongenial task of editorship, which suited him amazingly badly (it made him feel, he used to say, 'like a toad under a harrow') – he would stop dead in his flow of talk when a certain chief contributor of his came into the room, with 'Here's —— : now we must be serious.' Yet the man in question was genial, to the world at large. Thackeray was not of the men who 'have no enemies'.

> Who has no enemies, shall know no friends:
> 'A real good chap', men say. And there it ends.

A very good fellow may sometimes be a very bad man. The two key-secrets of Thackeray's great life, as I take it, were these – Disappointment, and Religion.[4] The first was his poison; the second was his antidote. And, as always, the antidote won. No wonder that he was disappointed. First a man of fortune, then a ruined and a struggling artist, then a journalist, recognised to the full as such even by the brothers of the craft, but, like them, very little beyond it – then at last the novelist and the famous man, he was thirty-eight before the first number of *Vanity Fair* was published. Till then he was not really known. He was but fifty-two when he died. . . .

Honoured and held dear by friends the choicest and the worthiest, he kept them in a sense so wonderful that after five-and-twenty years of death he is more alive with them than half the dwellers upon earth. . . .

[Merivale draws upon the reminiscences of one of his 'younger but closest friends', Follett Synge.[5]] 'I was an enthusiastic and, I like to think, a discriminating admirer of Thackeray [writes Synge]. But it was not until 1849 or 1850 that I first met him. It was at the old Fielding Club, in which, by accident, we found ourselves one evening alone. The great man fell into conversation with me, and I found his company delightful. Not knowing Thackeray by sight I had no idea who was talking to me. We left the Club together at the small hours, he walking home to his house in Kensington, and I turning down St James's Street on my way to my chambers. When we parted, my companion shook me by the hand very warmly, and said, "Young 'un, I like you; you must come to see me. My name is Michael Angelo Titmarsh." I continued to meet the great man occasionally, though our acquaintance never ripened into intimacy until 1852 in Washington, where I was for a couple of years attache to the English Legation. In that year Thackeray was lecturing in the United States, and I saw a great deal of him. I married in that country, and wrote to Thackeray, who was in New York, to ask him to be present at my wedding. From a long letter in reply I make the following extract:

> I married at your age with £400 paid by a newspaper, which failed six months afterwards, and always love to hear of a young fellow testing his fortune bravely in that way. If I can

see my way to help you, I will. Though my marriage was a wreck, as you know, I would do it once again, for behold, Love is the crown and completion of all earthly good. A man who is afraid of his fortune never deserved one. The very best and pleasantest house I ever knew in my life had but £300 a year to keep it....'

In 1853 the Synges came to England, and Thackeray, who with his daughters was paying a visit to his mother in Paris, saw their names in a list of passengers. He immediately crossed the Channel to see his young friend at the Foreign Office, then went to the wife in their lodgings and said, 'My dear, we English are a very fine people; but some of us are not so friendly and sympathetic as they are in your country. I cannot let you live here alone in lodgings, with no one to look after you, while your husband is at his work. You must come, if you kindly will, and take possession of my old barrack in Young Street. I must go back to Paris tonight, but my daughters and I will come to you as soon as we can. And remember that the house is yours and that we are your guests.' He would take no denial, and carried the young wife off with him. They remained in Young Street, enjoying their stay, and delighting in his affectionate intimacy, until the end of the year, when he would hardly let them go to take a flat of their own in Westminster.[6] For many years he was a constant visitor at their house, and they passed a great portion of their time in his. He never came without a visit to the infantry-quarters of the family, who well remember now how the 'lofty moralist' had to bend his head before he could come through the nursery-door.

[Merivale prints some of Thackeray's letters to Synge, but comments:] For letters under the visible seal of confidence this is not the place. Nor could their publication have any part in his friend Synge's wishes or his own. One's only desire must be to repeat nothing that could hurt the living or surviving friends of the dead.

'Not that Thackeray', as his old friend [Synge] says to me, 'would have deliberatively written or spoken a word to hurt anybody's feelings. My uncle Toby had not a more tender heart, but he never pretended to speak always by the card, or to be more free from prejudices than Charles Lamb, who called himself a man "with humours, fancies, craving heart, sympathy, requiring books, pictures, theatres, chit-chat, scandals, jokes, antiquities, whims, and what not". It must be remembered that I was often, and for long periods at a time, an inmate of Thackeray's family: that he spoke to me out of the fullness of his heart, and very often regretted that he had been led by misapprehension to write or speak things which on afterthought he considered unjust.'

A specimen of the poetry in which, at any moment the most unexpected, Thackeray liked to indulge may be added here on the authority of the same witness. A dinner-conversation falling appropriately on gastronomics, when opinions were being gravely given on the momentous matter, a fair neighbour appealed earnestly to him as to what such an authority as he thought to be the best part of a fowl. Gravely he looked at her, and said,

> Oh! what's the best part of a fowl?
> My own Anastasia cried:
> Then, giving a terrible howl,
>   She turned on her stomach, and died!

On another occasion his love of Lear-like rhyme led him, when he wanted as usual to help some poor soul in trouble, to translate some German verses to fit the drawings in the original book, and to get his daughters and his friend Synge to contribute some rhymes of their own, which combined to produce a popular nonsense-book, known to the initiate as Bumblebee Bogo's Budget.

And so, when he fell into Charterhouse talk one day before dinner at Richmond, he regretted for his friend's boy, who had just received a nomination for the school, that the days of breeches were over, and that the gown-boys had been consigned to trousers instead. After dinner, when the cheese was under discussion, Thackeray gave his vote for Brie. But there was none to be had. 'Bobby', said Thackeray, turning to Synge, 'will be like that waiter.' 'Why?' 'Because he will have no Brie cheese.' It was on the same day that a broken-down Irish gentleman, not unlike the great Costigan, fell into talk without being introduced. His brogue was thick and noble, and after a time he said, 'Ye might not believe it, Sorr, but I'm an

Irishman.' 'Good heavens! You don't say so!' answered Thackeray. 'I took you for an Italian.' This playful love of Ireland and the Irish was for ever with Thackeray, and many of his Irish ballads are little less racy of the soil than Lever's own. But it was not understood, as he always felt he never was. His good-tempered banter was set down as mockery, and one day, in Anthony Trollope's stables, a curious old groom who heard Thackeray's name said to him, 'I hear you have written a book upon Ireland, and are always making fun of the Irish. You don't like us.' 'God help me!' said Thackeray, turning his head away as his eyes filled with tears; 'all that I have loved best in the world is Irish.' Much did he love to talk of Irish oddities, and during his American lectures was delighted to tell how, dining at St Louis, he overheard one Irish waiter say to another, 'Do you know who that is?' 'No', was the answer. 'That', said the first, 'is the celebrated Thacker.' 'What's *he* done?' 'D——d if I know.'

For the story of his last parting with his friend Mr Synge, I prefer again to quote the latter's account to me textually: 'Just before I sailed for the Sandwich Islands,' he writes, 'and when I was staying in Thackeray's house in Palace Green, my host and I one day met in the library. He said, "I want to tell you that I shall never see you again. I feel that I am doomed. I know that this will grieve you; but look in that book, and you will find something that I am sure will please and comfort you." I took from its shelf the book he pointed out; out of it fell a piece of paper on which Thackeray had written a prayer, all of which I do not pretend to remember. I only know that he prayed that he might never write a word inconsistent with the love of God or the love of man: that he might never propagate his own prejudices or pander to those of others: that he might always speak the truth with his pen, and that he might never be actuated by a love of greed. I particularly remember that the prayer wound up with the words: "For the sake of Jesus Christ our Lord".'

NOTES

1. The South Bank ('transpontine') theatres of that period were rough and unsophisticated, and specialised in blood-and-thunder pieces.

2. *The Wolves and the Lamb*, presented 24–5 February 1862 at his new Palace Green house and later adapted into novel form as *Lovel the Widower*.
3. *Cornhill Magazine*, Feb 1864. See above, II, 331–2.
4. Thackeray, he remarks later (*Life of Thackeray*, p. 212), 'to whom the modern doubt had not come, held to the old faith, and thought of death not gloomily but with a cheerful trust and hope'.
5. William Webb Follett Synge (1826–91), diplomat and contributor to magazines. In 1853, while serving in Washington, he married an American girl, Henrietta Wainwright, 'a charming young creature a great deal too good for him', Thackeray commented (*LPP*, III, 210–11) – 'poor little Mrs Synge,' as he later called her (ibid., p. 539), and, by 1860, 'the best little mother' of 'ever so many dear little children' (*LPP*, IV, 201). Thackeray was a warm and very helpful friend to them. For his lending Synge £1000, in 1862, see above, II, 336–7, and *LPP*, IV, 262n.
6. The Synges were at Young Street for the autumn and winter of 1853; their first child was born in December.

A Man of Moods

BLANCHARD JERROLD

From *The Best of All Good Company: A Day with Thackeray* (1872) pp. 315–18, 327. William Blanchard Jerrold (1826–84), eldest son of Thackeray's *Punch* colleague Douglas Jerrold, was a prolific journalist, dramatist, novelist, biographer, and miscellaneous writer. *The Best of All Good Company* was a series of short paperback memoirs; Dickens had been the subject of its opening number. The Thackeray number is subtitled, 'And see the great Achilles whom we knew'. Much of it consists of quotations from other men's accounts of Thackeray, here omitted.

Who that has seen will ever forget the commanding figure and the stately head? Sauntering – usually a solitary man – through the hall of the Reform Club, or in the quietitudes of the Athenaeum, making up his mind to find a corner to work for an hour or so on the small sheets of paper in his pocket, in a hand as neat as Peter Cunningham's or Leigh Hunt's;[1] gazing dreamily, and often with a sad and weary look, out of window; moving slowly westward home to dinner on a summer's evening; or making a strange presence, as obviously not belonging to the place, in Fleet Street on his way to Whitefriars or Cornhill; who that knew him does not remember dear old Thackeray, as his familiars lovingly called him, in some or all of these moods and places? In Thackeray, as in Dickens, there was a strong and impressive individuality. No two men could be less alike, in person or mind, than these two writers who shared the world's favour together; and yet there was an equality and identity in their impressiveness. Dickens's strength was quick, alert, and with the glow of health in it; it seemed to proceed like that of a mighty engine from an inward fire. Thackeray's was calm, majestic by its ease and extent, as the force of a splendid stream. Hawthorne's figure and air has been described as 'modestly grand'; and the observation, it occurs to me, applies exactly to Thackeray. Indeed, I have often been struck with the idea that the two men must have affected society much in the same way, and by the same mental and physical qualities. Like Hawthorne, Thackeray 'Wandered lonely as a cloud' – a cloud, it should be noted and remembered, with a silver lining. In their solitude, when suddenly observed, both had a sad, a grave aspect; and each was 'marvellously moved to fun' on occasions. In both the boy appeared easily; and this was a quality of Dickens' genius, as it was of my father's....

If Thackeray cast upon the outer world an austere – almost contemptuous – look and walked the streets and paced the clubs self-contained, solitary, it was because he was an observer of human nature, indeed of all nature. You stand away to examine a picture. He who goes to observe the Downs on a Derby Day does not take three sticks at Aunt Sally. When Thackeray observed a child at play, he was touched by the natural flow of its movements and the natural philosophy underlying its prattle. Dickens put himself under the glossy plumes of the raven in the happy family and dwelt unctuously on the juiciness of the youngster's exposed calves. The difference, I have thought, having often come upon both at busy points of observation, was shown in their attitude towards the world when in the thick of it. Thackeray sailed majestically along, one hand thrust in his pocket, a cultivated, fastidious, high-bred man, deep-hearted withal. Dickens had a swifter headway, a more combative and a compacter air, and bore down with his bright eye that had (to use Doré's phrase to me applied to his own retentive vision) plenty of collodion in it, upon every human countenance, every beggar's limp, or groundling's daub of dirt. Brave and loyal workers both, who have laid the world under immeasurable debts of gratitude to them; they held along opposite sides of the way, and at each passing man and woman gazed, albeit they knew them not, feeling that there were no ordinary men abroad that day.

It was with Thackeray as with Hawthorne. The grand, sad mask could pucker in a moment, and break into hearty fun and laughter. A friend went laughing into the Reform Club one afternoon; he had just met Thackeray at the door of the Athenaeum Club. He had had a dispute with his cabman about the fare, which he had just proposed to settle by a toss. If Thackeray won, the cabman was to receive two shillings, and if the toss went against the author of *Vanity Fair* the cabman was to receive one shilling. Fortune was with the novelist; and he dwelt delightfully afterwards on the gentlemanly manner in which the driver took his defeat. Yet there were times, and many, when Thackeray could not break through his outward austerity, even when passing an intimate friend in the street. I and a mutual friend met him one afternoon in Fleet Street, ambling to Whitefriars on his cob, and a very extraordinary figure he made. He caught sight of us, and my companion was about to grasp his hand, but he just touched his hat with his finger, and without opening his lips or relaxing the solemn cast of his features, he passed on. My companion stamped his foot upon the pavement and cried, 'Who would think that we were up till four o'clock this morning together, and that he sang his "Reverend Dr Luther", and was the liveliest of us.'

But Thackeray was a sick man, as well as a hard-worked one. He was threatened by several disorders of long continuance; and against which he stoutly fought, turning his noble placid face bravely upon the world – this 'great Achilles whom we knew', and who was most loved by those who knew him best. Indeed by the outer world – by those with whom he came in contact for the first time – he was not loved, and not often liked. His address was as polished as a steel mirror, and as cold. In the *Hoggarty Diamond*, in that exquisite chapter [ch. 3] given to Mr Titmarsh's drive with Lady Drum, Mr Samuel observes, 'For though I am but a poor fellow, and hear people cry out how vulgar it is to eat peas with a knife, or ask three times for cheese, and such like points of ceremony, there's something, I think, much more vulgar than all this, and that is insolence to one's inferiors. I hate the chap that uses it, as I scorn him of humble rank that affects to be of the fashion; and so I determined to let Mr Preston know a piece of my mind.' And Mr Preston knew it accordingly. In this passage there is the keynote of the worldly side of Thackeray's character. He was beloved by his inferiors, and reserved his hottest scorn for those pretenders who, buffeted and cold-shouldered by those in whose society they aspire to mix, take their revenge upon their dependants. Thackeray was most deeply touched by any kindness or grace shown to him by one beneath him; and perhaps this honourable feeling (possible only in a cultivated being) is best shown in his whimsical dedication of the *Paris Sketch Book* to his tailor, M. Aretz....

And so, in his most gracious moods – gentle to the weak and lowly, beloved of women and children,[2] but grand and stern and silent, a mighty form crowned with a massive snow-haired head, 'see the great Achilles whom we knew'. [And various friends' reminiscences follow.]

Testimonies of love, of friendship, of admiration, in records of kindly acts, in anecdotes of tender heart, in passages from his works illustrating passages of his life, filled the papers at that mournful Christmastime when he died. The instances of his kindly and unostentatious help to many of his young literary friends, might be given by the score. I can remember many that came under my own observation. I was one morning at Horace Mayhew's chambers in Regent Street when Thackeray knocked at the door, and cried from without, 'It's no use, Ponny Mayhew: open the door.'[3]

'It's dear old Thackeray,' said Mayhew, instinctively putting chairs and table in order to do honour to the friend of whom he never spoke without pride, and without adding, 'I know dear good Thackeray is very fond of me.'

Thackeray came in, saying cheerily, 'Well, young gentlemen, you'll admit an old fogy.'

He always spoke of himself as an old man. Between him and Mayhew there were not many years. He took up the papers lying about, talked the gossip of the day, and then suddenly said – with his hat in his hand – 'I was going away without doing part of the business of my visit. You spoke the other day at the dinner (the *Punch* weekly meeting) of poor George.

Somebody – most unaccountably – has returned me a £5 note I lent him a long time ago. I didn't expect it: so just hand it to George: and tell him, when his pocket will bear it, just to pass it on to some poor fellow of his acquaintance. Bye-bye.' A nod and he was gone.

This was, we all agreed, very like 'dear old Thackeray'.

NOTES

1. 'Shortly before his death he spent a morning in the Reading Room of the British Museum, and there by accident left upon a table a page of the manuscript of the story he had in hand. The paper being found, the clearness and roundness of the writing at once suggested the owner to the attendant, and the precious missing leaf was forwarded to Kensington' [Jerrold's footnote].
2. 'During a small party at Horace Mayhew's, at which Thackeray had been in one of his heartiest, kindliest, and at the same time most whimsical moods, a young lady crept to the side of the host, and was unable to say less, by way of expressing her enthusiasm for the lion of the evening, than, "I should so like to kiss him." The host spoke to Thackeray: whereupon the great man advanced to the blushing damsel and treating her like a pet child, lifted her from the ground and kissed her forehead. It was one of the prettiest scenes imaginable' [Jerrold's footnote].
3. Horace ('Ponny') Mayhew (1816–72), brother of the more famous Henry Mayhew (1812–87): miscellaneous writer and member of *Punch* staff.

Glimpses

VARIOUS

A miscellany of encounters: sources in the Notes.

The first time I met Thackeray [writes R. H. Horne (1803–84), poet and journalist]... was at the office of the *Court Journal*, then [1837] edited by my admired and lamented friend Laman Blanchard. Thackeray was seated at the editor's desk. 'Oh! thank you!' exclaimed Blanchard, who was always glad to have to write as little himself as possible: 'what are you writing there?' 'I don't call it writing,' said Thackeray, without looking up, 'so much as squirting a little warm water down a page of your journal.' This compliment to his courtly readers delighted Blanchard more than it would have done most editors of a fashionable journal.[1]

I am, and always have been, a highly nervous, retiring, and modest person [explained the painter W. P. Frith, R.A. (1819–1909), recounting his first meeting with Thackeray, in his 'Titmarsh' days. Thackeray had written warmly about a painting by Frith, who was keen to meet him and was introduced to him at the Deanery Club. Thackeray was with 'a very convivial party' in the smoking-room.] I was very young at the time, although I had just been elected an Associate of the [Royal] Academy, and I sat in awestruck silence listening to the brilliant talk of those men. Someone called on Thackeray for a song, and he instantly struck up one of his own writing, as I was told. I forget the words, but I remember two individuals – Gorging Jack and Guzzling Jimmy – who seemed to be the presiding geniuses of it. No sooner had the applause accorded to it subsided, than Thackeray turned to me and said, 'Now then, Frith, you d——d saturnine young Academician, sing us a song!'

I was dumb before this address, and far too confounded to say anything in reply. Encouraged, perhaps, by my proving myself such an easy butt, the attack was renewed a little later in the evening: 'I'll tell you what it is, Frith, you had better go home; your aunt is sitting up for you with a big muffin.' Again I was paralysed, and shortly after I went home.

After this I contented myself with admiration for the works of the great author, without feeling any desire for a more intimate acquaintance with the man. Of course, I often met Thackeray afterwards, but I never gave him an opportunity for renewing his playful attacks. I know very well that Thackeray was much beloved by those who knew him intimately, and I have often been abused by some of his friends (notably by dear Leech) for my absurd anger at what was meant for a joke; but I submit that such attacks on an inoffensive stranger were very poor jokes, and even after the long lapse of time I feel humiliated and pained in recalling them.[2]

[Lady Louisa de Rothschild, *née* Montefiore (1821–1910), a noted beauty and hostess, of the Jewish banking family, met Thackeray on a Rhine river steamer in 1848. Her journals record this and subsequent meetings.] '... The second, but greater charm of our day's journey was Mr Thackeray's presence. Strange enough, we made acquaintance directly and he remained with us the whole day. We talked of literature, drawings, Jews, of whom he has a bad opinion,[3] politics, etc., and we parted very good friends – at least I fancy so. He seems a good and an honest man, with a kind heart, notwithstanding a large fund of satire. I like him better than his books.' [Her daughter] Lady Battersea remembered this meeting to the end of her life, as she was startled when Thackeray took her up in his arms and, poising her on his shoulders, walked up and down the steamer, telling her fairy-tales....

'On Sunday Thackeray called. He was amiable and agreeable, but when he talked of so many of the great, the beautiful and the clever who are all anxious to attract his notice and admiration, I felt that he must be a *little* spoilt, or at least that there was not much to attract him here....

'The dinner went off pretty well. I was very agreeably placed and perhaps Mr Thackeray's vicinity helped to make the dinner pass quicker and acted as a cordial upon my health. C. Villiers was my other neighbour, but amusing as he is, I greatly prefer Thackeray, because he joins to wit and humour and fun deep and good feeling, which he is never ashamed of showing and which makes one like, as well as admire him....

'Yesterday... in the afternoon Thackeray called – very agreeable as he always is *en tête à tête*. Singularly enough he expressed what I had been thinking all the morning, that love is short-lived and that without any apparent reason the being who has inspired us with passionate affection, at whose dear presence our heart has throbbed and our cheek turned pale, becomes perfectly indifferent to us. I had never experienced it, but I felt such might be the case, and with Thackeray it evidently has been the case'.[4]

[The philologist and orientalist Friedrich Max Müller (1823–1900) first met Thackeray in 1851, at an Oxford dinner, which was very constrained until Thackeray broke the ice with a 'horrible pun'.] The rest of our little dinner party was very successful; it became noisy and even brilliant. Thackeray from his treasures of wit and sarcasm poured out anecdote after anecdote; he used plenty of vinegar and cayenne pepper, but there was always a flavour of kindliness and good nature, even in his most cutting remarks.[5]

[Gordon Hake, a physician at Bury St Edmunds, was dining one day, together with his friend George Borrow, the author, at Hardwick Hall, near Bury, the seat of Sir Thomas and Lady Cullum. Thackeray was a friend of the Cullums, and was staying there; all the other guests were titled persons.] At that date, Thackeray had made money by lectures on the Satirists, and was in good swing; but he never could realise the independent feelings of those who happen to be born to fortune – a thing which a man of genius should be able to do with ease. He told Lady Cullum how it mortified him to be making provision for his daughters by delivering lectures; and I thought she rather sympathised with him in this degradation.... Thackeray, as if under the impression that the party was invited to look at him, thought it necessary to make a figure, and absorb attention during the dessert, by telling stories and more than half acting them; the aristocratic party listening, but appearing little amused. Borrow knew better how to behave in good company, and kept quiet; though, doubtless, he felt his mane.[6]

Thackeray I occasionally met in society [wrote Lady Dorothy Nevill (1826–1913), the celebrated Tory hostess].... In society Mr Thackeray was not nearly such a brilliant talker as Charles Lever, who was the life and soul of any party – joyous, good-humoured, and unrestrained. Thackeray, on the other hand, was inclined to be satiric and severe. On one occasion I recollect his administering a terrible verbal castigation to an unfortunate individual who had incurred his displeasure, and ever after I was rather afraid of him.[7]

[Charles Gavan Duffy (1816–1903), 'Young Irelander' journalist and politician, and later Prime Minister of Australia, was introduced to Thackeray by Thomas Carlyle in 1855.] He is a large, robust, fresh-looking man, with hair turning grey. The expression of his face disappointed me; the damaged nose and bad teeth mar its otherwise benign effect, and were imperfectly relieved by a smile which was warm but hardly genial. He is near-sighted, and said, he must put on his glasses to have a good look at me. He told me he had met some of my [Irish nationalist] friends in America, and liked them. John Dillon was a modest fellow, and Meagher pleased him by laughing at the popular ovations offered to him. They both said whatever they thought, frankly; rather a surprise to him, as in Ireland he had only met three men who spoke the truth; but then, he added, smiling, he had not made the acquaintance of the Young Irelanders.... He spoke of his intended lectures on the House of Hanover, and said he sometimes pondered the question whether every soul of these people he had to speak of was not d——d in the end. The Marquis of Hertford receiving London society in an attitude seen elsewhere only in hospitals, surrounded by smiling crowds, who ate his dinners and congratulated him on his good looks, was a story from which he shrunk, which could be told indeed nakedly only by Swift....

[Discussing current politics, Thackeray said that] the constitutional system was getting frightfully damaged in England, and we could not count on a long life for it in its present relations. I asked him how we were to get on in Ireland, where we had only the seamy side of the constitution? He said he had never doubted our right to rebel against it, if we had only made sure of success; but in the name of social tranquillity and common sense, he denied the legitimacy of unsuccessful rebellion.

I rejoined that it was no more possible to make sure beforehand that you were going to win in an insurrection than in a game of roulette. You had to take your chance in both cases.... I spoke rapidly of the Irish famine, the exportation of the natural food of the people to pay inordinate rents, the hopeless feebleness and fatuity of Lord John Russell's government, and the horrors of Skull and Skibereen, and I asked him to tell me, if he were an Irishman, what he would have done under the circumstances? He paused a moment, and replied, 'I would perhaps have done as you did.'

We afterwards walked out together towards Hyde Park. We met an Italian image boy who had a bust of Louis Napoleon among the figures he carried on his head. Thackeray took off his hat and saluted it, half, but only half, mockingly, and murmured something about a man who understood his business and mastered the art of government.... The talk turned upon books, and I told him I had noted with wonder the accuracy, or rather the fitness, of the Irish names of men and places in *Barry Lyndon* that being the point where a stranger usually blunders or breaks down. He said he had lived a good deal among Irish people in London and elsewhere....[8]

[The American actor and dramatist Lester Wallack (1820–88) met Thackeray in 1856. The novelist's New York lodgings were two doors away from Wallack's house. 'Our short and intimate associate association is one of the most delightful reminiscences of my life', he wrote, though initially] I thought him, with his great height, his spectacles, which gave him a very pedantic appearance, and his chin always carried in the air, the most pompous, supercilious person I had ever met; but I lived to alter that opinion, and in a very short time.... Thackeray, I suppose, took a fancy to me; at any rate it was understood every night when I came home from acting that if I saw a light in a certain window I was to go in, and if not it was a sign they had gone out to dinner or to bed. When I did find them in we never parted until half-past two or three in the morning. Then was the time to see Thackeray at his best, because then he was like a boy; he did not attempt to be the genius of the party; he would let [his host William Duer] Robinson or me do the entertaining while he would be the audience. It did not matter how ridiculous or impossible might be the things I said, he would laugh till the tears ran down his face; such an unsophisticated, gentle-hearted creature as he was.[9]

[Frederick Locker-Lampson (1821–95), author of *London Lyrics* and other *vers de societe*, first met Thackeray in the early 1850s, and wrote affectionate reminiscences of him. One day they were discussing Thomas Hood.] 'What a vigorous fellow Hood is' [said Thackeray]; 'what a swing there is in his verse!' I agreed with him, and then said something about Thackeray's own poetry. 'Yes,' he replied – 'yes, I have a sixpenny talent (or gift), and so have you; ours is small-beer, but, you see, it is the right tap.' ...

He spoke [on another occasion] with a lisp, as if his teeth were defective, and ended by, 'I am on my way from the dentist.' You will remember that towards the end of that little poem ['Mrs Katherine's Lantern'] he refers to his toothless condition. ...

Some people thank God that they do not set store by the smaller refinements and civilisations of life. Let me tell them that they are thanking God for a very small mercy. Such boons gave Thackeray a keen satisfaction. He was a man of sensibility: he delighted in luxuriously furnished and well-lighted rooms, good music, excellent wines and cookery, exhilarating talk, gay and airy gossip, pretty women and their toilettes, and refined and noble manners, *le bon gout, le ris, l'aimable liberte*. The amenities of life and the traditions stimulated his imagination.

On the other hand, his writings show how he equally enjoyed Bohemianism, and how diverted he could be by those happy-go-lucky fellows of the Foker and Fred Bayham type.

Thackeray expanded in the society of such people, and with them he was excellent company. But, if I am not much mistaken, the man Thackeray was melancholy – he had known tribulation, he had suffered. He was not a lighthearted wag or a gay-natured rover, but a sorrowing man. He could make you a jest, or propound some jovial or outrageous sentiment, and imply, 'Let us be festive', but the jollity rarely came. However, I ought to say that though Thackeray was not cheerily, he was at times grotesquely humorous. Indeed, he had a weakness for buffoonery. I have seen him pirouette, wave his arm majestically, and declaim in burlesque – an intentionally awkward imitation of the ridiculous manner that is sometimes met with in French opera.

I remember calling in Palace Gardens, and, while talking with all gravity to Thackeray's daughters, I noticed that they seemed more than necessarily amused. On looking round, I discovered that their father had put on my hat, and, having picked my pocket of my handkerchief, was strutting about, flourishing it in the old Lord Cardigan style. As I was thin-faced, and he, as a hatter once remarked of Thomas Bruce, was 'a gent as could carry a large body o' at', you may suppose he looked sufficiently funny.

Thackeray could be very amusing about the malice of kind and the perfidy of honest people; but still, in everyday life, and in spite of his *flair de cynique*, he was naturally inclined to believe that gossip false which ought not to be true.[10]

[*4 Apr 1858.*] Had a curious conversation with Thackeray at the Cosmopolitan [wrote the statesman and author Sir Mountstuart E. Grant Duff (1829–1906) in his diary] about a French invasion, *à propos* of the Fiery Colonels, with regard to whom there was a good deal of talk at this time. He said, alluding to his recent candidature at Oxford: – 'The chief reason why I wished to be in Parliament was, that I might stand up once a year, and tell my countrymen what will happen when the French invade us.' ... [Years later, the historian J. R. Green gave him] the most remarkable account of canvassing Oxford with Thackeray, whose want of power of public speaking seems to have been perfectly extraordinary. On the hustings he utterly broke down, and Green heard him say to himself, 'If I could only go into the Mayor's parlour for five minutes, I could write this out quite well.'[11]

[Another diarist, Sir William Hardman, noted particularly Thackeray's bawdiness: *19 Nov 1862.*] Meredith ... heard a story of Thackeray at the Garrick. The great humourist said the other day: 'I see the Queen has been erecting another xxxxxxxxmonial to the Prince!' Thackeray's conversation, I should tell you, is decidedly loose.

[*May 1864.*] 'I like those Guardsmen, their conversation is so interesting' [a favourite anecdote of Thackeray's ran]. 'I met one once in the smoking-room of the Club; we never spoke a word, but he was civil to me – he rang the bell for me, or he *didn't* ring the bell for me, I forget which – no matter. When I left, he left too, and we found we were both going in the same direction along Pall Mall. Silently we walked side by side – you must know I had not been *introduced* to him. At last we met a woman. I said, 'That's a nice-looking girl.' After a pause, he replied, 'Haw, yes, I have had her.' After a longer pause,

'Haw, my brother has had her.' After a still longer pause, 'Haw, haw, in fact we've both had her.' No more was said, and shortly afterwards we parted. I *do* like those guardsmen.'[12]

[In the early 1860s, writes the French critic Hyppolite Taine (1828-93)] I had a conversation with Thackeray, whose name I mention because he is dead, and because his ideas and his conversation are to be found in his books. He confirmed orally all that he had written about the snobbish spirit. I told him a trivial circumstance of which I was eye-witness. At a charity meeting the speaker set forth to the audience the importance of the work undertaken by remarking that the Marquis of——, 'a person in such a situation', had kindly consented to take the chair. Thackeray assured me that platitudes like these are common; he said that he admired our equality greatly, and that great people are so habituated to see people on their knees before them, that they are shocked when they meet a man of independent demeanour. 'I myself', he added, 'am now regarded as a dangerous character.'[13]

'Many a fine fellow has been buried at Kensal Green, but never a finer or a truer than Makepeace Thackeray' [said the artist George Cruikshank (1792-1878) to Moncure Conway, at Thackeray's funeral]. 'How little did they know the man who thought him a hard, cold, and cutting blade. He was much more like a sensitive, loving little girl.' I never was more impressed than at this moment with Cruikshank's genius for seeing; his phrase interpreted certain lines under Thackeray's eyes, lines of wondrous tenderness, as if their light were flowing out to all on whom he looked. 'Here is one picture I have in my mind of him', said Cruikshank; 'he was coming from Ireland across the Channel, with his wife and children, one an infant. There was a fearful storm all night, and the Channel horribly rough, and Mrs Thackeray was seized with brain-fever. And through all that terrible night, from shore to shore, sat Thackeray, motionless, bearing the infant in one arm, sustaining the wife with the other, utterly unconscious of the prevailing terror – for there was danger. His poor wife never recovered from brain-fever, and was worse than lost to him for ever.' Cruikshank had been Thackeray's teacher when the author aspired to be an artist; 'but', he said, 'he had not the patience to be an artist with pencil or brush. I used to tell him that to be an artist was to burrow along like a mole, heaving up a little mound here and there for a long distance. He said he thought he would presently break out into another element and stay there.' ... Nearly every literary man in London was present [at the funeral]. I particularly remarked the emotion of Charles Dickens.[14]

NOTES

1. Appendix to *Letters of Elizabeth Barrett Browing Addressed to Richard Hengist Horne*, ed. S. R. Townshend Mayer (1877) II, 274–5.
2. W. P. Frith, *My Autobiography and Reminiscences* (1889), I, 106–8.
3. A tactless remark, in the circumstances; but later, in *Pendennis* (ch. 2), he made her some amends: 'I saw a Jewish lady, only yesterday, with a child at her knee, and from whose face towards the child there shone a sweetness so angelical, that it seemed to form a sort of glory round both.'
4. Lucy Cohen, *Lady de Rothschild and Her Daughters* (1935) pp. 34–6.
5. F. Max Müller, *Auld Lang Syne* (1898) p. 108.
6. Gordon Hake, *Memoirs of Fifty Years* (1892) pp. 165–6.
7. *The Reminiscences of Lady Dorothy Nevill* (1906) pp. 279–80.
8. Sir Charles Gavan Duffy, *Conversations with Carlyle* (1892) pp. 192–5.
9. Lester Wallack, *Memories of Fifty Years* (1889) pp. 205–7.
10. Frederick Locker-Lampson, *My Confidences* (1896) pp. 300–5.
11. Sir Mountstuart E. Grant Duff, *Notes from a Diary 1851–1872* (1897) I, 102–3; ... *1873–1881* (1898) I, 112. Anti-British feeling ran high, in France in 1858, after Orsini's attempt to assassinate Napoleon III; the plot had been hatched in London. Congratulatory addresses to the Emperor, from French army regiments, bristled with bellicose remarks about 'the land of impurity' which harboured such 'monsters'.
12. *Letters and Memoirs of Sir William Hardman: Second Series: 1863–1865*, ed. S. M. Ellis (1925) pp. 184–5. Ellis fades out, into discreet ellipses, another improper Thackeray anecdote, in *The Hardman Papers: A Further Selection (1865–1868)* (1930) p. 300. Henry Silver's unpublished diaries about the *Punch* Table talk contain other samples of this racy side of Thackeray's conversation – the difficulty of finding a rhyme for 'snugger', etc.: see A. A. Adrian, *Mark Lemon: First Editor of 'Punch'* (1966) pp. 38, 68; and Ray, *Adversity*, p. 156 ('we know from many sources that Thackeray liked to talk and write bawdy to congenial company'), and *Wisdom*, pp. 347–8.
13. Hyppolite Taine, *Notes on England*, trs. W. F. Rae (1872) p. 242.
14. *The Autobiography, Memories and Experiences of Moncure D. Conway* (1905) II, 5–6.

Intimations of Mortality
ANNE THACKERAY RITCHIE

(1) from *Biog. Intros*, XII, xxv–xxxiv; (2) from *Letters of Anne Thackeray Ritchie*, ed. Hester Ritchie (1924) pp. 119–20. Thackeray began writing *Denis Duval* in May 1863; it was serialised, posthumously, in the *Cornhill*. For the kinswoman Mrs Warre Cornish, whom Anny quotes, see above, II, 193. Anny here describes him at work on his last novel, uncompleted at his death.

(1) My father used to talk about it all to us. . . . He was anxious about this novel. I can remember his saying that *Philip* had not enough story, and that this new book *must* be a success, if he could make it so. He used to carry the chapters about with him, and often pull them out from his coat pocket to consult. He said that it was a superstition of his to write at least one line in every day whether he was ill or well. Only once, to my recollection, did he try to dictate some pages of *Denis Duval*, but he very soon sent his secretary away, saying that he must write for himself. . . .

One pleasant impression still in my mind belonging to those days, is that of my father's return one summer's evening, pleased and in good spirits from a little visit he had paid to Winchelsea and Rye.[1] He came home delighted with the old places; he had seen the ancient gateways and sketched one of them, and he had seen the great churches and the old houses, all sailing inland from the sea. Winchelsea was everything he had hoped for, and even better than he expected. He was so often ailing in those latter days that when he was well and happy it seemed to be a general holiday in the house.

Another association which I have with *Denis Duval* is connected with almost the last page of the manuscript. One day he came down at luncheon-time in great spirits and excitement; he was quite carried away by what he had been reading and writing that morning concerning the splendid gallantry of Captain Pearson of the *Serapis*. Instead of eating his luncheon, he began describing the engagement with as much pride as if he had witnessed it, or as if he had had a son serving on board. His old friend and neighbour Admiral FitzRoy had looked up the papers and particulars and sent them to him from the Admiralty; my father followed them all with something beyond interest, until he seemed to be actually living through the events which laid hold of his imagination.

My sister-in-law, Mrs Warre Cornish, who was scarcely more than a child in those days, has written down some of her reminiscences of that time. 'Out of my girlish remembrances of visits at Palace Green,' she writes, 'the impression made by the creation of *Denis Duval* remains extraordinarily clear. It was in the summer of 1863, and I believe that Mr Thackeray was just then very happy, finding himself once more, after a long interval, in the full vein of historical romance. But I knew nothing of this at the time, only that the atmosphere of *Denis Duval* permeated everything.... The story progressed day by day, and reached us through his talk with his daughters, and with my sister and myself, whose father he had loved. The great world of London came and went past the quiet green precincts, and he went to the great world or came from it....

'The inspiration sometimes had to be waited for and caught at the flood. The carriage came to the door and waited, waited an hour, an hour and a half, two hours. Mr Thackeray wrote on. His daughters only said what a good thing it was that every ten minutes made a page of Papa's handwriting. At last he came, and got into the carriage with us, all in the best of spirits. As we drove towards Wimbledon or Richmond he would read *every* name on the small shops as we passed; he wanted Christian names for certain smugglers to come into the story. He commented on all the names. Every minute seemed brimful in his society; one never thinks, even when remembering what followed, of incompletion....'

Only a few days before his death my father came home one afternoon saying that he could not get accustomed to the number of people whom he did not know, who seemed to know him in the street, and took off their hats as he went along. His figure was so remarkable, and so little to be passed over, that no wonder people recognised him as they recognised Tennyson or Carlyle, or any other of the well-known characters of those days....

One bright afternoon in December 1863 we drove with him to the Temple. Our friend Lady Colvile came with us, and we went through the Park to pick him up at the Athenaeum, and then on to the Temple church, where the service was going on. The anthem was 'Rejoice, and again I say unto you, rejoice', and afterwards the evening hymn was sung. When we came out from the inner aisle, he was waiting for us, standing quite still with his back turned. He began to chant the anthem in an undertone, and then he praised the evening hymn, which he always liked; he said it was simple and unaffected, and entirely to the purpose, expressing just what was needful and no more. We walked with him along the Terrace and down some steps into the Garden. For a little while longer the sky was very bright and red, then the twilight began, and we went in to tea with Herman Merivale, who was expecting us in his rooms, up some twisting stairs. My father laughed and was in good spirits, and looked at the pictures upon the walls. Perhaps it all reminded him of his own Temple days – 'Ah, happy rooms, bright rooms, rooms near the sky,' he says in *Philip*, 'to remember you is to be young again.' . . .

He had no real illness, but he flagged all that last week and was more at home than usual. An old friend who came to see us told me that my father took him upstairs to his room to show him some book, and he noticed that he was quite tired and out of breath with the one flight of stairs.

He had so often been ill and rallied, that my sister and I clung to this hope; but our grandmother was more anxious than we were.

He was ill one morning and he sent for me to give me some directions, and to tell me to write some notes. He had *The Times* upon his bed. This was two days before Christmas. He died suddenly in the early morning of Christmas Eve, 24 December 1863. He was not sorry to go; only a day or two before he had said so. . . .

(2) [*Anny's journal, early 1864*.] I recollect how Papa took up my diary for 1864 and said: 'Next year begins with a Friday.' And I little thinking replied 'Papa, I assure you Friday is our lucky day. Indeed it will be a happy year.'

I remember now, only I can't bear to think of it, that all last year he was never well; he said 'Life at this purchase is not worth having.' He said 'If it were not for you children, I should be quite ready to go.'

One day not long ago, I came into the dining room and he was sitting looking at the fire. I do not remember ever to have seen him looking like that before and he said, 'I have been thinking in fact, that it will be a very dismal life for you when I am gone.'[2] He said, 'If I live, I hope I have ten years more work in me. It is absurd to expect a man to give up his work at 50.' He said too: 'When I drop, there is to be no life written of me; *mind this* and consider it as my last testament and desire.'[3]

Today I do not remember many things he has said. I can see him passing his hand through his hair, laughing, pouring out his tea from his little silver teapot. I can see him looking at his face in the glass and saying 'I am sure I look well enough, don't I?'

NOTES

1. Thackeray was doing his homework: these locations, like Captain Pearson and his ship *Serapis*, his reading about which is mentioned below, were to feature in the novel. Earlier in this Introduction (p. xiv) Anny had been discussing Thackeray's reading habits, and remarked, 'My father's memory, though partial, was very clear. I remember Mr Kinglake once saying that his quickness of apprehension was most remarkable, and equalled by that of very few people. If he read a book he turned page after page without stopping at all, in a rapid methodical way, and he used to say that from long habit he could glean the contents of each page as he glanced at it.'

2. In her manuscript reminiscences, 1864–5, Anny records that he went on to say, 'I have a great mind to put it in my will that you are not to live with Grannie' (*Wisdom*, p. 412). He discussed other new provisions in the new will he intended to make, but in fact he died intestate.

3. This determination was at least a year old. Henry Silver had recorded in his diary, 20 Nov 1862, that the effect upon Thackeray of reading a recent biography had been 'to make him tell his daughters "Mind, no biography" of himself' (*Adversity*, p. 1).

Some Obituaries

GEORGE VENABLES AND OTHERS

(1) [*The Times*, 25 Dec 1863, p. 7 (by E. S. Dallas[1]).] Suddenly one of our greatest literary men has departed. Never more shall the fine head of Mr Thackeray, with its mass of silvery hair, be seen towering among us. It was but two days ago that he might be seen at his club, radiant and buoyant with glee. Yesterday morning he was found dead in his bed. With all his high spirits he did not seem well; he complained of illness; but he was often ill, and he laughed off his present attack. He said that he was about to undergo some treatment which would work a perfect cure in his system, and so he made light of his malady....

[A survey of his career follows.] On the whole, as we look back upon these writings [before *Vanity Fair*], we do not think that if his fame at that time was unequal to his merits the public were much to blame. The very high opinion which his friends entertained of him must have been due more to personal intercourse than to his published works. It was not until 1846 that Mr Thackeray fairly showed to the world what was in him. Then began to be published, in monthly numbers, the story of *Vanity Fair*. It took London by surprise – the picture was so true, the satire was so trenchant, the style was so finished. It is difficult to say which of these three works is the best – *Vanity Fair*, *Henry Esmond*, or *The Newcomes*. Men of letters may give their preference to the second of these, which is indeed the most finished of all his works. But there is a vigour in the first-mentioned, and a matured beauty in the last, which to the throng of readers will be more attractive. At first reading, *Vanity Fair* has given to many an impression that the author is too cynical. There was no man less ill-natured than Mr Thackeray, and, if anybody doubts this, we refer him to *The Newcomes*, and ask whether that book could be written by any but a most kind-hearted man. We believe that one of the greatest miseries which Mr Thackeray had to endure grew out of the sense that he, one of the kindest of men, was regarded as an ill-natured cynic....

Highly polished as his style was, he wrote, at least in his latter days, with great ease. He wrote like print, and made very few corrections. What he had to say came naturally to him; he never made an effort in his writing; and he rather despised writing which is the result of effort. This naturalness he carried into his daily life. He had in him the simplicity of the child with the experience of the man. It was curious to see how warmly his friends loved him, and how fervently his enemies hated him. The hate which he excited among those who but half knew him will soon be forgotten; the warmth of affection by which he was endeared to many friends will long be remembered. He had his foibles, and so have we all. Some of his foibles, such as his sensitiveness to criticism, always excited the good-humoured mirth of his friends. But these foibles were as nothing beside the true greatness and goodness of the man. It was impossible to be long with him without seeing his truthfulness, his gentleness, his humility, his sympathy with all suffering, his tender sense of honour; and one felt these moral qualities all the more when one came to see how clear was his insight into human nature, how wide was his experience of life, how large his acquaintance with books, how well he had thought upon all he had seen, and how clearly and gracefully he expressed himself. A man in all the qualities of intellect, he was a child in all the qualities of heart; and when his life comes to be laid bare before the public in a biography we have no doubt that, whatever intellectual rank may be assigned to him, no man of letters with anything like the same power of mind will be regarded as nobler, purer, better, kinder than he.

(2) [*Illustrated London News*, XLIV (2 Jan 1864) 6.] But let us add [to this account of his literary character] that, as in the case of Sir Walter Scott, the personal merits of the man have aided to endear him to us all. The high moral nature, the ever-ready charity, the gentlemanly bearing of William Thackeray, are matters within the knowledge of thousands, and there is no intrusion upon private life in writing that the great author was

a good man. You cannot, if you would, keep the light of a true man's private life from the public eye. The authors of England – the journalists (he was long a newspaper writer, and graceful tribute to the ability he displayed has been promptly borne by those who had best means of knowing his power – were all proud of him, and justly proud. He was one of their noblest representatives; and it was good for their profession that a thorough gentleman, who lived by it, and took pride in it, and adorned it, should fill a grand place in the view of the world. The list of those who came to stand with bare heads and wet eyes while the earth fell upon his coffin will testify to the love and reverence felt for him by those who labour with the brain. There has never been such a gathering in our time as stood in the rays of that winter sun to hear the solemnest words ever spoken by man uttered over what but a few days before had been William Makepeace Thackeray.

(3) [*Punch*, XLVI (2 Jan 1864) 1, 17.] While generous tributes are everywhere paid to the genius of him who has been suddenly called away in the fullness of his power and the maturity of his fame, some who have for many years enjoyed the advantage of his assistance and the delight of his society would simply record that they have lost a dear friend. At an early period in the history of this periodical he became a contributor to its pages, and he long continued to enrich them, and though of late he had ceased to give other aid than suggestion and advice, he was a constant member of our council, and sat with us on the eighth day from that which has saddened England's Christmas. Let the brilliancy of his trained intellect, the terrible strength of his satire, the subtlety of his wit, the richness of his humour, and the catholic range of his calm wisdom, be themes for others; the mourning friends who inscribe these lines to his memory think of the affectionate nature, the cheerful companionship, the large heart and open hand, the simple courteousness, and the endearing frankness of a brave, true, honest gentleman, whom no pen but his own could depict as those who knew him would desire.

[On a later page, *Punch* carried some verses headed 'William Makepeace Thackeray (December 24th, 1863)'. Anthony Trollope, quoting its first three stanzas, remarked that 'The spirit and nature of the man have been caught here with absolute truth' – *Thackeray* (1879) p. 59.²]

> He was a cynic: By his life all wrought
>   Of generous acts, mild words and gentle ways:
> His heart wide open to all kindly thought,
>   His hand so quick to give, his tongue to praise.
>
> He was a cynic: you might read it writ
>   In that broad brow, crowned with its silver hair;
> In those blue eyes with child-like candour lit,
>   In the sweet smile his lips were wont to wear.
>
> He was a cynic: by the love that clung
>   About him from his children, friends, and kin:
> By the sharp pain, light pen and gossip tongue
>   Wrought in him, chafing the soft heart within.
>
> He was a cynic: let his books confess
>   His *Dobbin's* silent love; or yet more rare,
> His *Newcome's* chivalry and simpleness;
>   His *Little Sister's* life of loving care.
>
> And if his acts, affections, works and ways
>   Stamp not upon the man the cynic's sneer,
> From life to death, oh, public, turn your gaze –
>   The last scene of a cynical career!
>
> These uninvited crowds, this hush that lies,
>   Unbroken, till the solemn words of prayer
> From many hundred reverent voices rise
>   Into the sunny stillness of the air.
>
> These tears, in eyes but little used to tears,
>   These sobs, from manly lips, hard set and grim,
> Of friends, to whom his life lay bare for years,
>   Of strangers, who but knew his books, not him.
>
> A cynic? Yes – if 'tis the cynic's part
>   To track the serpent's trail, with saddened eye,
> To mark how good and ill divide the heart,
>   How lives in chequered shade and sunshine lie.
>
> How e'en the best unto the worst is knit
>   By brotherhood of weakness, sin, and care;

How, even in the worst, sparks may be lit
   To show all is not utter darkness there.
Through Vanity's bright-flaunting fair he walked,
   Marking the puppets dance, the jugglers play;
Saw Virtue tripping, honest effort baulked,
   And sharpened wit on roguery's downward way;
And told us what he saw: and if he smiled
   His smile had more of sadness than of mirth –
But more of love than either. Undefiled,
   Gentle, alike by accident of birth,
And gift of courtesy, and grace of love,
   When shall his friends find such another friend?
For them, and for his children God above
   Has comfort: let us bow: God knows the end.

(4) [*Saturday Review*, 2 Jan 1864, pp. 9–10, by Thackeray's former schoolfriend George Venables (on whom see above, I, 12).] Whatever Mr Thackeray wrote was obviously, and for the most part intentionally, tinged with individual peculiarity, and only the most careless readers can have failed occasionally to think of the author. The circumstances of his life, as well as his tastes and habits, brought him into contact with an extraordinarily large circle of acquaintances, and his striking personal appearance was still more widely known within and beyond the range of London society. By the friends who knew him best, Mr Thackeray was thoroughly beloved, and in the due proportion of nearer or remoter intercourse he inspired an affectionate regard in all who shared his conversation. All competent observers who have been brought by merit or good fortune into contact with men of genius know that, notwithstanding innumerable diversities of character, they are almost always distinguished by a fundamental simplicity and nobleness of nature. The course of Mr Thackeray's life was probably not unfavourable to his intellectual and moral development, but no perversity of training or exceptional obliquity of circumstances could have converted him into an intriguer, a fanatic, or a prig. Not affecting stoical elevation, liable to conscious and unconscious foibles, he satisfied the first condition of greatness or natural superiority by always remaining essentially the same. A certain largeness and

passivity of disposition left room for the undisturbed play of his intellect and fancy. It was not his mission to guide the opinions of men, or to direct their practical energies. The gift of humorous observation and of dramatic reproduction is subtler and rarer, and it is not less really useful.

Superficial critics often attributed to Mr Thackeray the bitter and sarcastic tendency which they imagined that they discovered in his writings. His friends, on the other hand, influenced perhaps by their knowledge of his personal character, received from his works an opposite impression. His satirical acuteness contrasted oddly, and yet pleasantly, with an invincible credulity in every form and every pretence of goodness. The hero of the day, especially if his merits were philanthropic or religious, always commanded his momentary belief and admiration. Innate diffidence or modesty inclined him to exaggerate the greatness of good men and of those who professed to be good. In real life, and sometimes in literary composition, he was unduly tolerant of impostors whom he was far too honest to imitate. The sarcastic quality of his writings represented the reaction of his judgement against his impulses, and it also arose, in part, from an almost feminine impatience of harshness and wrong. He might be said to be habitually angry because all the world was not as gentle and as genial as himself; and yet he was so far from entertaining excessive self-esteem that, if he could have denuded himself of his personality, he would probably have chosen an entirely different type of character, which would have been narrower and poorer than his own. If he had been a dull man, he would perhaps have submitted to the dictation of some presuming theorist or sectarian teacher; but a happy faculty of discerning absurdity secured him against the consequences of his unusual softness of disposition. To a certain extent, he was aware of his own amiable peculiarities, and several of his fictitious characters are partially copied from the simpler and less vigorous side of his own nature. The weakness which too often distinguishes the virtuous and benevolent personages of his novels indicates his unfounded suspicion that intellectual power is a moral drawback rather than an inappreciable advantage. He knew himself to be able and brilliant, and he never discovered that he was intrinsically good. He once accepted as a compliment the half-serious remark of one of his friends, that the principal feature of his character was a weak religious sentimentality.[3]

It was fortunate that Mr Thackeray failed in his attempt, some years ago, to obtain a seat in Parliament. For politics, and in general for either abstract or practical controversies, he was incapable of caring, and his consciousness of his true vocation was characteristically displayed in his hearty congratulations of the successful adversary, who, as the defeated candidate informed his supporters, was better qualified for the House of Commons than himself. It would perhaps have been better if he had never meddled with history, for some kinds of greatness irritated and repelled him, and his strong perception of personal obliquities blinded him to the great public interests which were often identified with imperfect kings or statesmen.... It would be unfitting at the present moment to notice even petty defects, except for the purpose of explaining the paradox of a benevolence which sometimes seemed to require a cynical expression. Mr Thackeray's friends were not perplexed by any similar inconsistency between his affectionate character and his kindly demeanour. The formidable satirist never sought to be feared either by his intellectual equals or by the most commonplace of his associates.

His knowledge of character was minute and accurate, but it was confined to the limits of his own experience. He had lived among artists, men of letters, native and foreign adventurers, and in the best society of London; but he knew nothing of peasants or artisans, and he never attempted to describe them.... In Becky Sharp, Mr Thackeray performed a feat which has rarely been accomplished in fiction, by endowing the creature of his imagination with a portion of his own genius and wit. Perhaps the reality of life which is imparted to the thoroughly commonplace George Osborne is almost an equally difficult achievement.... He always took pleasure in playing with the language of which he had obtained perfect mastery. His puns and his unexpected rhymes were surprisingly ingenious, and the flowing metre of his humorous ballads was not far removed from the music of genuine poetry. His ordinary style was in a high degree pure and idiomatic, and his habitual cultivation of the niceties of language taught him to appreciate, in his maturer years, the classical studies which he had too much undervalued in his youth. He sometimes said that his highest aspiration would be to produce a few short poems as finished and perfect as the Odes of Horace. Detailed criticism would be ill-suited to the occasion, but the memory of a great writer is inseparably, and for the world at large exclusively, associated with his works. To those who knew Mr Thackeray himself, it seems as if a sagacious stranger might construct his true character from a careful study of his writings. It would be evident that, while he had no pretension to learning, he possessed vast stores of miscellaneous knowledge, and that whatever he knew was available for his purposes. His gaiety and melancholy corresponded to the humour of his fictions, and to the pathetic element which they contained. The acrimony of his satire was but the form in which a sensitive nature sought at the same time concealment and utterance. The most common error in his conception of character proceeded from an excess of charitable forbearance. He made his amiable women almost silly, not because he despised feminine virtues, but because he had taught himself to be tolerant of folly if he fancied that it was combined with goodness. Exaggerating to himself his own conscious failings, holding that intellectual gifts afforded no security for moral excellence, he scarcely knew how large a possibility of error is abolished by the elimination of stupidity. His survivors understand better the essential purity of character which was intimately connected with his sparkling fancy and with his keen observation.

NOTES

1. Eneas Sweetland Dallas (1828–79) was a distinguished critic, and a frequent reviewer in *Blackwood's*, *The Times*, etc. I owe this attribution to the kindness of Mr Gordon Phillips, Archivist to *The Times*.
2. Trollope attributes these verses to Tom Taylor (1817–80), dramatist, journalist, and long-time contributor to *Punch*, of which he became Editor in 1874. Anne Thackeray Ritchie, however, attributes them to Shirley Brooks, Taylor's predecessor as Editor (*Biog. Intros*, VI, xxv). Miss Mary Anne Bonney, Librarian of *Punch*, tells me that no record remains which identifies the authorship of the verses or of the prose tribute.
3. 'In a letter to a friend Mr Venables wrote, "I once told him that the basis of his character was religious sentimentality, and he gravely said that I

understood him perfectly; but, like Horace, he gave warning that neither he nor his tastes, opinions, and feelings were to be attacked with impunity. His humorous pugnacity subsided at once in the presence of real or apparent goodness" ' (*Biog. Intros*, XII, xxii).

A Man Not Easily Summed Up
JOHN BLACKWOOD

From Mrs Gerald Porter, *Annals of a Publishing House: John Blackwood* (1898) pp. 98–9. Thackeray never published with the firm of Blackwoods nor contributed to *Blackwood's Magazine*, though as early as 1838 the Revd James White had commended him to Robert Blackwood as 'the cleverest of all the London writers, I think...; a gentleman, a Cambridge man. I told him he had better not waste his time with the inferior magazines... but to go at once to you. He is shy, I suppose, for he said he wished *you* would invite him to contribute...' – Mrs Margaret Oliphant, *Annals of a Publishing House: William Blackwood and his Sons* (1897) II, 196. Later however, a friendship developed between him and John Blackwood, whose letters often mention him and his works. Extract (1) is from a letter of 30 Dec 1863; extract (2), written soon afterwards, is to a contributor, and gives reasons for rejecting the paper about Thackeray which he had submitted to *Blackwood's Magazine*. Anne Thackeray Ritchie, quoting from these letters in her account of her father's death, remarked, 'Such words from those whom he trusted and who trusted him are *not* words, they are facts, and they represent what has been and is still for those of us who inherit these memories' (*Biog. Intros*, XII, xxii).

(1) Thackeray's death... is a real grief to me, and indeed to all my family; 'old Thack.' was a constantly recurring thought and subject of conversation with us. I am desperately distressed for the girls. Poor things, he completely made companions of them, and I cannot think how they are to recover from the blow.... Poor fellow, how often he has talked to me about them. To London literary men Thackeray's death is a very serious loss. He was a central figure, and his tone leavened and did good to the whole body. By all good fellows it will be thoroughly felt.

(2) I do not feel that [the paper that you offer] describes

Thackeray, and consequently I did not like to put it into the Magazine as our portrait and tribute to his memory. I do not much care for the stories you give. He used to tell such stories in a pitying half-mocking way in which it was impossible to say how much was sincerity and how much sham. But when he dropped that vein, and spoke with real feeling of men and things that he liked, the breadth and force of his character came out, and there was no mistake about his sincerity. None of the numerous sketches I have read give to me any real picture of the man with his fun and mixture of bitterness with warm good feeling. I have stuck in this note. Writing about old 'Thack.' has set me thinking about him, and all the scenes we have had together. I feel so truly about him that I am frightened to give a wrong impression of him to one who did not know him.

Suggestions for Further Reading

As has been evident throughout this collection, Gordon N. Ray's two-volume biography *Thackeray: The Uses of Adversity 1811–1846* (Oxford, 1955) and *Thackeray: The Age of Wisdom 1847–1863* (Oxford, 1958), and his four-volume *Letters and Private Papers of W. M. Thackeray* (Oxford, 1945–6), are indispensable. The biography is incomparably better informed and more sophisticated in understanding than any of its predecessors. Many letters came to light after the 1945–6 publication, and a further volume is expected. Ray's *The Buried Life: A Study of the Relation between Thackeray's Fiction and his Personal History* (Oxford, 1952) has much about the originals of his characters, a topic earlier explored, from less complete knowledge, in John Wendell Dodd's *Thackeray: A Critical Portrait* (New York, 1941). The processes of his art, more at the level of craftsmanship, are discussed in J. A. Sutherland's *Thackeray at Work* (London, 1974).

Anne Thackeray Ritchie was a scatterbrain and inaccurate, besides inevitably being an emotionally involved and protective commentator upon her father. Her various recollections of him nevertheless deserve reading *in extenso* (see above, I, 79). Other early biographical studies are unsatisfactory, but contain useful original material: the Merivale–Marzials biography (see II, 347) and the two-volume *Life* by 'Lewis Melville' (Lewis Benjamin) published in 1899 and rewritten in 1909. James Grant Wilson's huge compilation *Thackeray in the United States* (2 vols, London, 1904) is a splendid quarry. An earlier compilation, *Thackerayana: Notes and Anecdotes*, ed. Joseph Grego (London, 1875; rev. 1901; repr. New York, 1971) contains much miscellaneous material. Later biographies which, though falling short of Ray's in scholarship, remain useful are Malcolm Elwin's *Thackeray: A Personality* (London, 1932) and Lionel Stevenson's *The Showman of Vanity Fair* (London, 1947). J. Y. T. Greig's *Thackeray: A Reconsideration*

(Oxford, 1950) offers a sharply critical view of the man and his work. His early career is surveyed in Harold S. Gulliver's *Thackeray's Literary Apprenticeship* (Valdosta, 1934). E. Beresford Chancellor's *The London of Thackeray* (London, 1923) is a useful and well-illustrated companion to the novels. His illustrations to his own works are reproduced and discussed in John Buchanan-Brown's *The Illustrations of W. M. Thackeray* (London, 1979). An ingenious 'autobiography' has been compiled and created from Thackeray's letters and other writings by Margaret Forster in *William Makepeace Thackeray: Memoirs of a Victorian Gentleman* (London, 1978).

Critical discussion of the novels is not the task of this book, but a few studies might briefly be mentioned. His early reception is recorded in Dudley Flamm's *Thackeray's Critics: An Annotated Bibliography of British and American Criticism 1836–1901* (Oxford, 1967) and illustrated in *Thackeray: The Critical Heritage*, ed. Geoffrey Tillotson and Donald Hawes (London, 1968). 'Twentieth-century views' of his work are exemplified in *Thackeray: A Collection of Critical Essays* (Englewood Cliffs, N. J., 1968), and listed in John Charles Olmsted's *Thackeray and his Twentieth-century Critics: An Annotated Bibliography, 1900–1975* (New York, 1979). Major critical books on Thackeray include Geoffrey Tillotson's *Thackeray, the Novelist* (Cambridge, 1954), John Loofbourow's *Thackeray and Form of Fiction* (Oxford, 1964), Juliet McMaster's *Thackeray: The Major Novels* (Manchester, 1971), Barbara Hardy's *Exposure of Luxury: Radical Themes in Thackeray* (London, 1972), and John Carey's *Thackeray: Prodigal Genius* (London, 1977).

Further guidance may be found in the chapters by, respectively, Arthur Pollard, Lionel Stevenson and Robert A. Colby in *The English Novel: Select Bibliographical Guides*, ed. A. E. Dyson (Oxford, 1974); *Victorian Fiction: A Guide to Research*, ed. Lionel Stevenson (New York: Modern Languages Association, 1964); and *Victorian Fiction: A Second Guide to Research*, ed. George H. Ford (New York: Modern Languages Association, 1978). Lionel Stevenson also provides the bibliographical listing of Thackeray's works and commentators in *The New Cambridge Bibliography of English Literature*, Vol. 3, ed. George Watson (Cambridge, 1969).

Index

'A. Z.', on WMT, 178–85
à Beckett, Gilbert, 321, 322
Adams, Henry, on WMT, 185
Ainsworth, William Harrison, WMT on, xvii
Allen, John, on WMT, 19–21; 22, 23, 29
Allingham, William, on WMT, 282–4
Arcedeckne, Andrew, on WMT, 297; 130–2, 253
Ashburton, Lady, 34, 297
Ashburton, Lord, on WMT, xvi
Athenaeum, 298

Ballantine, William, on WMT, 45, 294, 298
Balzac, Honoré de, WMT on, 69, 90, 121; 101, 141
Baxter, Lucy, on WMT, 172–7; 137
Baxter, Sally (Mrs Hampton), WMT on, 172, 175, 184, 185; 173, 177
Bayne, Alicia, on WMT, 4–5, 85–8; 21
Beale, Willert, 228, 235–6, 250–1
Bedingfield, Richard, on WMT, 112–24
Berry, Mary and Agnes, 89, 92, 144
Bevan, Samuel, on WMT, 52–4
Bigelow, John, on WMT, 338–40
Blackwood, John, on WMT, xiii, xxi, 381–2
Blackwood's Magazine, 11, 381
Blanchard, Laman, 359–60
Boehm, Joseph Edgar, 17, Plates 1, 15
Borrow, George, 362
Boyes, John Frederick, on WMT, 7–12
Bradbury & Evans, 45–6, 301

Bray, Charles, 139, 214
Brimley, George, on WMT, 166
Brontë, Charlotte, on WMT, 70, 106–12, Plate 10; WMT on, 107
Brookfield, Mrs Jane, on WMT, 55–8, 93, 112; WMT on, 57; xxi, xxviii, 79, 88, 92, 205, 347
Brookfield, William, on WMT, 56, 58; WMT on, 27; 20, 92
Brooks, Shirley, on WMT, 321, 326; 155, 322, 380
Brotherton, Mrs Maria, on WMT, 6
Brown, John, on WMT, 145–51; 251
Browne, Hablot K., 305, 322
Browning, Robert and Elizabeth Barrett, on WMT, 103–6, 195, 306; WMT on, 103, 123, 283; 196, 222
Bryant, William Cullen, on WMT, 127–8
Buller, Charles, 34, 37
Burnand, Francis Cowley, on WMT, 130–3, 323–4
Butler, Mrs Harriet (WMT's maternal grandmother, formerly Mrs Becher), 5, 78, 82, 139

Carlyle, Thomas, on WMT, 33–9; WMT on, 33, 39, 116, 121, 179, 280; 2, 97, 112, 121, 328, 370
Carmichael-Smyth, Mrs Anne (née Becher; later Mrs Richmond Thackeray), on WMT, 4, 5; WMT on, 57, 114, 121, 139, 199–200, 218, 243, 247, 372; 2, 7, 62–3, 78, 82, 110, 117–18, 184, 371
Chapman, John, on WMT, 138
Chasles, Philarète, 1

385

386 INDEX

Coleridge, Arthur, 153
Collins, Charles Alston, 152, 201, 306
Collins, Wilkie, WMT on, xvii
Conway, Moncure D., on WMT, 36, 367–8
Cooke, John Esten, on WMT, xv, 256–64
Cooper, Charles, on WMT, 129–30
Cooper, Thomas, WMT on, 116
Corkran, Henriette, on WMT, 58–64
Cornhill Magazine, WMT as editor of, xxix, 35, 103, 163–5, 190, 222, 228, 233, 240, 251, 269, 274–5, 276, 304, 326, 331, 332–3, 336, 338, 339, 341–6, 350; monthly dinners, xx, 165, 222, 342–3
Courtiras, Gabrielle de ('la Comtesse Dash'), on WMT, 25
Cranch, Christopher P., on WMT, 216–17; 215
Croly, George, 247, 250
Crosse, Mrs Andrew, 301
Crowe, Amy, 133, 152–3
Crowe, Mrs Catherine, 141–2
Crowe, Eugenie, 83
Crowe, Eyre, on WMT, xxi, 54, 133–7, 177; WMT on, 133–4
Crowe, Sir Joseph, on WMT, 133
Cruikshank, George, on WMT, 367–8
Cundall, H. M., on WMT, 322

'D. D.', on WMT, 13–14
Dallas, E. S., on WMT, xiv, 373–4
Dana, Richard Henry Jr, on WMT, 128
Davies, Gerald S., on WMT, 14–17
Deville, J. S., 17, Plate 1
Dicken, Charles Rowland, on WMT, 13–14
Dickens, Alfred, on WMT, 305
Dickens, Mrs Catherine, 338
Dickens, Charles, on WMT, 75, 185, 291, 300, 301–6, 312, 318, 320, 368; WMT on, xvii, 114, 121, 122, 129, 138, 179, 224, 237–9, 242, 251, 275, 276, 278, 284, 290–2, 300, 307–10, 312, 317, 325, 326; WMT's envy of, 47, 75, 76, 134, 137, 159, 290–2, 299–300; compared with WMT, xvii–xix, xxv, 1, 34, 36–7, 125, 146–7, 152, 154, 161, 203–4, 217, 230, 238–9, 325, 328–9, 334, 356–7; reconciliation with (1863), 206, 208, 308–9, 312–13; David Copperfield, 206, 249, 251, 301; Dombey and Son, 38, 237–8, 305; Household Words, 239, 276; Little Dorrit, 318; Old Curiosity Shop, 47; Oliver Twist, 3; Pickwick Papers, 146, 179–80, 301, 302; xxvii, 153, 155, 167, 201, 202, 218–19, 276, 313, 324. See also Garrick Club row
Dickens, Charles, Jr 305
'Dignity of Literature' controversy, xxviii, 123, 209, 211, 301–2
Disraeli, Benjamin (1st Earl of Beaconsfield), on WMT, 75–8; WMT on, 118
Dixon, William Hepworth, 298
D'Orsay, Alfred, Count, 142
Doyle, Richard, 153, 214, 246; Plate 13
Duff, Sir Mountstuart E. Grant, on WMT, 366
Duffy, Charles Gavan, on WMT, 36–7, 362–4
Dürer, Albert, 266
Dwyer, Major Frank, on WMT, 66–71

Eliot, George, xix, 80, 123, 138, 139, 214
Elliotson, Dr John, 241–2
Elliott, Mrs Jane, 57, 88
Elwin, Malcolm, 298, 301
Elwin, Whitwell and Frances, on WMT, 20, 242–50; WMT on, 243, 245; xvi
Emerson, Ralph Waldo, on WMT, xix; WMT on, 116, 269
Espinasse, Francis, 33, 37–8

INDEX

Faucit, Helen (Lady Martin), 205–6
Féval, Paul, on WMT, 300
Field, Maunsell B., on WMT, 217–18
Fields, Mrs Annie, on WMT, 156
Fields, James T., on WMT, 156–67, 305
FitzGerald, Edward, on WMT, xv–xvi, xxiv, 27–33, 228; WMT on, 27, 32; 20, 23, 331
Forster, John, on WMT, xvi, 211; WMT on, xvii, 138; 139, 243, 249, 317, 318
Fox, W. J., WMT on, 121
Fraser, Thomas, 3, 40
Fraser, Sir William, on WMT, 140–5
Fraser's Magazine, on WMT, 72–3; WMT's association with, xx, 2, 3, 28, 33, 72, 137, 148, 236, 277
Frith, W. P., on WMT, 294, 360–1
Furness, Horace Howard, on WMT, 167

Garrick Club row (1858), xviii, 49–51, 206, 208, 289–90, 301, 308–9, 311, 312–20, 324. *See also* Thackeray, W. M.: HOMES AND HAUNTS.
Gaskell, Mrs Elizabeth, on WMT, 167; 110
Gore, Mrs Catherine, WMT on, 122

Hake, Gordon, on WMT, 362
Hallé, Sir Charles, 311–12
Hamstede, Frederick, 285–6
Hannay, James, on WMT, xxi, xxii, 96–101; WMT on, 221
Hardman, Sir William, on WMT, 306, 366–7
Hatton, Joseph, on WMT, 325
Hawthorne, Nathaniel, on WMT, 182, 185; compared with WMT, 356, 357
Helps, Sir Arthur, 91–2, 93
Hennell, Sarah, 214–15
Higgins, Matthew ('Jacob Omnium'), 195, 202, 222, 251–2
Hill, Frederic, on WMT, 93

Hodder, George, on WMT, xiv–xv, xxi, 228–42
Hole, Samuel Reynolds, on WMT, 251–3
Hood, Thomas, WMT on, 12, 121, 174, 364; 330
Horne, Richard Hengist, on WMT, 359–60

Illustrated London News, on WMT, xxi, 374–5
Illustrated Times, 50, 314
Innes, Harry, on WMT, 64–6
Irvine, J. W., on WMT, 16–17

Jeaffreson, John Cordy, on WMT, xvii, xxi, 284–99
Jerrold, Blanchard, on WMT, xvi, 168, 355–9
Jerrold, Douglas, on WMT, xv, xxv, 321; WMT on, xvii, 48, 116, 321; 42, 43, 154, 268, 276, 322
Jones, Mrs George B., 171

Keane, Deady, on WMT, 72–3
Kemble, Fanny, on WMT, 124–6, 346; 196
Kennedy, John Pendleton, on WMT, 282
Kenny, Charles Lamb, 23
Kenyon, John, on WMT, 301
King, Mrs Henry, 175–6, 177, 248, 338, 340
Kinglake, A. W., on WMT, 372; 2, 20
Kingsley, Charles, on WMT, 83
Knight, Charles, on WMT, 297
Knowles, James Sheridan, WMT on, 122

Lamb, Charles, WMT on, 32; 161
Laurence, Samuel, WMT on, Plate 10; portraits of WMT, 144, 147, Plates 10, 17; 39
Leech, John, WMT's association with, 10, 17, 40, 154, 155, 243, 251, 253, 306, 321, 322, 360; 148, Plate 8
Lehmann, Rudolph, on WMT, 26

Lemon, Mark, on WMT, 238, 324–5; 43, 154, 321, 322
Lennox, Lord William Pitt, on WMT, 299–300
Lever, Charles, on WMT, 73–5; WMT on, 68, 69, 73, 144–5; 64–71, 362
Lewes, George Henry, 23, 203, 222, 337
Liddell, Henry George, on WMT, 17–18
Linton, Mrs Eliza Lynn, on WMT, 202–5
Locker-Lampson, Frederick, on WMT, 213–14, 364–6
Lockhart, John Gibson, on WMT, 104–5
Lowell, James Russell, on WMT, 215–16
Lunt, George, on WMT, 167–71
Lytton, Edward Lytton Bulwer (1st Baron Lytton), WMT on, xvii, 99, 146, 159, 298, 300, 323; 97

Macaulay, Thomas Babington (1st Baron Macaulay), on WMT, xxii; WMT on, 122; 242
McCarthy, Justin, on WMT, 328–30
Mackay, Charles, on WMT, 40–3
Maclise, Daniel, 33, 148; Plates 2, 3
Macready, William Charles, WMT on, 121
Marochetti, Baron Carlo, 266, 273
Martin, Sir Theodore, on WMT, 151, 205–8
Martineau, Harriet, on WMT, 297, 299; 34–5
Marx, Karl, on WMT, xix
Masson, David, on WMT, xvii, 276–9
Mayhew, Horace, 322, 324, 325, 326, 358–9
Maynooth College, 66, 70, 71
Merivale, Herman (*père*), 347
Merivale, Herman Charles (*fils*), on WMT, 286, 298, 347–55; 79, 205, 222, 310, 371
Merriman, John Jones, on WMT, 93–6

Millais, Sir John Everett, on WMT, 151–3; 155, 222
Milnes, Richard Monckton (1st Baron Houghton), on WMT, 288, 331; 2, 20, 166–7
Montgomery, Robert, 116
Morning Chronicle, 40
Motley, John Lothrop, on WMT, 279–82
Müller, Friedrich Max, on WMT, 362
Mulock, Dinah (Mrs Craik), on WMT, 118; WMT on, 118

Napoleon, I, 162, 224
National Shakespeare Tercentenary Celebration Committee, xxix, 52, 298–9, 329
Nevill, Lady Dorothy, on WMT, 362
Newman, John Henry, WMT on, 139

O'Connell, Daniel, 118
O'Connell, Morgan John, 71, 216, 218
O'Connor, Feargus, 117
O'Donnell, journalist, 277–9

Paget, Charles, on WMT, 23
Palmerston, Viscount, 67, 338
Pappenheim, Jenny von, on WMT, 24
Pattle, Virginia, WMT on, 88
Payn, James, on WMT, 273–5
Perry, Kate, on WMT, 39, 57, 88–93
Perugini, Mrs Kate (*née* Dickens, then Mrs Charles Collins), on WMT, 306–11; 153, 155, 167, 201
Pictorial Times, 43
Planché, James Robertson, on WMT, 25–6
Pollock, Sir Frederick, on WMT, xxii
Prescott, William Hickling, 157, 178
Priestley, Lady, on WMT, 208, 276
Proctor, Bryan Waller, and wife, on WMT, 301; 112, 161

INDEX

'Prout, Father' (Francis Mahoney), 71, 283–4, 294
Punch, on WMT, xiii–xiv, 375–7; WMT's associations with, xv, xxviii, 3, 48, 54, 73, 75, 81, 117, 129, 134, 154, 160, 227, 233, 320–6, 375; Table conversations, xx, 321, 322–4, 368; 130

Quarterly Review, 242–3
Quin, Frederick, WMT on, 339, 340; 338

Rachel, Madame, 111, 112
Ray, Gordon N., xv, 39, 51, 84, 285, 314, 321, 383
Reach, Angus, 42, 49
Redesdale, Lord, on WMT, 151
Reed, William Bradford, on WMT, 186–91
Reeve, Henry, on WMT, 24–5
Rigby, Elizabeth (Lady Eastlake), on WMT, 107, 145
Ritchie, Lady: *see* Thackeray, Anne Isabella
Ritchie, William, WMT on, 199; 193, 198
Rothschild, Lady Louisa de, on WMT, 361
Ruskin, Mrs Euphemia (later Lady Millais), on WMT, 151, 153
Russell, Sir George, on WMT, 311–13
Russell, Dr John, WMT on, 6; 12, 13
Russell, William Howard, on WMT, 153, 154–6; 225, 337, 339

Sala, George Augustus, on WMT, xvi, 218–28; WMT on, 218, 239, 242; 240
Samuelson, James, on WMT, 130
Sand, George, WMT on, 69, 121
Saturday Review, on WMT, 375–81; 30, 33, 218, 225
Scott, Sir Walter, WMT on, 8, 182, 206–7, 261, 312, 323; 1, 31, 101, 374
Shawe, Isabella: *see* Thackeray, Mrs Isabella

Shawe, Mrs Matthew, WMT on, 216
Shee, William Archer, xxv
Silver, Henry, on WMT, 321, 322–3, 326, 368, 372
Sinclair, John, on WMT, 94–6
Smith, Albert, on WMT, 52; WMT on, 49; 220, 317
Smith, Elder & Co, 49, 341
Smith, George, on WMT, 108, 110–11, 341–5; WMT on, 164, 211; 107, 209, 218, 221, 269, 302, 337
Spectator, on WMT, 126–7
Spedding, James, 20, 29
Stanley, Lady, of Alderley, 279, 280, 282
Stephen, Mrs Leslie: *see* Thackeray, Harriet
Sterling, Edward, 3
Sterling, John, 20, 34
Stoddard, Richard Henry, on WMT, xxv, 128
Stoddard, William Wellwood, 12
Stone, Frank, on WMT, 28–9; Plate 5
Story, Emelyn and Edith, on WMT, 254–6
Story, William Wetmore, 215, 254
Stowe, Mrs Harriet Beecher, WMT on, 135, 174, 177, 191
Sturgis, Russell, on WMT, 185
Sumner, Charles, 224
Synge, William Webb Follett, on WMT, 351–3; 337, 355

Taine, Hyppolite, on WMT, 367
Taylor, Bayard, on WMT, 264–73
Taylor, Sir Charles, 222, 223, 343
Taylor, Sir Henry and Lady, 299
Taylor, Tom, 322, 380
Tennyson, Alfred (1st Baron Tennyson), WMT on, 114, 323; 20, 27, 29, 102, 214, 370
Tennyson, Frederick, 20, 28, 31
Thackeray, Anne Isabella ('Anny', later Lady Ritchie), on WMT, xxi, xxiii–xxiv, xxvi, 6, 18, 23, 27, 78–84, 105, 112, 208–13, 251, 280, 311, 321–2, 339–40,

Thackeray – *continued*
345–6, 369–72, 381; writings, 79, 197, 298, 340, 344–5; WMT's pride in these, xxix, 79, 165, 252, 339, 345, 346; WMT's affection for, 234, 254, 381; WMT dictates novels to, 81, 212–13, 215, 369; xx, 31, 33–4, 105, 157, 196–7, 205, 279, 280, 286, 305, 308, 331, 347, 383

Thackeray, Francis St John, on WMT, 101–3

Thackeray, Harriet ('Minny', later Mrs Leslie Stephen), xx, 78–80, 105, 196–7, 205, 280, 308, 381

Thackeray, Mrs Isabella (*née* Shawe), WMT on, 2–3, 78, 119, 122, 188, 352, 354; courtship of, 25, 78; married life with, xxvii, 2, 28, 78, 80, 352; insanity, xx, xxi, 3, 119, 149, 188, 287–8, 367

Thackeray, Jane (died in infancy), xxvii, 78, 149, 182, 184, 305

Thackeray, William Makepeace

LIFE

summary, xxvii–xxix
childhood, 1–2, 4–6
schooldays, 2, 5, 6–19, 113, 322–3, 325, 353
at Cambridge, 19–23
at Weimar, 23–4
law-student, 2
Paris, 2, 24–5 (*see also below*)
journalism, 2–3, 24, 29 (*see also under magazines' titles*)
marriage, *see under wife's and daughters' names*
finances, xxvii, 2, 19, 30, 44, 45, 49, 51, 52, 117, 118, 122, 130, 162, 207, 233, 235–6, 248, 250–1, 253, 288, 342, 351–2
novels, *see under their titles, below*
lecturer, as a, *see below*
parliamentary candidate, as a, xxviii, 116–17, 119–20, 303, 366, 379

death, 95, 105–6, 150–1, 152–3, 155, 304, 305–6, 328, 371
funeral, xxix, 153, 155, 206, 208, 242, 303, 305, 312, 325, 367–8, 375

HOMES AND HAUNTS

America, 42, 85, 161 (*see also* America (ns), opinion of, *below*)
Athenaeum Club, 75, 85, 166, 190, 206, 208, 302, 309, 312, 355
British Museum, Reading Room, 113, 118, 231, 281, 359
Cider (or Cyder) Cellars, 52, 185, 215, 216
Evans's Supper Rooms, 40, 49, 218, 293, 348–9
Fielding Club, 230–1, 351
Garrick Club, 25–6, 56, 85, 102, 108, 131, 155, 215–16, 253, 314, 349
  See also Garrick Club row *above*
Great Coram Street, 51, 78, 134
Jermyn Street, 43, 51
Kensington, Palace Green, 86–8, 94, 100, 183, 184, 196, 224, 249, 340
Onslow Square, 85, 231
Our Club, 276–7, 285–6
Paris, 24–5, 58–64, 78, 84, 163–4, 193, 202, 204, 282
Reform Club, xxv, 85, 224, 226, 355
Rome, 104–5, 255
Young Street, 79–83, 93, 95, 117, 162
Weimar, 23–4

PERSONAL QUALITIES, OPINIONS, ETC.

Addison, Joseph, admiration for, 11, 78, 98, 139, 146, 180
America (ns), opinion of, 85, 135, 167–8, 187, 191, 224, 265–6, 269; Civil War, 184, 269–70, 323, 326
appearance, 7, 17, 21, 24, 25, 43–4, 59, 72, 74, 80, 85, 87, 99,

INDEX

appearance – *continued*
107, 127, 128, 136, 144, 146, 169, 178, 258, 279, 315, 328, 355, 364. *See also* face, *below.*
bawdiness, xx, 28, 366, 368
best work, his?, 83, 95, 97, 144, 157, 169, 311
biography, wished for no, xxii–xxiii, 79, 347, 372
Bohemian, xxi, 171, 217, 227, 244, 260, 286, 365
candour, openness, xvi, xxiii, 1, 63, 99, 146, 229, 243, 261, 265, 291, 297, 299, 327, 333, 334
capital punishment, views on, 119, 124
Cervantes, *Don Quixote*, aversion to, 262
changeable nature, moodiness, xvi, 70, 175–6, 219, 222, 225–6, 229–30, 271, 288–9, 294–5, 297, 309, 334, 357
children, love of, xxii, 16, 58–64, 65, 79, 90, 94, 102, 187, 193–5, 254–6, 302, 303, 305, 306, 347–9, 361
clubman, a, xx, xxi, 75, 85, 99, 112, 119, 120, 144, 293
conversation, 25, 34, 35, 38–9, 46, 95, 99, 107–9, 130, 142, 147, 168–9, 180–2, 187–8, 195, 201, 221, 229, 244–5, 252, 255, 258, 264, 279, 298, 315, 323, 325, 334–5, 350, 362, 368
cynic, a?, xiii, xv, 8–9, 38, 40, 42, 51, 63, 74, 75, 94, 98, 108, 109, 119, 122, 129, 142, 152, 165, 175, 176, 182–3, 188, 220, 226, 254, 257, 264, 265, 272, 315, 326, 336, 366, 373–4, 376, 378, 379
dictating, practice of, 81, 136, 212–13, 215, 217, 223, 231–2, 235, 241, 248, 259–60, 369
diffidence, 9, 28, 333, 334
drawings, 2, 5, 6, 10, 14, 18, 20, 24, 25–6, 37, 44–5, 64, 81, 83, 97, 117, 161, 167, 171, 194, 197, 210–11, 246, 252–3, 271–2, 273, 320, 367–8, 384; Plates 4, 6 and 7
drinking, fondness for, xx, 21, 63, 115, 123, 167, 241, 258, 283, 295–6, 339, 343, 365
Dumas, Alexandre (*père*), enjoyment of, 69, 115, 261–2
eating, pleasure in, 8, 29, 56, 74, 123, 160, 241, 258, 267, 288, 295, 339, 365
Englishness, 101, 115, 121, 128, 168, 268, 279
exercise, dislike of, 7–8, 12, 119, 159
exhaustion of his genius, 30, 77, 103, 114, 237, 244, 250, 292, 331, 334
face, nose, 12, 14–15, 59, 72, 74, 93, 107, 120, 127, 143, 144, 146, 151, 156, 178, 181, 232, 258, 315, 363
Fielding, Henry, love of, 14, 22, 113, 122, 144, 157, 312
foreign languages, proficiency in, 25, 26, 221
France, views on, 24, 69, 121
fun, jollity, 24, 25, 113, 143–4, 160–1, 167, 222, 225, 229, 335, 350, 357, 361, 364, 365, 380
generosity, kindness, xiii, xv, 15–16, 28, 30, 42, 51, 53, 54, 59, 61, 66, 91, 92, 97, 98, 102–3, 122, 125, 145, 175, 189, 203, 220, 225, 230–1, 235, 237, 255, 268, 286, 297, 298, 303, 336–7, 348, 352, 358–9, 361, 374, 376
gentleman, a, xviii, 22, 35, 37, 75, 85, 86, 123, 128, 168, 169, 179, 182, 227, 279, 287, 315, 321, 375
Goethe, respect for, 23–4, 116, 162
health, ill-health, xvi, xxviii, 29, 57, 82, 84, 94, 95, 96, 104, 105, 113, 119, 120, 134, 152, 159, 180, 183, 198, 229, 233–4, 241, 256, 268, 270, 271, 288, 295–6, 297, 298, 302, 312, 327, 340,

health – *continued*
342, 345, 354, 357, 369, 371, 373. See also death *above*.
Horace, knowledge of, 9, 17, 19, 98, 100, 101, 380, 381
indolence, procrastination, xviii, 2, 5, 17, 22, 46, 77, 109, 116, 157, 158, 161, 162, 266, 288, 333, 335
Irish, opinion of the, 67, 68, 71, 74, 122, 143, 277–8, 353–4, 363–4
Jews, attitude to, 361, 368
Keats, John, admiration of, 10
lecturer, as a, xviii, 29, 30, 34–5, 39, 41, 80, 100, 110, 111–12, 124–30, 132, 133, 135–6, 138, 156, 158, 161, 166, 172–3, 175, 179, 186–9, 216–17, 232–3, 236, 240–1, 247–8, 250, 272, 281, 315, 329–30, 362; Plate 8. *See also English Humourists and Four Georges below.*
Londoner, a, xix, xx, xxi, 65, 74, 318, 381
melancholy, 25, 105, 127, 145, 146, 148–9, 183, 225, 258–9, 265, 277, 286, 327, 335, 365, 380
Milton, a bore, 116, 146
observation, powers of, 4, 102, 170, 245–6, 248, 356
political opinions, 1, 66, 67–8, 117, 119, 122, 147, 321, 323, 326, 363, 379
portraits and photographs of, 17, 31, 144, 147, 178
publishers, dislike for, 140
puns, love of, 26, 94, 312, 322, 349, 353, 362, 379
reading, 2, 11, 22, 63, 68–9, 97–8, 113, 115, 118, 120, 141, 146, 372. *See also under authors' names.*
real: the 'real' Thackeray, xiii–xv, 87, 98, 146, 220, 229, 256–8, 264, 265, 288, 326–7, 382
religious convictions, 21, 57, 80, 87–8, 116, 120, 121, 123, 138–9, 149–50, 182, 198–201, 243, 245, 286, 351, 354, 355, 379, 380–1
scenery, no interest in, 42
science, on, 252
sensitivity, 9, 13, 34, 41–2, 47, 50, 90–1, 159, 165, 182, 185, 213–14, 229, 234, 277, 298, 332, 336, 337, 342, 350, 365, 367, 374, 380
servants, attitude to, 115, 182–3, 185, 233–4
Shakespeare, remarks on, 99, 114, 163, 167, 182; 18
singing, proclivity for, 22, 133, 166, 188, 258, 286, 360
smoking, indulgence in, 2, 41, 55, 84, 108, 179, 184, 231, 241, 252, 259, 273–4, 280
sociability, xx–xxi, 7, 78, 95, 104, 180, 274, 281
snob, a?, 29, 37, 67–8, 75, 76–7, 93–4, 111, 123, 160, 182, 204, 220, 227, 297, 299, 321, 330, 358, 361, 367
speaker, public, as a, xviii, 8, 95, 96, 120, 158–9, 223, 229, 238–9, 272, 287, 366
Swift, opinion of, 36, 98, 128, 180–1
taverns, inns, frequenter of, 293–4
theatre, love of, 5, 8, 348
undervalued his art, 36, 64, 75, 105, 237, 246, 302
voice, 19, 63, 72, 105, 127, 128, 147, 172, 186, 188, 216–17, 223, 232, 241, 245, 258, 264, 268, 329, 365
weeping, capacity for, 35, 90, 93, 165, 185, 195, 209, 218, 234, 255, 342, 345, 346, 347, 354
women, taste in, attitude towards, xxi–xxii, 47–8, 57, 63, 71, 79, 88, 114–15, 118, 119, 121, 156, 170, 204, 215, 226, 257, 344, 361, 365
Wordsworth, opinion of, 117
working methods, 9, 36, 63, 83,

INDEX

working methods – *continued*
115–16, 134, 136, 157–8, 197, 208–18, 231–2, 235, 243, 248, 250, 259, 281, 285, 369–70, 374
young men, helpful to, 48, 101, 288, 358

WORKS
Barry Lyndon, 364
Book of Snobs, The, WMT on, 280; 3, 23, 46, 49, 95, 227
Catherine: A Story, 3, 219
'Charity and Humour', 136, 177, 303, 305
Cornhill to Cairo, 37, 39, 44
Denis Duval, composition of, 196, 253, 333, 369–70; 304, 313
English Humourists, xxiii, 32, 34, 97, 110, 125, 128–9, 175, 180–1, 315, 341
Esmond, composition of, 133, 259; publication of, 49, 341; WMT on, 157–8, 169, 177, 209, 280, 311, 334; 70, 103, 173
Four Georges, The, 41, 92, 100, 117, 125, 129, 132, 147, 175, 228, 231–2, 240, 267, 281, 315, 329–30, 331
Irish Sketch Book, The, 3, 34, 64–5, 71, 143
Kickleburys on the Rhine, The, 109, 341
Lovel the Widower, 271, 355
Miscellanies, 234
Mrs Perkins's Ball, 44
Newcomes, The, composition of, 195, 212–18, 248; WMT on, 244; Colonel Newcome, 13, 14, 16–17, 215, 226, 246, 247, 251, 331; his death, 185, 195, 212–13, 215–17, 218; Ethel Newcome, 173, 177, 185; other characters, 207, 215–18, 278; 17, 18, 31, 103, 243, 305, 311, 373
'Novels by Eminent Hands' ('*Punch's* Prize Novelists'), 69, 73, 75, 144, 264, 301
Paris Sketch-Book, The, 219, 358

Pendennis, composition of, 260; WMT on, 29, 116, 206, 260; Arthur Pendennis, xxii, 18, 20, 23, 111, 154, 173, 247; Helen Pendennis, 218; her death, 209, 350; Laura, 213; Warrington, 23, 111, 141; 20, 29, 31, 130, 131, 133, 140, 211, 311, 313, 368
Philip, composition of, 250, 340; WMT on, 250, 369; 18, 109, 371
projected works, 141, 244, 262, 272, 280
Rose and the Ring, The, 194, 210, 255–6, 271, 341
Roundabout Papers, The, xxiii, 19, 107, 150, 228, 269–70, 273, 340, 344
Vanity Fair, composition of, 10, 45–6, 51, 56, 69–70, 84, 89, 98, 134–5; publication of, 39, 45–6, 51, 82–3, 140, 145, 152; 'makes' WMT, xvii, 3, 29, 97, 260, 373; WMT on, 83, 95, 97, 118, 140, 162, 252, 260, 273; Amelia, 18, 56, 58; Becky, 83, 98, 114, 140, 145, 260–1, 379; Dobbin, 18, 20, 23; Jos Sedley, 295; 23, 24, 96, 104, 142, 237, 274, 299
verses, 12, 40–1, 54, 90, 94, 95, 113, 169, 171, 175, 188, 211, 249, 303, 304, 309–10, 321, 335, 353, 365, 379
Virginians, The, composition of, 158, 237, 249, 262–3, 281, 282, 283, 317; WMT on, 280; 50, 178, 224
Wolves and the Lamb, The, 271, 349, 355
Yellowplush Papers, The, WMT on, 117, 261; 2

Times, The, on WMT, xiv, 225, 243, 319, 373–4; 3, 34, 155, 162, 269
Town Talk, on WMT, 314–16
Trollope, Anthony, on WMT, xiv, xvi, xix, 96, 331–7, 349–50, 375–6; 12, 222, 342–3

Trollope, Mrs Frances, WMT on, 122

Venables, George Stovin, on WMT, xiv, 12–13, 36, 377–81; 14–15, 23

Vizetelly, Henry, on WMT, 43–52; 314

Walker, Frederick, 197, 222, 310; Plate 13

Wallack, Lester, on WMT, 364
White, James, on WMT, 381
Wills, William Henry, WMT on, 275, 276; 317

Yates, Edmund, on WMT, 50–1, 257, 258, 264, 294, 313–20; WMT on, 51, 289–90, 324, 326
Yorke, Grantham, WMT on, 139